Applied Doughnut Economics and Neuroeconomic Psychology for Business and Politics

Torben Larsen
DEALs Online Collaborative Platform, Denmark

A volume in the Advances in Finance, Accounting, and Economics (AFAE) Book Series

IGI Global
PUBLISHER of TIMELY KNOWLEDGE

Published in the United States of America by
IGI Global
Business Science Reference (an imprint of IGI Global)
701 E. Chocolate Avenue
Hershey PA, USA 17033
Tel: 717-533-8845
Fax: 717-533-8661
E-mail: cust@igi-global.com
Web site: http://www.igi-global.com

Library of Congress Cataloging-in-Publication Data

Names: Larsen, Torben, 1946- author.
Title: Applied doughnut economics and neuroeconomic psychology for business and politics / by Torben Larsen.
Description: Hershey, PA : Information Science Reference, 2021. | Includes bibliographical references and index. | Summary: "This authored book investigates the concept that psychological and ecological research has eroded the foundation of mainstream economics and introduces readers to a promising new approach called Doughnut Economics (DE) "-- Provided by publisher.
Identifiers: LCCN 2020054395 (print) | LCCN 2020054396 (ebook) | ISBN 9781799864240 (hardcover) | ISBN 9781799864257 (paperback) | ISBN 9781799864264 (ebook)
Subjects: LCSH: Economics--Psychological aspects. | Neuroeconomics. | Environmental economics.
Classification: LCC HB74.P8 L28 2021 (print) | LCC HB74.P8 (ebook) | DDC 330.01/9--dc23
LC record available at https://lccn.loc.gov/2020054395
LC ebook record available at https://lccn.loc.gov/2020054396

This book is published in the IGI Global book series Advances in Finance, Accounting, and Economics (AFAE) (ISSN: 2327-5677; eISSN: 2327-5685)

British Cataloguing in Publication Data
A Cataloguing in Publication record for this book is available from the British Library.

Advances in Finance, Accounting, and Economics (AFAE) Book Series

ISSN:2327-5677
EISSN:2327-5685

MISSION

In our changing economic and business environment, it is important to consider the financial changes occurring internationally as well as within individual organizations and business environments. Understanding these changes as well as the factors that influence them is crucial in preparing for our financial future and ensuring economic sustainability and growth.

The **Advances in Finance, Accounting, and Economics (AFAE)** book series aims to publish comprehensive and informative titles in all areas of economics and economic theory, finance, and accounting to assist in advancing the available knowledge and providing for further research development in these dynamic fields.

COVERAGE

- Microeconomics
- Interest Rates and Annuities
- Finance
- E-finance
- Ethics in Accounting and Finance
- Finance and Accounting in SMEs
- Entrepreneurship in Accounting and Finance
- Investments and Derivatives
- Economics of Risks, Uncertainty, Ambiguity, and Insurance
- International Economics

IGI Global is currently accepting manuscripts for publication within this series. To submit a proposal for a volume in this series, please contact our Acquisition Editors at Acquisitions@igi-global.com or visit: http://www.igi-global.com/publish/.

The Advances in Finance, Accounting, and Economics (AFAE) Book Series (ISSN 2327-5677) is published by IGI Global, 701 E. Chocolate Avenue, Hershey, PA 17033-1240, USA, www.igi-global.com. This series is composed of titles available for purchase individually; each title is edited to be contextually exclusive from any other title within the series. For pricing and ordering information please visit http://www.igi-global.com/book-series/advances-finance-accounting-economics/73685. Postmaster: Send all address changes to above address.

Titles in this Series

For a list of additional titles in this series, please visit:
http://www.igi-global.com/book-series/advances-finance-accounting-economics/73685

Financial Management and Risk Analysis Strategies for Business Sustainability
Joaquín Enríquez-Díaz (University of A Coruña, Spain) Laura Castro-Santos (University of A Coruña, Spain) and Félix Puime-Guillén (University of A Coruña, Spain)
Business Science Reference • © 2021 • 320pp • H/C (ISBN: 9781799876342) • US $215.00

Theory of Shocks, COVID-19, and Normative Fundamentals for Policy Responses Emerging Research and Opportunities
Olga Ivanovna Pilipenko (The Russian Presidential Academy of National Economy and Public Administration, Russia) Zoya Andreevna Pilipenko (Bank of Russia, Russia) and Andrey Igorevich Pilipenko (The Russian Presidential Academy of National Economy and Public Administration, Russia)
Business Science Reference • © 2021 • 250pp • H/C (ISBN: 9781799843092) • US $165.00

Handbook of Research on Theory and Practice of Financial Crimes
Abdul Rafay (University of Management and Technology, Pakistan)
Business Science Reference • © 2021 • 650pp • H/C (ISBN: 9781799855675) • US $345.00

Comparative Research on Earnings Management, Corporate Governance, and Economic Value
Elisabete S. Vieira (University of Aveiro, Portugal) Mara Madaleno (University of Aveiro, Portugal) and Graça Azevedo (University of Aveiro, Portugal)
Business Science Reference • © 2021 • 433pp • H/C (ISBN: 9781799875963) • US $215.00

Examining the Intersection of Circular Economy, Forestry, and International Trade
Badri Narayanan Gopalakrishnan (University of Washington, USA) Taranjeet Duggal (Amity University, India) and Tavishi Tewary (Amity University, India)
Business Science Reference • © 2021 • 315pp • H/C (ISBN: 9781799849902) • US $195.00

Influence of FinTech on Management Transformation

For an entire list of titles in this series, please visit:
http://www.igi-global.com/book-series/advances-finance-accounting-economics/73685

IGI Global
PUBLISHER of TIMELY KNOWLEDGE

701 East Chocolate Avenue, Hershey, PA 17033, USA
Tel: 717-533-8845 x100 • Fax: 717-533-8661
E-Mail: cust@igi-global.com • www.igi-global.com

Table of Contents

Preface

INTRODUCTION

The starting point of this book was an Alumni Conference 2017 for Economists graduated from Aarhus University. The former Danish Prime Minister and Secretary General of NATO Anders Fogh Rasmussen gave a guest lecture where he concluded that future economists should learn more psychology and sociology. At that time, I had just published my article on Homo Neuroeconomics with IGI, wherefore my proposal was that Neuroeconomics could provide the link between Economics and Psychology. Anders Fogh Rasmussen immediately supported this idea and after the lecture, I was invited by Professor Alexander Koch to give a lecture for teachers of Behavioral Economics November 30, 2017.

The essence of my lecture was that Homo Neuroeconomicus - in contrast to Homo Economicus - supports the Florida thesis of the rise of the creative class as a long-term demographic trend after WWII. This perspective was considered interesting, but already Economics has recognized differentiated consumer preferences for a long time in the format of the von Neumann thesis on expected utility, so, what's the game changing novelty by Homo Neuroeconomicus?

THE CHALLENGE

Actually, there is a gap between "laboratory" findings on Homo Neuroeconomicus and the issues in contemporary behavioral economics. In this background, my subsequent research has focused on bridging this gap in a series of neuroeconomic follow up papers. Central is my 2019 paper in the International Journal of Patient-Centered Healthcare, respectively the Encyclopedia of Organization Knowledge. These studies link my neuroeconomic model to personality psychology that of the `Big Five´ developed by Goldberg. This Neuroeconomic Psychology provides a new approach to behavioral economics:

- Links to the von Neumann thesis of expected utility improve options of predicting behavior
- Psychological rooting of the Saraswathy Pilot-in-plane model of entrepreneurial ingenuity improves guidance towards better education for entrepreneurship
- Human resource development (HRD) gets a neural foundation for broad personal guidance of new issues such as Cognitive Training and Stressmanagement.

SEARCH OF SOLUTIONS

On the background of the above development IGI has addressed me regarding a book proposal. The first strategic consideration was to develop a specific Textbook in Behavioral Economics. However, it became clear that consequences of Neuroeconomic Psychology are that comprehensive that a novel approach to Economics is required.

Contemporary Economics must have a far broader scope than the classical originating from Smith`s `On the Wealth of Nations` 1776. The classical phase of Economics faced general poverty as the central problem of the population in the Christian part of the world. Today, poverty is a minority problem in the industrialized world and economic transactions have become so dominant in the life of modern man that it has become a threat to the stability of the Ecosystem. A broader scope of Economics for the 21. Century is provided by Doughnut Economics (DE). DE presents Economics as an *embedded* discipline between the social foundation and the Ecosystem that requires a cybernetic approach with stronger political management than seen before. The state of DE primo 2021 is that the general framework is successfully disseminated to the general public by Raworth. Already DE has got attention from leading decision-makers in a number of countries, for instance in relation to application of the general framework for city planning where Amsterdam is the prototype.

So far DE is a novel stand-alone framework for people searching for an alternative to the teaching of Economics in the universities, often termed Mainstream Economics (ME). To clarify the relationships between ME and DE, it must be clarified how DE relates to the Laws of liberal market development who have been the core of Economics since Marshall. The challenge of this book is therefore to develop a synthesis of DE and ME.

ORGANIZATION OF THE TEXTBOOK

Writing Model

The book text is only 150 pages specific economics where typical textbooks in Economics use 500 pages. The shortening is due to skipping normative economic reasoning as outdated, focusing a strict positivistic format with an emphasis on clarification of the boundaries to related scientific disciplines. It is structured in accordance with the "5S" of effective learning in Lean Management developed by Japanese Toyota. Lean Management applies as follows:

First Survey the essence of the book reading the Plain-language Summary
Then, Select your preferred starting Part
Now, Study your Top priority Chapter and continue with that which complements it
Take your time to Structure learnings for practical use, answering the review questions
Finally, Share the learnings with other persons to consolidate your own ultimate understanding

Regarding References, the APA system is applied as a common standard in Textbooks, however, the general consideration has been to minimize use of references due to simplicity of reading. So, regarding what's considered common knowledge among economists are only briefly referenced mentioning a few pioneers in the historical development of the profession. However, in the case of conclusions that are questioned professionally, the opposite point of view is presented too.

Finally, the writing style is reviewed within the local sparring group with PhD Erik Frandsen, economist Leif Justesen and cand. Art Anne-Stine Larsen with a preference for a simple fluent language around key points rather than detailed cover up for criticism. So, the most hardcore neuroeconomic documentation of the Neuroeconomic Psychology is placed in an Appendix to Chapter 5 Cognitive Training.

The short version of core Economics enables that a series of specialists in neighbor disciplines can complement the economic learnings with independent mini reviews of their specialty to provide the reader with direct access to complementary know-how from both sides of the boundary fields:

- The development of neuroeconomic psychology is complemented by a Review in Chapter 5 of research in the "Big Five" by PhD (Psychology) Anna Vedel.
- Modern research in "Meditation and stress" is reviewed by Professor emeritus Are Holen to complement Chapter 6 Stressmanagement.
- The focus on Entrepreneur-like working styles complements Chapter 1 by both a portrait of the serial entrepreneur Martin Thorborg and a review of the state of Simple Living by Ole D. Nielsen.
- Chapter 3 on New Welfare Economy is reviewed by Professor, Emeritus Terkel Christiansen.
- Chapter 4 on Economic Ecology is complemented by a Review of the Danish Plan for 70% reduction of CO2-emission 2030 by Ulla B. Bendtsen and Louis B. Stewart, Danish Council of Climate.
- Director, MSc (Econ) Michael Juul-Sørensen has given his second-opinion on the practical relevance for economists of the Human Resource Development Part in the Chapters 5-6.
- The plain language summary of the history of Economics is complemented by paintings of key points by PhD, Artist Hiltrud Schinzel.

Structure

Plain-Language Summary

The body text begins with a Plain-language Summary that explains economic history from the Stone Age towards modern creative man by 5 quantum leaps all which are complemented by paintings by artist Hiltrud Schinzel. This gives the reader a platform to choose which of the 3 Parts he/she prefers to begin with. Further, each Chapter begins with an Abstract.

Section 1: Business Economics

Chapter 1: Pluralist Behavioral Economics

Firstly Neuroeconomic Psychology is presented as a synthesis of Neuroeconomics and `Big Five` psychology. This identifies Open-mindedness as an economic key quality in the 21st Century. 4 Heuristics for Open-minded behavior are developed: 1) Profiler, 2) Guide to `Simple Living`, 3) Entrepreneur-like business behavior and 4) Collaborative democracy towards common threats.

Chapter 2: From Local to Globalized Markets

The classical market as a self-stabilizing mechanism approaching an optimal allocation of resource is presented in 2.1. The overwhelming technological progress by globalization is explained in 2.2. Further, 2.3 gives a global statistical outlook that leads to an individual pension investment guide. Finally, a SWOT-analysis of liberalist market growth in 2.4.

Section 2: Doughnut Economics

Chapter 3: New Welfare Economy

7 Nobel Laureates recommend a tax system with negative income. The size, entitlement to, meeting out, and finance of Universal Basic Income (UBI) are concluded in accordance with other social security legislation. Further New Public Management 2.0, including national accountancy with multinational companies. An Index on Social Vulnerability builds on Covid-19 experiences.

Chapter 4: Economic Ecology

Reviews the global state of the human Footprint based on IPCC Reports. Then 2.2 reviews the state of alternatives to fossil energy. Pigouvian CO2 Tax is identified as the core intervention to prevent climate tipping-points. A complementary multilevel strategy structures the key tasks at different levels of society for the practical transition to a carbon neutral and circular economy.

Section 3: Human Resource Development (HRD)

Chapter 5: Cognitive Training

Modern economics must reflect that most modern people strive for personal development for self-actualization (HRD). Referring to scientists as Kahneman and Baddeley, Heuristics are developed for `Long-term Memorization` respectively `Reinforcement of Cognitive Performance`.

Chapter 6. Stress Management

WHO warns about epidemic job-related stress as a probable oncoming Pandemic. A review of medical research in de-stressing by classical meditation concludes that it's effective to cope with stress. It's recommended that meditation courses become an integrated part of public health.

Introduction

PLAIN-LANGUAGE SUMMARY: 5 QUANTUM LEAPS TOWARDS CREATIVE MAN

The start of human history is difficult to date. The prehistory termed the Stone Age when man learned himself to use stone tools went on for millions of years. The exact start of humanity during the Stone Age depends on the definition. From the first footprints of man emerging millions of years ago, we have artistic expressions in French cave paintings on hunting 73.000 years ago, see Picture. The original culture of `Hunting and Gathering` was that of sharing within small groups.

Figure 1. French Cave Painting 15-17.000 B.C.

In this ultrashort survey of economic history, the peaks of human progress beyond simple farming are summarized in order of breakthrough. Further, the information on origin enables identification of the long periods of incubation between origin (birth) and breakthrough (maturation) characterizing bio anthropological progress. It shows up, incubation periods of specific elements of human economic development are that long, that the term cultural quantum leap is appropriate. In the explanation of the quantum leaps a series of Figures in the Chapters are previewed with the prefix “P”. In these previews only the main idea is explained while more elaborated explanations must wait for the respective Chapters.

1 Agriculture

In the Younger Stone Age about 10.000 years ago, man began to mold the earth with more sophisticated tools to improve productivity in the `Mesopotamian Half Moon` as Ploughing with a Yoke of Cattle that earlier exclusively were subject to hunting, see picture.

Figure 2. Plough with a Yoke of Cattle in Egypt 1.200 B.C.

This initiated, too, a change of human relations from *sharing to privatization* as persons farming a particular piece of land were allowed, to keep the outcome for themselves. Thus, the first stage of Economics is that of giving gifts as those with the better outcome of farming could give better gifts at social celebrations. This implicated about 3.000 B.C. the invention of money as indicators of value for *trade* and facilitating *hoarding* or storing of wealth as basics of monetary economics. The change from sharing to privatization of goods appears as the strongest cultural change so far.

2 Christianity

Human equality is a specific Christian endeavor that challenges the hierarchical order introduced by agriculture as illustrated in Picture HS1. The Roman Catholic Church, is the largest Christian church, with approximately 1.3 billion baptized Catholics worldwide as of 2018. As the world’s oldest and largest continuously functioning international institution, it has played a prominent role in the history and development of the Western civilization. The head of the Catholic church is the Bishop of Rome, known as the pope and other bishops are acknowledged as successors of Christ's apostles. In this way, the Roman Catholic Church becomes itself a hierarchy. So, the formation of Protestantism, when Luther 1537 in Germany published his 95 Theses for direct guidance of Christians without an intermediate hierarchy, is the breakthrough or maturation of Christianity. The breakthrough of Protestantism is the second quantum leap in the development of man originated by agriculture forming the Younger Stone Age.

Figure 3. Picture HS1. "Doctor and Patient" by Hiltrud Schinzel

3 Empirical Science

The Renaissance was a glowing period of European cultural, artistic, political, and economic `rebirth` following the Middle Ages. It originated in the 14th century rediscovering classical philosophy, literature and art. Some of the greatest thinkers, authors, statesmen, scientists, and artists in human history thrived during this era, opening up new lands and cultures to European commerce.

The Renaissance is credited with bridging the gap between the Middle Ages and modern-day civilization. In the Antique (4th Century B.C.) Aristotle discovered that looking out in the world all objects above the Moon had a regular predictable movement while all objects on the Earth below the Moon seem to move rather disorderly. Aristotle advanced his Geocentric world to install Cosmic order on Earth. Aristotle explains all movements on Earth by the basic elements which he identifies as land, water, fire and air. For this purpose, Aristotle devoted most of his life to the natural sciences, contributing with original observations and classifications to physics, astronomy, chemistry, zoology, etc.

The Renaissance interest in Aristotle inspired British Empiricism in the 17th Century to expand the understanding of the natural sciences with the notion that the understanding of nature depends not exclusively on nature itself but as well on the eyes that observe nature. Empiricists as Bacon and Hume showed that cognitive biases associated with tradition, emotional illusions, language and Temper influence human judgement very much. To prevent cognitive biases and failures, falsification of expectations (theories) before execution, is a must for good decision-making. Positivist science by falsification, has from the 18th Century experienced an unprecedented economic growth that since WWII is termed the 3rd Industrial Revolution. Positivist science rejects the classical logic with absolute contraindications and installs a new logic with 4 different outcomes, based on statistics, as shown in the Table 1, and further elaborated in Chapter 5.

Table 1. Options of positivist dialectics

Expectation	Supported by Data	Rejected by Data
True	**Business Plan**	*Experimental Failure*
False	*Theoretical Bias*	**Worst-case-alternative**

Positivist science rising the natural sciences including engineering, biology including healthcare and Economics, represent a third quantum leap in human economic development. Until recently, the progress in behavioral economics has been based on the paradigm of `bounded rationality` (BR) advanced by Simon 1955. BR has not the same positivist rooting as that of the natural sciences. However, combining neuroeconomics and the psychology of the “Big Five” feeds an Economic Psychology, identifying the Open-minded as a key person in the breakthrough of innovative goods and services due to the ability to “translate” innovations into a rationalist framework, see Figure 8 as elaborated in Chapter 1.

Figure 4. Neuroeconomic psychology

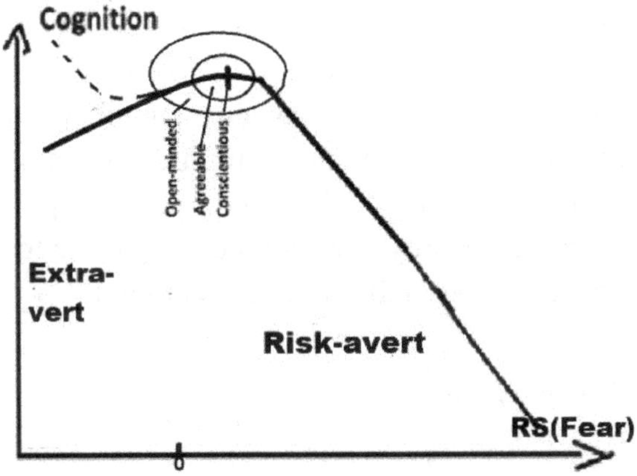

The founder of the market-based economic growth model, Adam Smith (1776), was himself a Scottish Protestant wicker. Figure 4 explains economic growth by invention of the plough in the Younger Stone Age. Before the plough, man could choose between producing 5 units of corn or 20 fish. With an optimal combination corresponding to E1. With the plough, man could redouble his harvest of corn to 10 units and reach the optimal product combination E2 with a far better overall level of satisfaction (from Utility level U2 to U3). This improves human survival to an extent that increased world population many fold and enabled construction of the Egyptian pyramids.

Figure 5. Simple economic growth

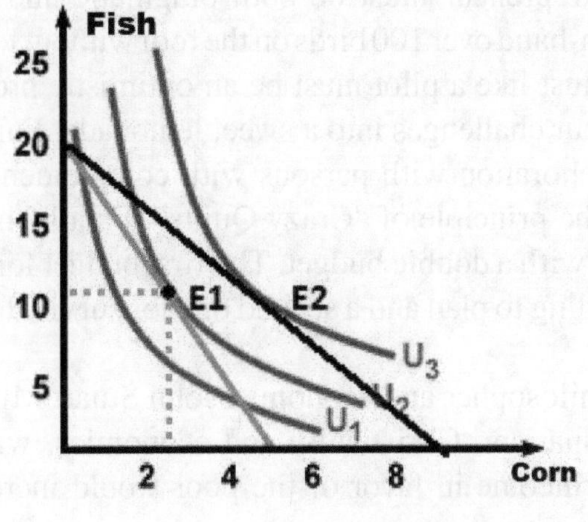

The level of economic growth is quantified as the Gross Domestic Product (GDP) per capita.

The liberalist market model has guided human economic development so far. The average income in the Industrialized world (G7), is now 15 times higher than in the Feudal rural village society. The liberal market economy represents a third quantum leap in human economic development representing the peak of the Renaissance. The special mindset of entrepreneurial pioneers is in accordance with Saraswathy explained by analogue to a Pilot-in-plane as illustrated in Figure 16 and elaborated in Chapter 1.

Figure 6. The modern entrepreneur

Firstly, an entrepreneur must be both pragmatic and visionary, giving priority to Bird-in-hand over 100 birds on the roof without losing his visionary target. Too, he must like a pilot must be an optimistic problem-solver with the gift to turn sour challenges into a sweet lemonade. Further, he must like a pilot seek collaboration with persons with complementary competences as expressed in the principle of "Crazy Quilts". Finally, he must secure the project economy with a double budget. The first budget for carrying through the project according to plan and a second one for survival of the worst-case-scenario.

The British philosopher and economist John Stuart Mill integrated 1861 in his book Utilinarism, Christianity and economics, with the thesis that redistribution of income in favor of the poor would increase total welfare due to the decreasing marginal utility of income illustrated in Figure P8 and in this way contribute to fulfilment of Christian values.

Figure 7. Definition of relative poverty

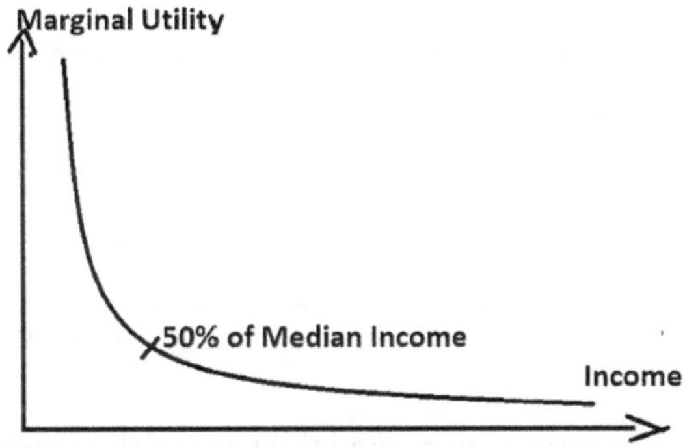

After WWII, a series of Nobel Laureates in Economics have recommended Universal Basic Income (UBI), as the best means of economic equalization. Entitlement, finance, and benefits from UBI, suspending poverty are investigated in Chapter 3. UBI is a realistic option in industrialized countries supporting human health in the bottom by social security and redistributing income to the benefit of the middle-class strengthening democracy. Moreover, UBI simplifies an over-complex public tax system.

Figure 8. Local markets

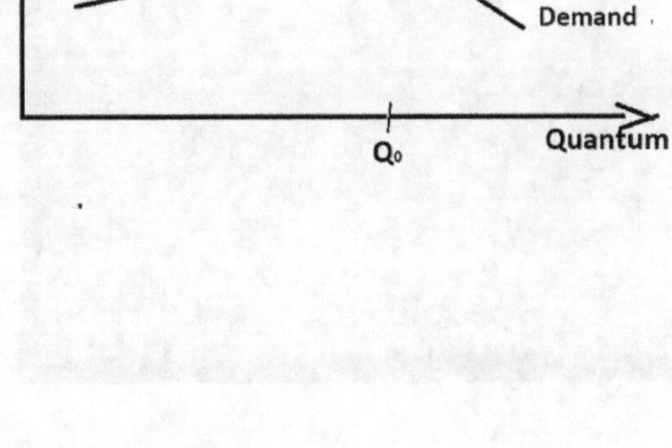

Figure 9. Globalized markets

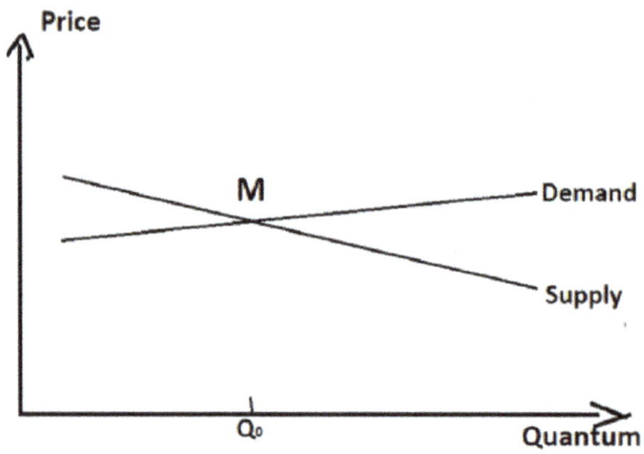

Since 1970, globalization has turned the laws of the market upside-down, as illustrated in the development from Figure 7 to 8. In local classical markets (Figure 7), profit is minimized by competition due to decreasing economies of scale as less productive resources, for instance less fertile land must be cultivated to meet increasing Demand. Globalization increases economies of scale (Figure 9) with excessive Monopolist gains (beyond M) as elaborated in Chapter 2 concluding a self-pension guide. The accumulation of monopolist gains since 1970 threatens today the subsistence of a large share of the middle-class in technologically advanced countries, for instance USA. So, UBI is no longer simply an idealist equalization endeavor, but a necessity for the low- and middle- income majority to counteract reinforcing monopolist gains by globalization.

Figure 10. Picture HS2. "The Machine" by Hiltrud Schinzel

Figure 11. Picture HS3. `Complementary Relationships` by Hiltrud Schinzel

The over-all mentality of Industrialization is illustrated as that of machines in Picture HS2.

4 Rise of The Creative Class

Ultrashort, the surface of the Hippie Culture originating in the 60s is peace, love and Rock'n'roll. Rock music is basically progressive, rhythmic, and explorative breaking fundamentally with the classic music tradition centering controlled expressions. The new free and happy lifestyle is a good appetizer for youngsters wherefore the Hippie Culture became the Culture of youth communities for instance around Festivals whereof that of Woodstock 1968 became iconic. A major motivation for the Hippies was the recognition that their parents lived a superficial alienated life without engagement in emerging international threats as the risk of nuclear confrontation between the superpowers USA and USSR and the emerging disruption of the environment.

The societal effect of the Hippie Culture manifests in the 21th Century, as the `Rise of the Creative Class`. So, the group of Open-minded people has risen from a minority of 10% through a dominant group of 40% of the adult population as documented by job classification statistics and elaborated in Chapter 1.1. This represents a sociodemographic change with implication for the democratic function beyond that of individual job functions.

In all, the youth criticism of the Grand Ma – culture of their parents represents a folkloristic protest towards the *Economic Fundamentalism* framed as Neoliberalism. A fourth quantum leap in human development with an incubation period nearly as long, as that of agriculture illustrated as complementary relationships in Picture HS3.

Figure 12. Tipping points by global warming

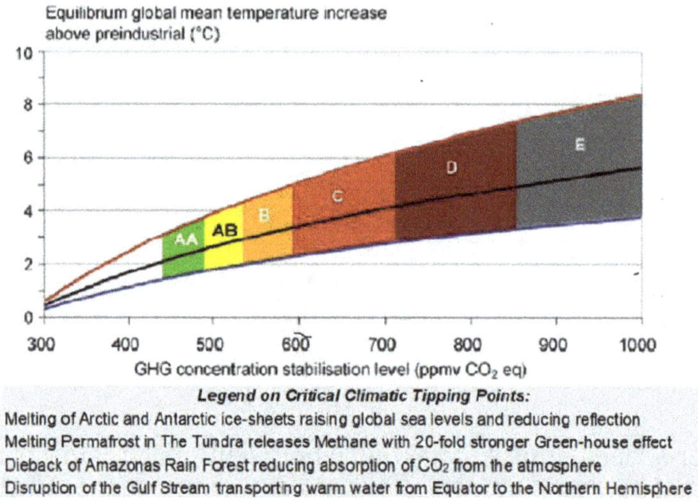

About 1.500 B.C., the Indo-European Vedas describe meditation as a pathway to reinforcing cognition, but meditation was known already at the time of construction of the Egyptian Pyramids 4.000 years B.C. The principle of cognitive reinforcement by meditation – as a key element of the Hippie Culture – is explained by neuroscience as minimization of fear responses. Sitting relaxed, quiet, and mentally passive, biological homeostasis releases stress and anxiety to the benefit of health and a slower and more deliberate thought process as demonstrated in more scientific trials. Chapter 6 reviews medical research and concludes a Health Technology Assessment (HTA).

5 GreenTec By Democratic Coalitions Across the Center

Since Meadows et al. published "Limits to Growth" 1972, ecologists have regularly warned about the catastrophic consequences of continued global warming. Today, the mechanism of global warming is documented by the Intergovernmental Panel on Climate Change (IPCC), see Figure 12. The crucial point is that global warming beyond 2°C, elicits a series of reinforcing warming changes, e.g. melting of Arctic ice, which have no point-of-return with catastrophic rising sea levels, long periods of droughts and frequent extreme weather. The crucial point of no return is about 450 ppmv CO2 eq in the atmosphere. The level before COVID-19 was 417 raising 3 ppmv per year.

The most effective economic intervention towards global warming is simply to make the polluter pay as humans respond to financial incentive. However, imposing new tariffs is extremely difficult to implement in democratic politics as it hits many people. Most economists agree that the best climate intervention is a Pigouvian Carbon Tax at the root of CO2-emission eq (ET) as elaborated in Chapter 4. The unique effectiveness of ET is that it immediately changes the price relations between production factors according to high respective low carbon emission. This gives a strong incentive to companies and entrepreneurs to restructure the composition of production factors towards carbon neutral production as documented by empirical research. Further, ET is simple to administer too, compared to specific political interventions towards a large variety of different end-user products with low consumer price elasticity. As stand-alone intervention, ET is estimated to substitute about 80% of contemporary CO2-emission. However, the political problems regarding accelerated transition to carbon neutrality are complex as known from research in social change.

Simple human conservatism is a challenge to all progress and not at least to global agreement on ET as any other important change. The most effective means to overcome this mental challenge is visible results within an accountable time horizon. The positive aspect is that the state of implementation of ET 2020 according to World Bank statistics is that 20% of the global CO2-emission is counteracted by a kind of ET. According to marketing experiences this level of penetration is close to a global breakthrough of ET.

More sophisticated resistance to change can be verbalized as a creed in continued liberalist entrepreneurial ingenuity or compassion with the poor segment of society. However, none of these verbalizations are supported by independent science. Neither is a non-fossil technological shortcut on the doorstep nor need ET to hit the lowest incomes. A second-best alternative to ET as broad subsidies to non-fossil infant-industries as wind and sun is neither recommendable because the transition effect is much weaker. Such subsidies are useful to accelerate the development of new fuels for air- and sea transport where non-fossil energy alternatives still are from being competitive.

Figure 13 shows the spectrum of economic ideologies from social liberalism across green center-parties to social democrats that represents a population majority in most industrialized democracies except the US. A center-coalition can agree on ET as a hybrid that combines liberalist entrepreneurial ingenuity with social responsible policies. The rising probability of this new complementary position on democratic political opposites, relies on the historical improvement in human creativity over 10.000 years by qualitative factors as simple agriculture, Christian equality, cognitive falsification integrated with entrepreneurship.

Figure 13. Post-industrial spectrum of complementary economic-political ideologies

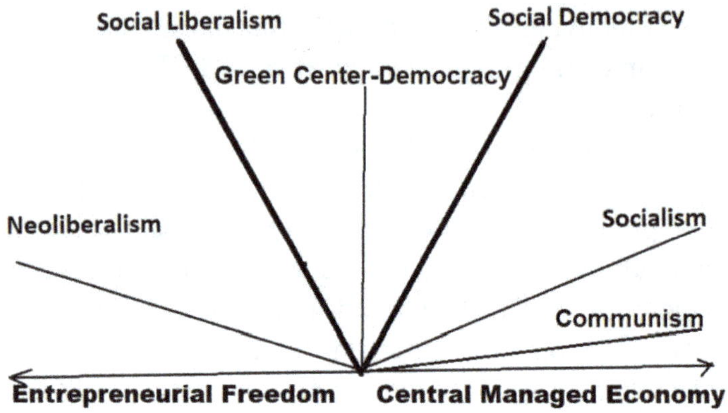

Center-oriented democratic collaboration, based on a logic of long-term complementarities on challenges facilitated by rising political influence of the creative class, is the potential fifth and final quantum leap towards implementation of Homo Sapiens Creatus as illustrated in picture HS4.

Figure 14. Picture HS4. `Janus Head` by Hiltrud Schinzel

A key global player towards carbon neutrality in the coming years are definitely China followed by more steps behind India and the EU. These Top players are dedicated to implement the Paris Agreement and the new Biden Administration in the US re-enters the Paris Agreement 2021. A relevant criticism of any cautious optimism is that leading Asian economies do not share the Western tradition of Christian striving for the Common Good. China for example, is not a Western-like representative democracy, but a socialist market economy ruled by a Top managed communist party and the Chinese tradition of Confucianism implicates respect for authorities.

Table 2. Modules of pluralist doughnut economics

Unit	Scope	
	Local	**Global**
Individual	**Business Economics** (Chapter 1-2) **1**	**Economic Ecology** **2b** (Chapter 4)
Social	**Welfare Economy** (Chapter 3) **2a**	**Human Resource Development** **3** (Chapter 5-6)

ULTRASHORT READER GUIDE

A biological approach to economic history identifies 4 quantum leaps in the development from Homo sapiens sapiens towards an optional Homo sapiens creatus (Creative man). The fate of Homo sapiens sapiens seems to be decided by the fifth quantum leap expecting stronger social-liberal democratic coalition across the center. The structure of *Pluralist Doughnut Economics* is summarized in Table 2 showing 3 modules to study in accordance with individual preference:

1 Business Economics deals with almost all the problems of the manager
2 Doughnut Economics (inspired by Raworth (2017) that expands the scope to include both `Social Foundation` (Welfare Economy) and `Ecological Ceiling` (Economic Ecology)
3 HRD serves people making up the workforce of an organization, business sector, industry, or economy. A narrower concept is human capital, the knowledge which individuals embody.

Similar terms include manpower, labor, personnel, associates or simply people.

Table 3. Example of productivity per man per year (Euro)

Goods	UK	DK
Steel	300	200
Bacon	200	300
Total production: without trade with free trade	500 600	500 600

INTRODUCTION

1 Classical Economics and the Modern Criticism

The origin of economics is visionary! The Scottish professor Adam Smith noticed that new technical inventions as the "Spinning Jenny" in the making of clothes and the `Steam Engine` to power machines in mines, manufacturing and transport (railways) revolutionized production options! For the Protestant wicker Adam Smith, this inspired a new vision of easing the material conditions of life for ordinary people by technological progress as it was already the case for well-off persons with servants. 1776 Smith edited his vision in `Inquiry into the Nature and Causes of the Wealth of Nations` (Smith, 1776). The term economics – rooted in the Greek word for household – was established in the late 19th century, primarily due to Political Economy to `Economics` as a shorter term for an `economic science` that must be independent of special interests unless the specific interest is clearly specified (Marshall, 1890). Economics focuses on the behavior and interactions of economic agents regarding production, consumption, distribution and finance of scarce goods:

- Microeconomics analyzes basic elements in the economy, including individual agents and markets, their interactions, and outcomes. Individual agents include in general households buying goods and services and firms producing and selling goods and services
- Macroeconomics analyzes the economy as an aggregated system where firms, households and public institutions interact with financial institutions on saving and investment. Macroeconomic elements are: income, labor market, capital market, currency, inflation, economic growth, and public policies that have impact on these elements.

An early theory of economic growth advances the principle of *comparative advantage under free trade* as illustrated in Table 3 (Ricardo, 1807).

Figure 15. Economic Rationality as Maximization of Utility
Note: *Curves are indifference levels (U) in the consumption of Corn and Bacon while Budget lines indicate the substitution of in production at market prices. Feudal peasants can rise satisfaction from U_1 to U_2 with the best possible distribution between Corn and Bacon. Supposing farmers become independent they can redouble productivity Corn from 5 to 10 units by individual planning raising satisfaction from E1 to E2.*

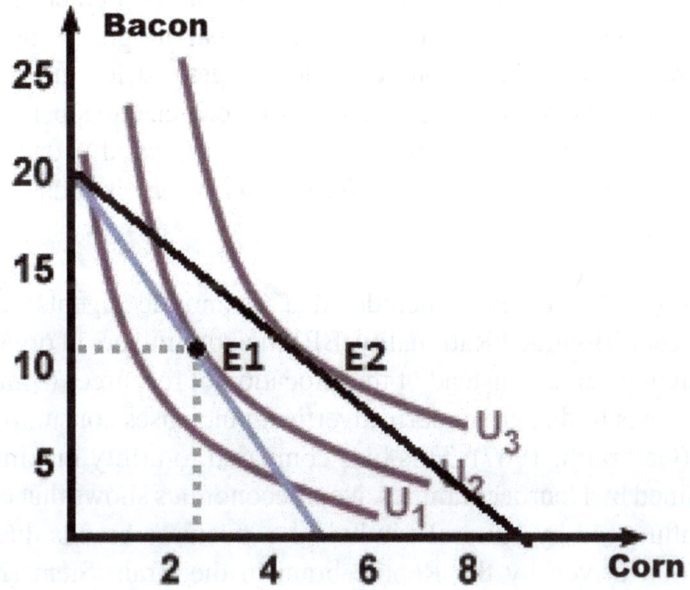

Suppose Denmark and the UK are in a state of no mutual trade and equal wages to all workers internally as well as across countries. Then the countries agree on free mutual trade. In the state of free trade both countries gain 20% in productivity according production in accordance with their respective comparative advantage and abandoning the less productive branch:

- UK can increase total production from 500 to 600 specializing in steel – a 20% gain
- DK can also increase total production from 500 to 600 specializing in bacon – a 20% gain, too

This simple prototype of the comparative advantage of globalized free trade explains the rise of productivity and income in the industrialized world. The original formulation of the principle of comparative advantage in trading was generalized for international trade by the Swedish economist team Heckscher-Ohlin and awarded with the Nobel Prize 1977. However, the essence of this basic trade principle is still that of *comparative advantage*. The global assumption by the principle of *comparative advantage* of free trade is, that rational decision-making means *maximization of individual utility* in all aspects of production, trade and consumption. Figure 1 illustrates the simple paradigm of individual maximization of utility in the relative consumption of scarce economic goods e.g. corn and bacon. Economics predicts the outcome of all kinds of decisions on scarce resources as that of optimal integration of emotion (*Preferences*) and resources under budget restriction (*Rationality*).

Since WWII, the Western culture has been criticized as parted between Humanities and Natural Sciences (Snow, 1958). The validity of the classical economic rationality-paradigm (*Utility maximization*) is today challenged from more angles:

- Sociological studies conclude that economic agents are rather satisficers (Bounded Rationality, BR) than optimizers in organizations, optimizing careers instead of the allocation of resources (Simon, 1958)
- Economics finds that modern advertising increases consumption about 20% (Galbraith, 1967). This bias compared to utility maximization is explained by Neuroeconomics. Neuroeconomics shows that consumers are influenced by cultural symbols e.g. business brands due to status imitation driven by the Reptile brain in the Brain Stem (Erk et al., 2002)
- Economic studies of American top-managers show too that complacency is an important source of basic cognitive errors. This fallacy is today explained by Neuroeconomics as rooted in dominance of the left Hemisphere far from classical economic utility maximization (Goel, 2006)
- Psychologists claim the role of anxiety in economic decision-making especially in times of economic crisis. This criticism claims broader fear-based loss aversion related to the individual loss history (Kahneman & Tversky, 1979)

Due to this criticism, behavioral economics (BE) was presented as a pluralistic research program. In the 60's, BE was organized around four groups of economists situated respectively at Carnegie, Michigan, Oxford and Stirling universities and united by their shared willingness to redirect economics towards new research directions. BE has turned disciplinary economics heterodox in the sense that mainstream economics as taught by most universities, recognizes limitations and fallacies in the paradigm of economic rationality wherefore non-orthodox contributions to economics as socialism are welcomed, too (Sent, 2005). Other attempts to renew BE are reviewed . A special review of the criticism of paradigmatic economic rationality proposes "Nudging as a new social relationship. Nudging is based on the *libertarian paternalism* that elbowing a kind way as an alternative to simple emotional kindness helps to improve rational decision-making at the level of ordinary people without clarifying what rationality is (Thaler, 2008). In all, this shows an admirable professional tolerance among economists. However, it is a crucial weakening of the prognostic value of BE for economic agents needing to preview the economic consequences of their choices before action.

A novel study clarifies the issue of `Pluralist Economics` (Graebner & Strunk, 2020). Already, Economics can claim pluralism in the object of study. However, the research methods applied must fulfil the criteria of positivist science which is a problem regarding behavior that so far has been based on subjective interpretations. In order to solve this dilemma a Neuroeconomic Psychology is presented in Chapter 1 with reference to an early idea (Davis, 2006).

2 The Doughnut as an Expanded Scope of Economics

Besides the weakening of simple economic rationality (Figure 15), Economics is also accused of considering the Ecosystem as an externality that requires political action outside the scope of economics. A novel expanded scope of economics, based on 7 principles, is presented as "Doughnut Economics" (DE), see Figure 2 (Raworth, 2017):

1. Change the goal of economics from GDP growth to the inner-outer balance of the Doughnut
2. See the big picture expanding the scope from self-contained markets to the embedded economy
3. Nurture human nature and develop from rational economic man to social adaptable humans
4. Get savvy with systems and develop from mechanical equilibrium to dynamic complexity
5. Design goods to be distributed away from 'growth will even it up again' to distributive by design
6. Create to recirculate materials from 'growth will clean it up again' to regenerative by design

7. Be Agnostic about Growth changing attitude from growth-addicted to growth-agnostic

Figure 16. Doughnut economics, Illustration by Hiltrud Schinzel
Legend: *A Doughnut is something you eat as a strong association to the Object of Economics. Economics must expand the scope to include Both the "Ecological Ceiling" and the "Social Foundation"*

Ad Guideline 1: From Liberalist Market Growth towards Sustainable Development

Radical expansion is required of the scope of economics from liberal economic growth in Gross Domestic Production (GDP) to an embedded positivist discipline with crucial borderlines (Figure 16):

- Social Foundation in relation to economics is studied in behavioral economics, see Chapter 1
- Ecological Ceiling specific to economics is studied in Economic Ecology, see Chapter 4

Ad Guideline 2: The Overall Purpose of Economic Development

The introductory `Plain Language Summary` is an ultrashort economic history from the Elder Stone Age until today. This historical approach identifies implementation of `Creative Man` as the ultimate goal of Economics.

Ad Guideline 3 and 7: Neuroeconomic Psychology for Social Adaptability

The expanded scope of Economics requires stronger economic-political planning, but how should that be accomplished? Raworth argues that the urbanization associated with industrialization by itself increases human interaction, interdependence, and reciprocity. This appears as the critical point against DE as mainstream economics considers the presupposition of such extra social adaptability as a line of wishful thinking without justification in BE. From this critical point of view, DE appears as a modernist version of the type of new human-relations management that was expected to bring extra economic growth in the 60s but showed up to fail in the 70s. However, in support of DE, the Florida thesis on "Rise of the Creative Class" implicates stronger cognitive collaboration on the level of society, too (Florida, 2012). Recent neuroeconomic research explains how the rise of the creative class by changes in the distribution of the `Big Five` Taxonomy improves social adaptability (Larsen, 2019). So, Chapter 1 presents a novel pluralist BE that radically changes consumer and producer behavior as well as the understanding of democratic voter preferences.

Further, Raworth calls a new generation of Agnostic economists to strengthen adaptability. An agnostic is according to the Greek tradition a person, who believes that the existence of a greater power, such as a god, cannot be proven or disproved. Therefore, an agnostic wallows in the complexity of the existence of higher beings. The gnostic fallacy is explained by neuroeconomics as that of Left Hemispheric dominance of cognition (Goel et al., 2006). Early, a study identified cognitive fallacy as due to *complacency* in American Post-War Top-Management (Galbraith, 1967).

Ad Guideline 4: From Simple to Systemic Logic

Classical Economics, as illustrated in Figure 1, is simple enough to be explained in plain language by simple (linear) cause and effect. The

Neoclassical modification to BR has enabled widespread use of complex econometric models to forecast the outcome of economic transactions regarding production, consommation, distribution and finance. Even the most prominent econometric models to guide macroeconomic stabilization of business cycles are basic linear. However, the ecological crisis requires coordinated macroeconomic adaptation to the conditions of the Ecosystem. This implicates a rapid transition from the present `linear` model of liberalist market growth to that of a `circular` economic model with recirculation of materials and non-fossil energy sources. In all ways, this means much stronger long-term economic-political interference with the market sector than that of short-term recovery from business recessions. This new way of managing macroeconomics is based on cybernetics which is rooted in Greek and means *First mate* (Wiener, 1948). The *First Mate* sets the goal onboard a sail ship, see Figure 17.

Figure 17. Qualitative growth in living systems
Note: *The growth of human species follows a universal pattern where a growth phase is incubated some time in advance. For instance was the invention of Stone Age tools prepared in many thousand of years before it within a relative short time span enabled an increase in global population from 3 to 100 million*

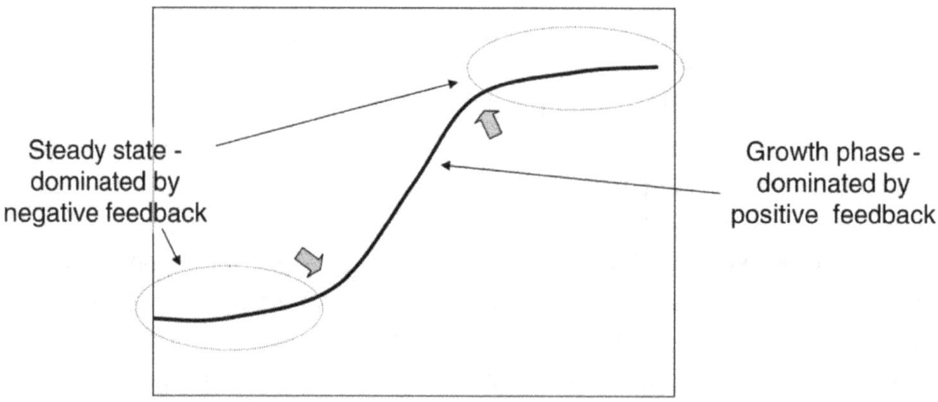

The development of fiscal policy after WWII aims to stabilize recurrent business cycles in Neoliberalist market economies (Keynes, 1936). So, Macroeconomics represents a transitional state between mechanical and cybernetic systems, as the target is limited to stabilization of the market economy presupposing special macroeconomic laws, for example multiplicator effects. The general principles of cybernetic development demands strong positive feedback from the target area. This is online with the experience that the adoption of Keynes fiscal policy required an extraordinary optimism as demonstrated by the winning side after WW2.

The methodological key to implementation of DE is on this background democratic acceptance of the relevant macroeconomic interventions at the new cybernetic peak. The new enlarged cybernetic macroeconomic targets are:

1. Social cohesion whereof the Pluralist Behavioral Economics is developed in Chapter 1 while the Socioeconomic Welfare Economics is elaborated in Chapter 3
2. Ecological sustainability where Economic Ecology is crucial is elaborated in Chapter 4

Ad Guideline 5-6: Ecodesign for Advancement of Circular Economy

Most modern products contribute to CO_2-emission driving global warming as the Top threat to continued economic growth. Redesign of products with a view on carbon neutrality has more bottom-up tracks to complement the top-down effect of cybernetic macroeconomics. However, the relative prices of production factors set narrow boundaries for bottom-up Eco-design of most market products outside the fashion-industry.

3 Doughnut and Market Economics

DE claims to present a comprehensive view on Economics. How does the expanded view interfere with fundamental principles of market function? The first Textbook in Economics appeared 100 years after Smith in Principles of Economics (Marshall, 1890). Marshall recognizes that market economy is associated with competition and award of self-interest which challenges Christian morality. However, the essence of market economy is not religious values but the cognitive ability to respect the logic of the market for the higher goal of economic growth for ordinary people. The following 5 typical behavioral `Laws of the Market` express a pragmatic common-sense on market transactions (James, 1907) adopting Doughnut Economics:

1 Opportunity Costs

The world has unlimited wants but limited means, wherefore a choice must be made. Economic agents must give up one thing to have another which requires ex ante calculation of value and cost of both alternatives to find out which option is most beneficial. In this process "Sunk Costs" from previous activity is without significance. Economics is per se pragmatic forward looking!

For example, the world has a limited beef supply. There are only that much cattle that farmers can raise in any given year, but where that beef goes is not to be foreseen. It can be turned into ground beef and mass-marketed in supermarkets or It can be put in Slim Jims and other beef jerky products. It can be transformed into beef broth and canned or sent to a local butcher. That many different beef products can be made but still there is only a limited amount of beef, so, how to decide which one is the best. In a market economy everyone is expected to choose the cheapest option to buy and the highest price for sale.

The law of opportunity cost is still valid in DE on both the consumer and the corporate levels. However, the distinction between private and social costa is crucial. In DE, the use of social costs including eventual costs to the environment is mandatory as the environment is internalized in contrast to the externalization in mainstream economics. However, economic pragmatism implies that private decision-makers cannot be expected to include negative social costs, for instance CO2-emission, in their private transactions. It requires political legislation to ensure that social costs are included in private market transactions. Chapter 4 focuses on the social costs of pollution, especially in the format of global heating.

2 Marginalism

Marginal or additive, rather than categorical changes, are basic and dealt with every single day when running a business. You increase the level of an activity as long its marginal benefit exceeds its marginal cost. In other words, it is not a wise business decision to spend more money than you are taking in if you do not have an overarching plan for profitability. You might spend three years with startup costs and rely heavily on investors, but no one is willing to invest, if they do not see a pathway towards some Return-of-investment (ROI).

Say you run a doughnut shop. The flour, sugar, eggs and butter you put into the doughnuts cost around $.10 per doughnut. You sell each doughnut for $1.50. That is a huge profit, so it seems like the marginal benefits do outweigh the costs. Unfortunately, your store has poor ratings and you barely have any customers. Your rent starts to pile up, and even though your doughnuts themselves are profitable, the marginal benefit does *not* end up exceeding the costs. You ultimately shutter your business. That is the marginal principle in its most cruel form.

A prototype example is when a store may choose to keep expanding their business as long as they see increased revenue. When a company sees the revenue has started to drastically shrink, it will in turn, scale down or close altogether. The classical marginalism applies to DE as well.

3 Declining Marginal Consumer Utility

The general mainstream law of diminishing returns is in DE limited to that of declining marginal consumer utility. In modern economics, the classical assumption of declining returns in production is replaced by modern experiences of increasing economies of scale by globalization as elaborated in Chapter 2.

The law of declining marginal utility applies more than ever to consumer behavior as elaborated in Chapter 1. When you have consumed a certain amount of a nutrition good, extra consumption has a declining marginal utility, for instance in the form of overweight.

4 Real – Not Nominal - Value

The real/nominal principle is one of the fundamentals of economics. Basically, it states that people are not interested in the face (nominal) value of money. They are interested in the actual (real) value of money. The real value is how much goods money can buy and how much money is actual worth in the scheme of real consumer options. This is specifically important when people must decide whether to buy or rent a dwelling. Owning your dwelling may have large expenses in the early years but lower expenses in the long run.

To find the best choice of dwelling in accordance with the real value principle, it is necessary to have a minimal competence in financial calculation of compounded interest. A simple case requiring financial calculation is comparison of payments at different points of time. The Real/nominal principle applies in the same way in Doughnut and mainstream economy.

5 Legislative Protection against Monopolist Exploitation

Already at the end of the 19th Century it became clear that a typical failure of liberal market economy is that of development of monopolistic markets where a single or a small group of suppliers are capable of distorting the normal market regulation of ROI or profit. If this case was an exception during the First Industrial Revolution, it has become the normal case during the ongoing Fourth Industrial Revolution with extremely globalized digital technology and even Artificial Intelligence (AI). In the globalized economy, systemic national accountancy with multinational companies (MNC) and active redistribution policies, are developed in Chapter 3.

For example, in international trade each country has products they specialize in. Taiwan is a huge manufacturer of microchips. American companies buy these chips to make computers. These computers can then be sold back to Taiwanese consumers. Basically, we import the products we do not specialize in and sell off the ones we do. Sometimes, things are deeply intertwined. The core is that such exchange is voluntary and not imposed due to illegal exploitation of monopolization.

DE values current protection against monopolistic exploitation as fundamental and recommends that established corporate ROI is complemented by formal targets of employee rights and environmental protection along the lines administered by B-lab for B-corporations as elaborated in Chapter 1.

4 A Model of Pluralist Doughnut Economics

The expanded scope of DE, modern research in pluralist behavioral economics as well as elements maintained and modified from mainstream economics frame *Pluralist Doughnut Economics*. It is structured in 3 modules within 6 Chapters as shown in Table 4

Table 4. Modules of pluralist doughnut economics (PDE)

Unit	Scope	
	Local	Global
Individual	**Business Economics** (Chapter 1-2) **1**	**Economic Ecology** **2b** (Chapter 4)
Social	**Welfare Economy** (Chapter 3) **2a**	**Human Resource Development** **3** (Chapter 5-6)

The modules 1 *Business Economics* and 2 *Doughnut Economics* are basic. Besides, module 3 *Human Resource Development (HRD)* focuses the unfoldment of human abilities in a neurobiological framework as DE Guideline 2. Chapter 5 reviews tools for *Positivist Dialectics* as the central methodology of Economics, while Chapter 6 focuses tools for Stressmanagement.

Compared to mainstream economics PDE requires a much stronger political regulation of the economy than ever seen in liberalist market economies to overcome evidenced market failures. In this way PDE represents a post-Keynes approach beyond simple stabilization policies demanding effective implementation of long-term structural changes in both 1) Distribution of income and 2) Protection of the environment. This requires a methodological transition from stochastic to cybernetic systems in Socioeconomic planning with a solid rooting in empirical science.

In all, the Textbook presents PDE as the core knowledge base on Economics for mutual communication of economics between decision-makers at all societal levels: private households, managers in both private and public enterprises as well as both local and national politicians.

Explain the Figures

Figure 18.

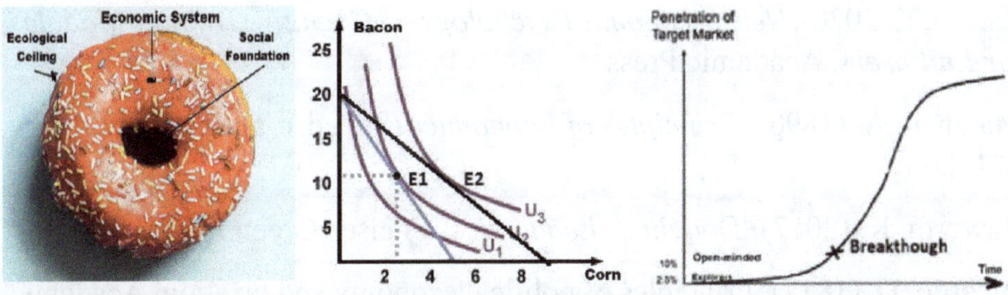

Doughnut Economics **Classical Growth Model** **Qualitative Growth**

REFERENCES

Davis, J. B. (2006). The Turn in Economics: Neoclassical Dominance to Mainstream Pluralism. *Journal of Institutional Economics*, *2*(1), 1–20. doi:10.1017/S1744137405000263

Erk, S., Spitzer, M., Wunderlich, A. P., Galley, L., & Walter, H. (2002). Cultural Objects modulate reward circuitry. *Neureport*, *13*(18), 2499–2503. doi:10.1097/00001756-200212200-00024

Florida, R. (2012). *The Rise of the Creative Class-Revisited: 10th Anniversary Edition*. Basic Books.

Galbraith, G. (1967). *The New Industrial State*. Houghton Mifflin.

Goel, V., Tierney, M., & Sheesley, L. (2006). Hemispheric Specialization in Human Prefrontal Cortex for Resolving Certain and Uncertain Inferences. *Cerebral Cortex (New York, N.Y.)*. Advance online publication.

Gräbner, C., & Strunk, B. (2020). Pluralism in economics: Its critiques and their lessons. *Journal of Economic Methodology*, *27*(4), 311–329. doi:10.1080/1350178X.2020.1824076

James, W. (1907). *Pragmatism's Conception of Truth. Lecture 6 in Pragmatism: A New Name for Some Old Ways of Thinking*. Longman Green and Co. doi:10.1037/10851-000

Kahneman, D., & Tversky, A. (1979). Prospect Theory: an analysis of decision under risk. *Economet*, 263-91.

Keynes, J. M. (1936). *The General Theory of Employment, Interest and Money*. Palgrave MacMillan.

Larsen, T. (2020). *Neuroeconomic Psychology – 3 Cognitive Training Modules for End-users*. Academic Press.

Marshall, A. (1890). *Principles of Economics* (8th ed.). The Online Library of Liberty.

Raworth, K. (2017). *Doughnut Economics*. Chelsea Green Publishing.

Ricardo, D. (1817). Principles of political economy and taxation. Academic Press.

Sent, E. M. (2005). Behavioral economics: How psychology made its (limited) way back into economics. *History of Political Economy*, *36*(4), 735–760. doi:10.1215/00182702-36-4-735

Simon, H. (1957). *A Behavioral Model of Rational Choice in Models of Man, Social and Rational: Mathematical Essays on Rational Human Behavior in a Social Setting*. Wiley.

Smith, A. (1776). *Inquiry into the Nature and Causes of the Wealth of Nations*. doi:10.1093/oseo/instance.00043218

Snow, C. P. (1959). *The Two Cultures and the Scientific Revolution*. Rede Lecture.

Thaler, R., & Sunstein, C. (2008). *Nudge*. Penguin Books.

Wiener, N. (1948). *Cybernetics Or Control and Communication in the Animal and the Machine*. MIT Pr.

Section 1
Business Economics

Chapter 1
Pluralist Behavioral Economics

ABSTRACT

Open-minded is identified as an economic key quality in the 21st century due to special abilities in the dissemination of innovations. The impact of dissemination is increasing due to the rise of the creative class including the open-minded. The long-term consumer profile—the most open-minded state of cognition—is identified as simple living contrasting consumerism. The modern prototype of an entrepreneur is "pilot-in-plane" à la Saraswathy, who fits best to the open-mindedness personality. Open-minded entrepreneurs strive for revenue of capital (ROI). A simple ROI formula is presented for business check by entrepreneurs. In all, four heuristics are presented for the doughnut agent. The chapter is complemented by a portrait of the serial entrepreneur Martin Thorborg and a minireview of the author and specialist of "Simple Living" Ole D. Nielsen.

DOI: 10.4018/978-1-7998-6424-0.ch001

INTRODUCTION

The Scope of business economics is almost all the economic problems of the manager.

Chapter 1 Pluralist Behavioral Economics is based on integration of Neuroeconomics and `Big Five` psychology into Neuroeconomic Psychology (NeP).

NeP identifies a broad set of positivist guides of business behavior respectively as

- Consumer 1.2
- Specialist in any occupation 1.3
- Democratic Voters 1.4

Chapter 2 From Local to Globalized Markets explains laws of the market at both the local 2.1 and the global 2.2 levels. An outlook on the globalized economy 4.3 peaks with an individual guide to pension investments.

Finally, a SWOT-analysis of Market Economics 4.4 points towards Part 2 Doughnut Economics.

1.1 NEUROECONOMIC PSYCHOLOGY

1.1.1 Neuroeconomics and the `Big Five` Psychology

With the new Millennium new hypersensitive brain scanners have appeared. Combining the new scanner technology with the solution of economic tasks gives rise to the new discipline Neuroeconomics that in plain language enables an objective `Mind Reading` as alternative to verbal questioning on economic motives as further elaborated in Appendix to Chapter 5.

A review of Neuroeconomics concludes a neuroeconomic model of economic decision-making (Larsen, 2017). The dynamics of cognitive integration is tripartite as illustrated in Figure 2. The X-axis represents the ambivalent state of passion as internally inhibited by fear which is represented by the Autonomic Nervous System (ANS). The Y-axis represents Cognition as indicated by the degree of Lateralization (Hemispheric asymmetry in the EEG). The basic parameter of economic decision-making is the typical resting position on the integration curve that represents individual Temper or `Risk-aversion`. Neuroeconomic trials on Complex (Intertemporal) respective Explorative choices show that the best cognitive integration is accomplished for a moderate autonomic arousal of ANS. In this way Risk-willingness or Temper is a basic economic decision-making parameter.

"Willingness to take risks in general" or the reciprocal to Risk-aversion is studied in a representative survey on 'risk attitudes' with 20,000 respondents (2Dohmen et al., 2012). A simple personal question on 'General risk attitude' is answered on a scale from 0 through 10 giving a good explanation of individual performance. The correlation for a on important life domains are: 1) Car driving (r=0.49), 2) Financial matters (r=0.50), 3) Careers (r=0.61), 4) Sports/leisure (r=0.56), and 5) Health (r=0.48). The Dohmen-scale has an average of 4.4 with SD=2.25. More factors affect the 'General risk willingness', however, the single far most important factor is gender as females are moderately more risk-averse than males (Average: Male=5 and Female=4). The wiring of the brain shows gender differences in the way that males have strong Frontal-Posterior connections which promote stringent logical thinking while females have better interhemispheric connections promoting collaborative and balanced thinking.

Figure 1. Neuroeconomic Model of Economic Choices
Legend: *The cognitive Peak is evidenced by:*
1 Intertemporal Choices demonstrate dominance of risk-aversion with low cognition.
2 Explorative choices demonstrate dominance of passion.

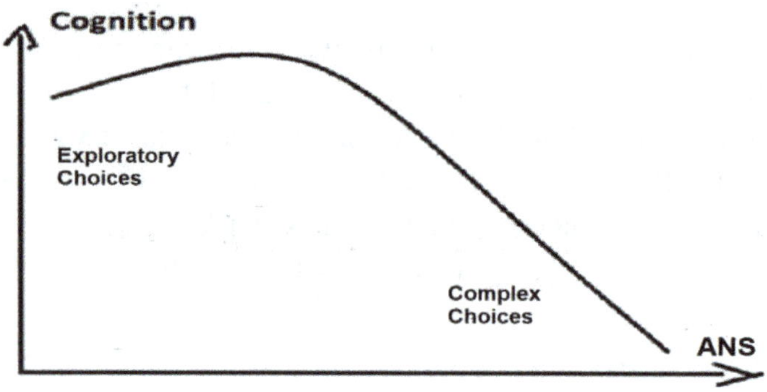

Behavioral psychology identifies five different groups of personality ('Big Five') by statistical correlation studies (Goldberg, 1993). Originally, the theory of 'Big Five' was advanced by two Air Force psychologists, who published a technical report in 1961 which was very little known among psychologists until the 80s. 1993 Goldberg published a multifactor statistical correlation study which confirmed the 'Big Five' as the common denominators of five groups of statistical related personality characteristics, see Figure 3.

Figure 2. `Big Five` Personality Traits
Note: *The psychological term `Neuroticism` is replaced by `Risk-averse` in Economics.*

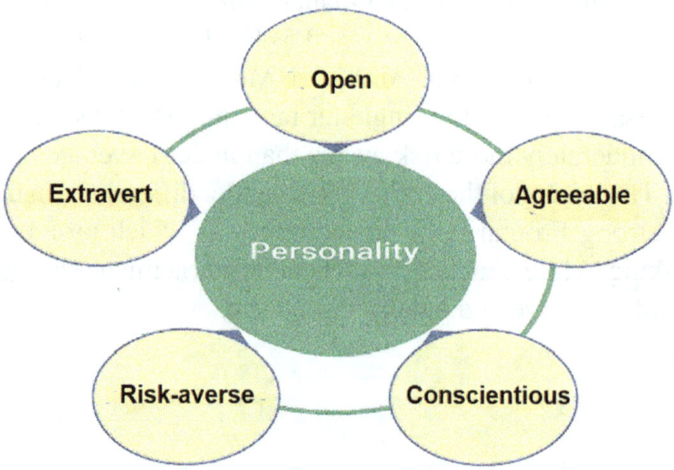

The relation between 'Risk Willingness' and the 'Big Five' is investigated in a correlation study (Becker et al., 2012). The overall conclusion is that there is a positive correlation between risk willingness and personality traits as extraversion and open-mindedness and on the other side a negative correlation between risk-willingness and personality traits as agreeable/ conscientious and pragmatism. The general of Neuroeconomic Psychology is presented with five different behavioral profiles (whereof three in the center) and ordered in accordance with the correlation-study, see Figure 4. As it covers all the normal psychological profiles, it represents a pluralist approach to behavioral economics.

Figure 3. Neuroeconomic Psychology
Source: *Larsen 2019: Neuroeconomic Psychology.*
Legend: *Neuroeconomic Psychology orders the 'Big Five' by Risk-willingness:*
1 Extraverts are definite the most Risk-willing known as Risk-lover in Economics
2 Risk-averters (Neuroticism in APA) are also well-known in Economics
3 The center group divides in 3 according to flexibility:
Open-minded are the most flexible
Conscientious are the least inflexible
In between, Agreeable are somewhat flexible in personal relations

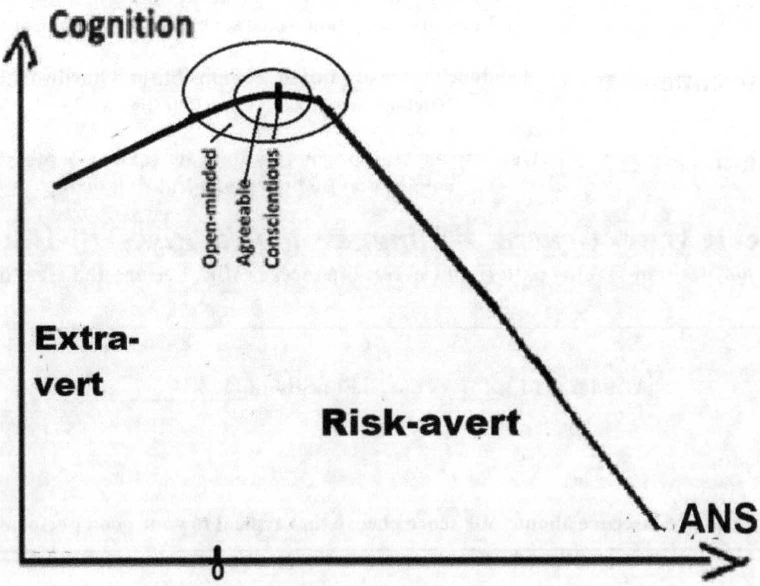

The relation between psychometrics by the Dohmen-scale and sensitivity to the 'Big Five' is complementary rather than parallel. The Dohmen-scale is useful for quick identification of extreme Tempers in either the negative or the positive spectrum. Based on the skewness of the distribution of risk-preferences <3 indicate a risk-averse personality while scores >6 indicate a risk-willing personality. Center-oriented scores between the poles (3 through 6) indicate classical rationalists (Conscientious and Agreeables). The level of Risk-willingness (X-axis) associated with peak cognition is rather risk-neutral and deviations from the center implicate reinforcing emotional biases in the format of either over-optimism or risk-aversion in accordance with the Prospect theory (Kahneman, 2003).

Figure 4. Heuristic 1 for Profiling

Which of these Groups do you resemble the most?	
Extravert ◻	**Seek stimulation in the company of others and talkativeness** **Outgoing/energetic vs. solitary/reserved!**
Open-minded ◻	**Open to new aesthetic, cultural and intellectual experiences** **Inventive/curious vs. consistent/cautious**
Agreeable ◻	**Tendency to act in a cooperative, unselfish manner** **Friendly/compassionate vs. challenging/detached**
Conscientious ◻	**Tendency to be organized, responsible and hardworking** **Efficient/organized vs. easy-going/careless**
Risk-avert ◻	**Get easy unpleasant emotions (anger, anxiety, depression, vulnerable) Bad psychological well-being**

Indicate your *´General Willingness to take Risks`* (0-10):
(Your decision-making pattern in Career, Finance, Traffic, Leisure and Health)

1 2 3 4 5 6 7 8 9 10

Age:____ Gender (M/F):____ Education: ____________

Comment:

Note: If you are insecure about your score choose that typical to your good performance

The identification of the Open-minded is the most difficult in practice because this type belongs both to the center (Agreeables) and the positive pole (Extraverts). However, social skills to identify different psychological profiles must become a standard competence for future economic agents. Print Heuristic Profiler and try-and-error your psychological sensitivity among friends/colleagues/contacts. When you have applied the Heuristic Profiler to yourself and a dozen other people you know much more about your own profile and sensitivity to that of other persons.

Qualification of the social significance of the new Pluralist Behavioral Economics is demonstrated in a study of students in different Academic Majors using the `Big Five` Taxonomy (Vedel, 2016). Academic Majors divide historically in the natural sciences, for instance physics, chemistry and the Humanities (theology and language). Social science has developed in between the classical Majors from the beginning of the 19th Century. The psychological differences across Majors are often moderate (about 0.5 standard deviation), but especially open-mindedness differentiates strongly among Majors. It is a strong support of the neuroeconomic psychology model that open-minded, the theoretical most flexible personality, also is the most representative to students of Majors. Further data analysis indicates that the differences primarily are due individual temper and only secondarily affected by socialization. Relevant findings are:

- Students of political science score high on both Open-mindedness and Extraversion
- Students of economics, law and medicine score high on Extraversion
- Students of science (including engineering) score high on Agreeable
- Students of psychology/arts/humanities score high on Open-mindedness and neuroticism (Risk-aversion)

Students of economics are Extraverted in comparison with students of other majors. As Extraverts are more individualistic than the average this finding is online with the classical concept of Homo Economicus as an isolated Robinson Crusoe making sovereign decisions. A later study elaborates the characteristics of students of Economics/Business as more infected by the `Dark Triad` (Narcissism, Psychopathy and Machiavellianism) in contrast to students of psychology (Vedel & Thomsen, 2017). The historical background and actual state of the 'Big Five' Taxonomy is elaborated in Vedel`s Appendix to Chapter 5.

Further, an fMRI-study of management styles compares Entrepreneurs with other managers. Entrepreneurs are less dominated by the Left Hemisphere (Logic), have stronger associations (Frontopolar Cortex) and better effectiveness than other Academic educated managers (Laurie-Martinez &

Carinessa, 2003). This shows strong similarity between entrepreneurs and Open-mindedness.

The Open-minded is the most flexible of the different personality characteristics. The broad scope of experiences explains the advantage regarding the human adaptability required to meet future challenges. Open-mindedness characterizes the best economists according to the most brilliant modern economist Keynes. He stated 1924 that a good economist like Marshall should be '*as aloof and incorruptible as an artist, yet sometimes as near the earth as a politician*'.

1.1.2 The Rise of the Creative Class

Definition of the Creative Class

Florida defined as members of the creative class, those who are employed in occupations that are, to a significant extent, associated with 'the creation of meaningful new forms' (Florida, 2002). Florida rejects the option of defining the creative class in terms of human capital (e.g. college graduation), pointing out that not all college graduates work in creative occupations, and many who are employed in creative occupations never attended college or dropped out prior to graduation. The creative class, though, typically do tend to be college graduates.

Most members of the creative class are not 'super-creative'. Florida subdivides the creative class into a super-creative core that includes those whose work constitutes 'directly creative activity', creative professionals, and others whose work is constituted by a significant creative component. Members of the super-creative core include those classified by the BLS (Bureau of Labor Statistics, in their Occupational Employment Survey) as working in `Computer and mathematical occupations,` `Architecture and engineering occupations,` `Life, physical, and social science occupations,` `Education, training, and library occupations`, and `Arts, design, entertainment, sports, and media occupations`). Artists are classified under the BLS categories, `Judicial occupations,` `Health care practitioners and technical occupations,` and `High-end sales and sales management`. Florida, furthermore, maintains that there are others whose work, at least to some extent, involves the creation of meaningful new forms (e.g. shopkeepers, chefs, creatively oriented factory workers1), and should thus be thought of as part of the creative class. Florida estimates that the creative class comprises roughly 33% of the US workforce, whereof the super creative is about one third. A European follow-up shows the creative class accounts for 40% of the work force in Denmark (Anderssen & Lorentzen, 2005).

For comparison, the traditional working class (e.g., most factory and construction workers) comprises roughly 20% in the USA and the service class (e.g., retail store clerks, house cleaners, security guards) comprises roughly half of the working force.

Florida`s Thesis on the Rise of the Creative Class

The values of the creative class are summarized as the three `T`s` talent, tolerance and technology. Qualities that are most dense in larger cities and especially in quarters rich in `Street level culture` as cafes, sidewalk musicians, small galleries and bistros representing an *Introverted* minority of Extraverts.

Florida claims that *cities that fail to attract, maintain, and facilitate the activities of the creative class are much less likely to achieve high levels of prosperity and economic growth*, and generate a high tax base. Members of the creative class, especially those whose work is 'super creative' (e.g. software designers) tend to prefer, and generally thrive within cities constituted by an advanced technological infrastructure (e.g., major universities and research institutes), and a people climate that is conducive to creativity. Cities with creative people climates are culturally tolerant and diverse, thus making creative people in general feel welcome, and creative innovators and eccentrics in particular (e.g., eccentrics like Steve Jobs, Apple). Such cities, furthermore, consist of cultural amenities that stimulate creative expression, creative conversation and opportunities for social networking (e.g. galleries, artsy shops, cafes, hip bars, trendy nightclubs and restaurants). They also tend to contain neighborhoods with (physical) structural characteristics that stimulate creativity and creative nonconformity. Drawing on Jacobs's (1961) classic work, the Death and Life of Great American Cities, Florida argues that such neighborhoods are walkable, constituted by a substantial amount of mixed-use space (residential/commercial), and offer ample opportunities for creatively stimulating social interaction. Florida illustrated, and offered anecdotal support for his creative class thesis by pointing to cities such as Austin, San Francisco, and Seattle. These cities achieved high economic growth rates that were arguably due, in large part, to the fact that their creative amenities and reputation for cultural tolerance attracted talented innovators and eccentrics (e.g., software designers and High-tech entrepreneurs).

Florida also supports his thesis via correlational research. This research finds relationships between urban economic growth and the presence of the creative class. It also found relationships between the presence of the creative class, and the presence of gays as well as 'bohemians' (operated as those employed in an artistic occupation). These relationships held up even after Florida controlled for a variety of relevant variables. He explained these relatively counterintuitive relationships by positing that a strong gay or 'bohemian' presence can help a city to attract the creative class by signaling that it offers a culturally tolerant people climate that makes creative types feel welcome. He further argued that 'bohemians' often play a particularly important role with respect to enhancing a city's creative appeal, creating cultural amenities (for instance edgy art galleries and hip music venues) that attract and stimulate the larger creative class.

Evaluation of Florida`s Thesis with a View on Neuroeconomics

Florida's creative class approach to urban economic development has generally been well received by urban politicians in the U.S., Canada, and Western Europe, and has become an integral part of urban policy making in nations throughout the western world. In most cases, this approach informed and amplified existing efforts of cities to offer culturally stimulating milieus for creative production and consumption. By the 1970s, numerous cities had already adopted 'creativity agendas' designed to attract those who Florida later called the creative class. An agenda that has multiplied since the 1980s, as a growing number of cities throughout the world endeavored to cope with post-Fordist restructuring and deindustrialization. In many cases, how-ever, cities initiated new creativity agendas in response to Florida's ideas. Efforts by cities to enhance their creative milieus have generally focused on large-scale, top down projects such as new museums and cultural centers but have also included support for small-scale projects that encourage art and culture to blossom within walkable, mixed use neighborhoods. Through his writings and consulting activities, Florida encouraged cities to offer new (or additional) support for the small scale, neighborhood-based efforts. He has also encouraged cities to enhance their creative people climates by offering an atmosphere of tolerance (e.g., by supporting gay rights and welcoming immigrants), and by finding new ways to promote themselves as creative cities.

However, the rise of the creative class is that surprising, that it has been object to numerous criticisms from economists and other social scientists (Peck, 2005):

1. The whole concept of the creative class is criticized as being too heterogeneous, combining as different personalities as engineers and artists in one and the same group?

From the point of view of economics and social science, the kind of change of human creativity within a timespan from 1970 through 2000 presupposed by Florida`s thesis is contradicted by a biological rooting of the kind of talent constituting human creativity. However, Table 1 – based on recalculated data - shows that up to 40% of the adult population represents a center-group, oriented towards Open-mindedness. Since the 60s, liberal patterns of elevation of offspring and a rising level of disciplinary education have enabled a large part of the center-group to adopt Open-mindedness, raising the 'Creative Class' due to identification with the creative core group rather than other rationalists. This implicates a broader understanding than before of the potential of the creative class. A simple sign of the new mindset associated with the rising creative class is "Nudging" beyond verbal emotional support. The neuroeconomic psychology provides a plausible explanation of a real improvement in human adaptability within a relative short time span. Ultrashort, it indicates that classical rationality based on a logic of contradictions is replaced by a dialectic process to improve the integration of Ratio and Expectation.

Table 1. Demographic distribution of economic agents (%)

Group (Score)	Risk-averter (0-2)	Conscientious (3)	Agreeable (4-6)	Open-minded (7)	Extravert (8-10)
Males	5	5	23	9	8
Females	17	8	20	3	2
All (1970) **All (today)**	22	13	**43** **23 --**	**12** **-> 32**	10

Source: Recalculation of data from Dohmen et al. 2012 and Andersen & Lorentzen 2005.
Note: Over time 'Agreeables' move to 'Open-minded' by breeding and education as the center-profiles are culture based while the extreme poles are associated with genetics. Further, the rise
of protest movements explained by stress among Risk-averters with low risk-preference.

The impact of the dissemination capacity of open-mindedness in modern economics is consolidated by the finding that productivity is more than the technical interaction of labor and capital. Dissemination of Know-How on production is an independent growth factor termed human capital (HC). The open-minded is the veritable Homo Economicus that raises economic productivity to a new level by better dissemination of HC. HC is the stock of habits, knowledge, social and personality attributes (including creativity) embodied in the ability to perform labour so as to produce economic value (Becker, 1990). HC is an independent econometric growth factor that accounts for 12-15% of GDP (Schutt, 2003). Further, HC is closely associated with the study of human resources development (HRD), as found in the practice of business administration and macroeconomics.

2. The creative class is exacerbating instead of moderating inequalities in large cities?

The expectation from mainstream economics and social science is that improved human creativity should enforce less economic inequality at the level of society. However, in the period with the rise of the creative class, the development is characterized with the contrary, rising economic inequality. The fast rise in profit in fast growing companies, that have enabled them to recruit the most creative staff, is actually a solid proof of the productivity improvement by the creative class.

1.1.3 Technological Impact of the Creative Class

The Fourth Technological Revolution

2020 mankind is in the middle of a technological revolution by the creative class that will fundamentally alter the way people live, work, and relate to each other. The scale, scope, and complexity of this transformation is unlike anything humankind has experienced before. In order to unfold it, it must be seen in the proper historical context where an important contribution that has inspired this section is 'The Fourth Industrial Revolution' announced by the World Economic Forum (Schwab, 2017).

The First Industrial Revolution as previewed by Adam Smith in his 1776 'Inquiry into the Growth of Nations' was simply to mechanize production. This industrial breakthrough was characterized by novel inventions as the

'Spinning Jenny' and the 'Power loom' that enabled increasing production with fewer man-hours. However, in a broader sense the new mechanical machines followed from the development of new energy sources such as coal, the steam engine and petroleum for use in combustion-engines.

The Second Phase of Industrialization in the 19th Century established Industrialization in Europe and North America. It was based on electric power to create mass production factories with highly specialized employees and far more complex products.

After World War II, a Third Phase of Industrialization arose from increased collaboration between industry and science. This collaboration invented electronics and information technology to automate production, pharmaceuticals, and other chemicals as Plastics.

Now a Fourth Industrial Phase builds according to Schwab on the Third. The Fourth Digital Revolution is symbolized by the Internet invented by Berner Lee in 1983. It is characterized by a fusion of technologies that blurs the lines between the physical, digital, and biological spheres. There are three reasons why today's transformations driven by the creative class represent not merely a prolongation of the Third Industrial phase but rather the arrival of a Fourth and distinct one: *velocity*, *scope*, and *systems impact*. The speed of current breakthroughs has no historical precedent. When compared with previous industrial revolutions, the Fourth is evolving at an exponential rather than a linear pace. Moreover, it is disrupting almost every industry in every country. And the breadth and depth of these changes herald the transformation of entire systems of production, management, and governance.

The possibilities of billions of people connected by mobile devices, with unprecedented processing power, storage capacity, and access to knowledge, are unlimited. These possibilities will be multiplied by emerging technology breakthroughs in fields such as artificial intelligence, robotics, the Internet of Things, autonomous vehicles, 3D printing, nanotechnology, biotechnology, materials science, energy storage, and quantum computing.

Like the revolutions that preceded it, the Fourth Digital Revolution has the potential to raise global income levels and improve the quality of life for populations around the world. To date, those who have gained the most from it have been consumers able to afford and access the digital world; technology has made possible new products and services that increase the efficiency and pleasure of our personal lives for instance remotely ordering a cab, booking a flight, buying a product, making a payment, listening to music, watching a film, or playing a game.

In the future, digital innovation can be a game-changer of the supply-side, with long-term gains in efficiency and productivity. Transportation and communication costs will drop, logistics and global supply chains will become more effective, and the cost of trade diminishes, all of which will open new markets and drive economic growth. At the same time, it can yield greater inequality, particularly in its potential to disrupt labor markets. As automation substitutes for labor across the entire economy, the net displacement of workers by machines might exacerbate the gap between returns to capital and returns to labor. It is also possible that the displacement of workers by technology will, in aggregate, result in a net increase in safe and rewarding jobs.

In addition to, being a key economic concern, inequality represents the greatest societal concern associated with the Fourth Industrial Revolution. The largest beneficiaries of innovation tend to be the providers of intellectual and physical capital—the innovators, shareholders, and investors—which explains the rising gap in wealth between those dependent on capital versus labor. Technology is therefore one of the main reasons why incomes have stagnated, or even decreased, for the majority of the population in high-income countries: the demand for highly skilled workers has increased while the demand for workers with less education and lower skills has decreased. A winner-takes-all economy that offers only limited access to the middle class is a recipe for democratic malaise and dereliction.

Discontent can also be fueled by the pervasiveness of digital technologies and the dynamics of information sharing typified by social media. Most of the global population now uses social media platforms to connect, learn, and share information. In an ideal world, these interactions would provide an opportunity for cross-cultural understanding and cohesion. However, they can also create and propagate unrealistic expectations as to what constitutes success for an individual or a group, as well as offer opportunities for extreme ideas and ideologies to spread.

Specific Impacts on Economic Behavior

According to interviews with business executives, the acceleration of innovation and the velocity of disruption are hard to comprehend or anticipate and these drivers constitute a source of constant surprise, even for the best connected and most well informed. On the supply side, many industries are seeing the introduction of new technologies that create entirely new ways of serving existing needs and significantly disrupt existing industry value chains.

Disruption is also flowing from agile, innovative competitors who, thanks to access to global digital platforms for research, development, marketing, sales, and distribution, can oust well-established incumbents faster than ever by improving the quality, speed, or price at which value is delivered.

On the demand side a key trend is the development of technology-enabled platforms that combine both demand and supply to disrupt existing industry structures, such as those we see within the "sharing" or "on demand" economy. In addition, they lower the barriers for businesses and individuals to create wealth, altering the personal and professional environments of workers.

To empower decision-makers to find their economic identity the following sections review important research findings regarding behavioral economics as dominated by the creative class:

Box 1. Determinants of individual consumption

1. The **utility** (usefulness) of the product: The utility of a product is its ability to satisfy some needs of the consumer. Utility may depend on the quality of a product, its design, size, color, etc., all of which are mainly the objective properties of the product. **2.** The **consumer's preferences**: Preferences describe the consumer's subjective opinion, attitude towards the goods. Even if the product has useful properties, the consumer may not be aware of it, or may simply dislike it. Advertising is aimed at increasing consumer preferences. On this background a strong impact is here put on empowering consumer rationality. **3.** The **buyer's income**: With higher incomes the consumer is able, and usually willing, to purchase larger amounts of the goods. Income is definitely a limiting factor over consumer demand. **4. Prices of alternative and complementary products**: Consumers usually find several goods in the market that can be used for the same purposes. Various brands of coffee, milk, or consumer electronics satisfy nearly the same wants. The consumer may substitute one product by another similar product if the latter is cheaper. Complementary goods are usually consumed together and therefore the demand for one also influences the demand for the other e.g. CDs and CD-players. **5. Consumer's expectations about the future**: When the buyers expect that the price of the goods rise in the near future, they may buy larger quantities today, bringing ahead the purchases planned for the near future. The opposite is true when the consumers expect future price decreases. Similarly, when consumers expect increased wages they may start to consume more now, which leads to increased demand, but if they expect to lose their jobs, they may start to save for the hard times, decreasing their current demand. **6. Number of buyers** (the size of the market): The total market demand depends on the number of buyers present in the market. With more consumers demand is usually higher.

- 1.2 Reviews modern consumer behavior as a post-industrial lifestyle
- 1.3 Reviews modern business behavior with a view on a prototype of entrepreneurship
- 1.4 Discusses economic-political dynamics with dialectics as alternative to binary logic

1.2 HUMAN NEEDS, DEMAND AND GROWTH

1.2.1 The Criteria of Economic Growth

Definition of Human Needs with a View on Biological Evolution

Behavioral economics aims to guide people maximize utility from their income. Neuroeconomics has identified the Orbitofrontal Cortex as the Neocortical root of preferences. This means our needs are rooted in our biological nature. The basal part of our nature is pro-mammal with needs similar to other primates e.g. monkeys. Beyond the basal level, man has advanced biological needs.

The basal costs of living are estimated to 5 USD/day or 2000 USD/ Year (WB, 2015) which represent an absolute level of poverty to cover the physiological needs. The global state of absolute poverty is according to WB 10% of the world population. In contrast to the intuitive view of many people this is a dramatic progress compared to 1980 where it was 50% of the world population.

Absolute poverty is no longer an important issue in industrialized countries because it is suspended due to at least minimal social economic security even in Neoliberalist countries. Social equality is as important as economic effectiveness in most industrialized economies. The actual discussion of poverty focuses on relative poverty in the industrialized world, which beyond basal physical survival must enable an acceptable social living. Relative poverty in industrialized countries is typically defined by economists as 50% of the median income. In 2017, the median individual personal income in the USA was 32.000 USD indicating 16.000 USD or 12.000 EURO as the relative poverty threshold. Thus, relative poverty is about 8 times higher than absolute poverty. About 80% of the pre-industrial population lived in absolute poverty in Feudal, rural villages, a growth factor 8 illustrates the crucial impact of industrialization. Further, the definition of relative poverty implicates that the poverty limit rises with economic growth. However, an essential part of economic growth is declining prices for goods and services while human nature is the same. So, over time the definition of poverty becomes more and more generous.

The concept of relative poverty is illustrated in Figure 5 where the X-axis indicates the level of personal income. It is a classical prediction that man has great or even vital utility of small quantities. As the quantity of consumption increases of specific goods, the marginal utility gradually declines which is expressed in the common saying 'A little of everything is good, while too much spoils everything'. This presupposes a utility function which approaches a ceiling asymptotical in accordance with modern physiology of the digestive system. The marginal utility function (Y-axis in Figure 5) – the first derivative of the utility function – is continuously declining from a vital initial level, as income rises, and the quantity consumed increases. Relative poverty means that basal physical and social needs are just covered wherefore further consumption beyond that level has a marginal utility below 1.

Figure 5. Relative poverty boundary as $MI_{50\%}$

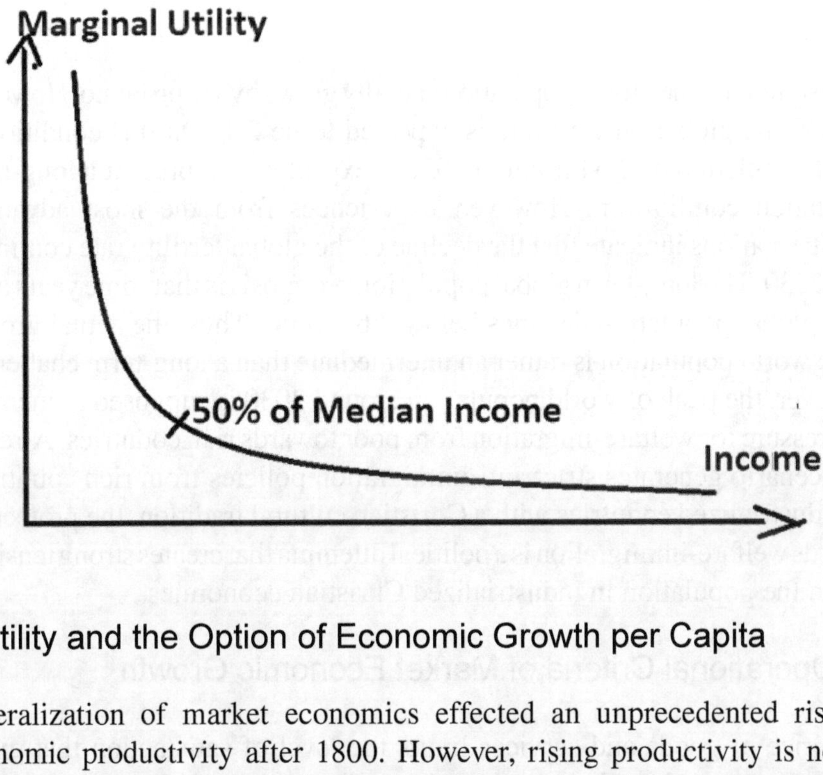

Fertility and the Option of Economic Growth per Capita

Liberalization of market economics effected an unprecedented rise of economic productivity after 1800. However, rising productivity is not in itself an assurance of rising long-term income per capita, as some classical economists expected, the population would grow exponentially due to human fertility while fertile land only can grow linearly (Malthus, 1826). Malthus clarified that in order to raise the general level of income, productivity growth must be accompanied by declining fertility rates. Table 2 gives key statistics on the development of the global fertility rate since 1960. The global rate of fertility was as high as 4.7 in 1960. Since 1960 the global rate of fertility has been halved to an actual level of 2.3 due to the family planning associated with economic growth all over the world. A fertility rate of 2.15 is required to maintain a population. In many advanced industrialized economies, the fertility rate has declined far below 2. This applies to all G7-members and China as well. The Indian fertility rate corresponds to the global average.

Table 2. Key figures on global population growth

Item	1960	1980	2000	2020	2030-Prognosis
Global Fertility Rate	4.7	3.6	2.7	2.3	2.1
Global Population in Billions	3	4.5	6.1	7.8	8.6

Source: World Bank Database.

In summary, the global population actually grows by 1% pro anno. However, in 2030 the global fertility rate is expected to be 2.1. On this condition, a world population of 8.6 billion in 2030 is expected to represent a long-term population equilibrium. However, experiences from the most advanced industry nations indicate that the decline of the global fertility rate continues after 2030. The long-term global population prognosis is that some years after 2030 global population declines below 8.6 billion. Thus, the actual growth of the world population is rather an intermediate than a long-term challenge. However, the peak of world population around 2030 is supposed to increase the pressure for welfare-migration from poor towards rich countries. Already this scenario generates strict anti-immigration policies from rich countries. As industrialized countries with a Christian cultural tradition, the protection towards welfare-immigration is a political dilemma that creates strong tensions within the population in industrialized Christian economies.

An Operational Criteria of Market Economic Growth

The price of goods and services limits the level of satisfaction that given the income and the relative prices determine which of alternative buying options is chosen. An economic key indicator of the flexibility of demand is the price elasticity which is explained in Figure 6 which shows that the difference between `Flat` (Fossil Energy for Power Plants) and `Steep` (Bread) Demand curves vary a lot.

Figure 6. Price elasticity of demand

Note: *The law of Demand states that if the price of a commodity falls the quantity demanded increases but much or little? The* elasticity of demand *indicated the relative change in Demand in response to a relative change in price.*

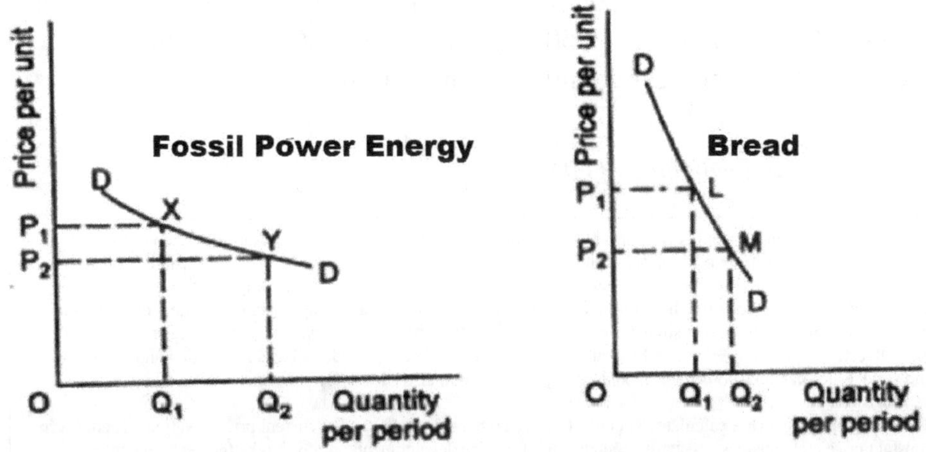

The total national production is aggregated as the Gross Domestic Production (GDP). Thus, economic growth increases consumer options and operates as increases in GDP as deflated with increases in the price level from the base year to the actual year. The statistical criteria of growth in consumer options summarizes as follows:

$\Delta GDP = GDPt1 * Pt0 / (GDPt0 * Pt1)$

Where GDP is Gross Domestic Product and Pt is average consumer prices and ΔGDP indicates growth in consumer options from period t0 to t1 as ΔGDP is deflated by price changes. ΔGDP indicates simply the growth in consumer options which is only one of more indicators of sustainable growth. Other indicators are 'Life Expectancy' and the Footprint (see Chapter 4)

The quantitative comparison of productivity in the pre-industrial, Feudal Village production with the Post-industrial, digitized economy is not straightforward due to substantial changes in the composition of consumption during the different phases of industrial development. A broad indicator of overall economic growth in the industrialized world for instance G7 is employment in agriculture. In the pre-industrial economy 80% of the working population was poor copyholders in agriculture. In the Post-industrial digitized economy <5% of the working force is required in agriculture and the agricultural refinery industries to feed the population. This indicates a gross 15-fold increase in labor productivity corresponding to an average growth of production capacity during ups and downs as well as peace and war of about 1.2% pro anno. Since 1980 emerging economies such as China, India, Brazil and South Africa have grown >5% pro anno, too. In 50 years or about 2030, most of them seem to catch up with the pioneer countries in industrialization.

Box 2. National Accounting of GDP

The aim of the national accounts is to provide an overall picture of the economy. The National Accounts system is a logical and coherent set of definitions and classifications, without which it would not be possible to obtain an overview of the immense number of financial transactions that take place in the economy during a period. The National accounts describe the economic cycle. The setting is a consistent and balanced system of economic transactions and definitions that show how productive activity (when we go to work) creates income, which is then allocated (e.g. as wages) and redistributed (e.g. as taxes) before it provides a basis for the demand for goods and services for personal consumption and savings. The system also shows how savings are placed (e.g. as a bank deposit). The National accounts are calculated at constant prices (chained values) and at current prices. National accounts in constant prices (chained values) have been adjusted for price developments. Accordingly, the development in real GDP (chained values) expresses the real economic growth. In order to describe the economic cycle, the economic transactions and economic stakeholders are divided into different types and detailed classifications that are coherent and consistent with each other and over time. The annual national accounts have the most detailed accounting and consistent time series dating back to 1966. National accounts are compiled according to international guidelines (ESA2010) making it comparable between countries. An advanced application of national accounting data is in macro econometric models serving policy development in different economic ministries, stakeholder organizations and financial institutions.

In summary, an illustrative benefit to ordinary quality of life by economic growth is redoubling of life-expectancy from 40 to 80 years. However, it must be emphasized that the primary significance of GDP in pluralist doughnut economics (PDE) is only that of an index of the economic capacity of the market-based economy. In PDE, the wider significance of GDP must be seen in relation to the stated macroeconomic targets, support of the social foundation and respect of the ecological ceiling as elaborated in Part 2 DOUGHNUT ECONOMICS.

1.2.2 Social Processes in the Shape of Consumer Behavior

The satisfaction of specific economic needs of a population is not a linear process but strongly influenced by social processes. The market penetration process, as illustrated in Figure 7, follows the general growth shape. The S-shape is explained by the differentiation of customers in accordance with neuroeconomic psychology. General marketing studies show that *open-*

mindedness plays a key role in *opinion-making* about the value of an innovation at an early stage and possessing the ability to communicate the utility to other rationalists in a sensible way. This is a game-changing novelty compared to the classical sovereign consumer (Robinson Crusoe).

Figure 7. Market penetration curve
Note: *The basic law of Biological Growth applies to marketing, too. Vast experience (Rogers, 1962) as well a study (Kern et al., 2019) identifies Open-minded as the key person in the formation of consumer standards.*

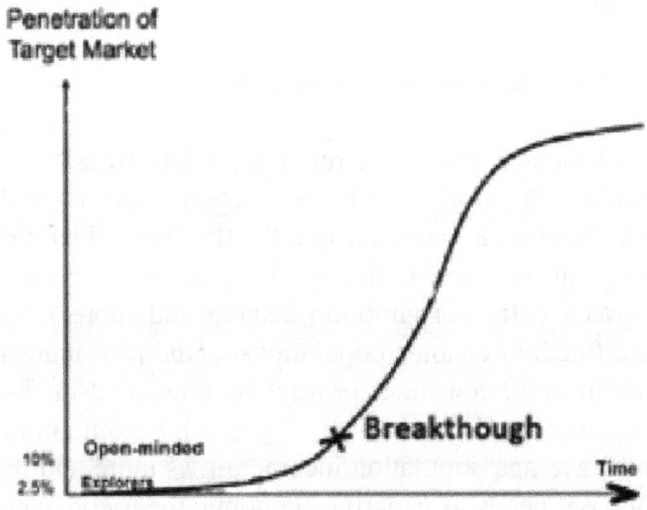

A study of 128.218 Twitter users representing 3.513 occupations is linked to psychology profiles (Big Five) (Kern et al., 2019). The study confirms Open-mindedness as especially characteristic to development occupations in industry. In contrast Top performers in sports, e.g. Tennis, score low in Open-mindedness but high in Conscientiousness, Agreeableness and Extraversion.

A neuroeconomic study of consumer behavior reveals the special neural characteristic of the Open-minded as that of a relative balance between the Hemispheres wherefore they become `early movers` inspiring rationalist consumers dominated by the left Hemisphere (Agreeables/ Conscientious) (Gountas & Corciari, 2010). Risk-averters have relatively few brain connections making consumer choices with minimal cognition wherefore they typically follow the Rationalists. `Extraverts`, with a moderate number of brain connections, are the earliest movers but are considered so imaginative that the spin-off to others is limited. So, NeP is pluralist BE integrating all types of economic profiles. The crucial marketing effect of Figure 9 arises, when a critical mass of Open-minded has grasped the essence of a novelty, and the market easily becomes multiplied by advertising.

In summary, Open-minded are usually at the center of extensive communication networks, for instance internal management circles, industry fora, or are very sociable individuals in their private sphere. When a critical mass of informed Open-minded has developed, the process of technology diffusion becomes self-sustaining like a snow-ball effect. Other rationalists are usually happy to wait and see until a mainstream has materialized before they allocate a budget.

1.2.3 Advanced Consumer Patterns

Persons with an income below the relative poverty threshold (Steep part of Figure 5 with high marginal utility of income) have no real economic freedom, while those with income above the threshold (Flat part of Figure 5 with low marginal consumer utility) get more and more personal freedom to choose between extra consumption, saving and more labor freedom. This economic freedom enables populations in the post-industrial society to differentiate in more consumer profiles as illustrated in Figure 8. The influence of open-minded trendsetters (Figure 7), become more and more important as the average population income grows more and more beyond satisfaction of basal needs. A tripartite economic theory on expected utility during insecurity has long influenced the theory of consumer behavior (von Neuman & Morgenstern, 1944). The von Neuman- Morgenstern theory is that consumer behavior differentiates between convex, concave and linear marginal utility of income. The following connection between personality and shape of utility function is identified:

- Risk-averters, cautiously following social norms as defined by Rationalists, represent a rather linear relationship between income and consumption
- Extraverts, responding strongly to status symbols, represent a strongly concave curve, Consumerism
- Rationalists in the center search value-for-money. Today, they split between status maximizers that follow the strongly concave pattern of Consumerism set by Extraverts and a weakly concave alternative pattern of `Simple Living` set by the most Open-minded recognizing the declining marginal utility.

Figure 8. Advanced alternatives in consumer behavior
Note*: The middle class disposes today over the double of what is needed to satisfy basal physiological and social needs. This makes the split between `Consumerism` and `Simple Living`for health and ecology with economies on household spending an existential choice.*

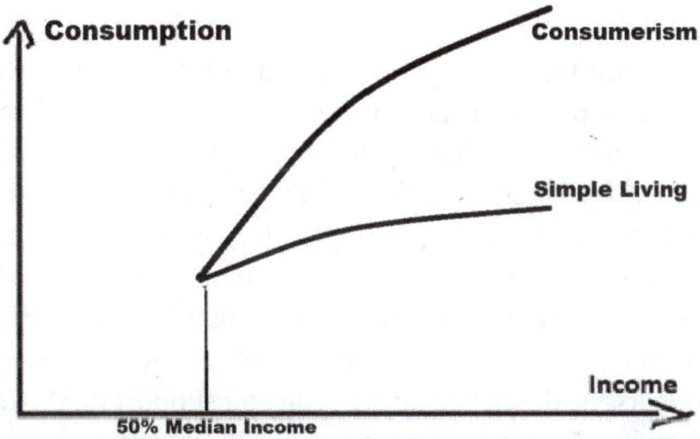

Simple Living originated in California 30 years ago aiming to turn around *Consumerism* (Luhr, 1997). Earlier it required a deep change e.g. moving from the city to a small local community. Today, it unites a triple motivation of economic, slow and ecological living with at least 10 different operational issues enabling implementation step-by-step. Appendix by O. Nielsen reviews the contemporary state of the `Simple Living` movement.

Figure 9. Maslow's hierarchy of needs

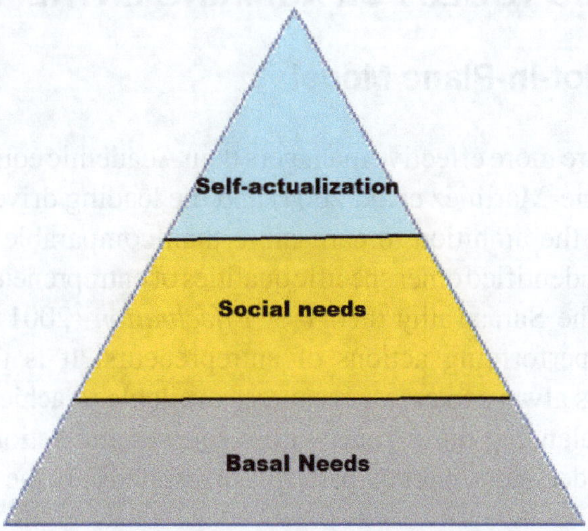

After WWII a dominant psychological alternative to mainstream Consumerism, has been Maslow's thesis of the hierarchy of needs (Mazlow, 1962). Figure 9 illustrates the stratification of `Basal needs` as physiological and security needs in the bottom, `Social needs` in the middle and Self-actualization on top.

Self-actualization represents the highest-order motivations, which drive us to realize our true potential and achieve our 'ideal self'. Self-actualization needs are also referred to as our 'being' needs; these include personal and creative self-growth, which are achieved through the fulfilment of our full potential. Maslow studied `exemplary` people, or individuals considered to have realized their full or near to their full potential in their special area of expertise or focus. These individuals included Mahatma Gandhi, Viktor Frankl, and Albert Einstein, who `personify a reality of self-actualization`. The rise of the creative class as described above is strong support to Maslow`s thesis of growing focus on self-actualization as broad economic growth reduces the marginal utility of consumption.

Neuroeconomic Psychology (NeP) reveals limitations in human self-actualization, too. Self-actualization presupposes, according to Maslow, a positive risk-will (Dohmen Score >6) wherefore it is only an issue for half of the population. The prototype for self-actualization is definitely the Open-minded personality balancing passion and Ratio in a dialectic way. The Extravert personality identifies typically self-actualization with status symbols and needs social disciplining to find a creative balance.

1.3 BUSINESS TOOLS FOR ASPIRING ENTREPRENEURS

1.3.1 The Pilot-In-Plane Model

Entrepreneurs are more effective managers than Academic educated business managers (Laurie-Martinez et al., 2004) and the leading drive to become an entrepreneur is the ambition to earn more than comparable employees. A dissertation has identified other specific qualities of entrepreneurs (Saraswathy et al., 2001). The Saraswathy theory of *Effectuation* (2001) identifies the decisions and performing actions of entrepreneurs. It is that where the next, best step is always to assess resources available to achieve goals while continuously balancing these goals with resources and actions like a Pilot-in-plane. This decision-making pattern corresponds to the Open-minded personality already identified as the prototype of modern Economics. The entrepreneurial decision-making pattern differs markedly from that of linear logic, where the goal is predetermined and the process to reach it is carefully planned in accordance with given resources.

Box 3. Heuristic 2 for Rationalization of Consumption

- Reduce the number of belongings in exchange of a few ones of high quality
- Slowing down the pace of life to find more meaning in your doings and preserving health
- Reduce the ecological footprint in private consumer behavior

The key points 1-3 are particularly relevant to young consumers, where experience shows they are easy-going with "Impulse" buying by quick loans with extreme rates of interest:

1 Create a stable rhythm in your daily activities

Books on "Simple Living" agree that establishing a stable rhythm in the daily lifecycle is a cornerstone because it frees extra energy from the subconscious level for cognitive tasks.

The key is to clarify and scheduler recurrent needs:

- Get a Morning Routine .... □
- Drink water during the day .... □
- Calm down before going to Bed .... □
- Clean-up and pay bills .... □

2 Review important household expenses with a view on reduction

To most families the easiest way to improve household finances is to reduce expenses.

More families follow this lesson after the Financial Crisis 2008. The following posts cover half of typical expenses:

- Move eventually to a smaller dwelling or rent out part of your dwelling e.g. during travel .... □
- Reuse clothes, furniture and co-used cars .... □
- Check your Mortgage, other Loans and Insurances with a view on renegotiation .... □
- Challenge shopping/buying and travel habits with a view on minimization, health and ecology .... □

3 Complete a "Magical" Reordering and Simplification of your personal Things

The most dramatic step towards "Simple Living" is often a sweeping simplification of your relation to personal things. The KonMari-method is to get rid of as many things as possible beginning with the easiest ones to be without. .... □

4 Prioritize quality for quantity in your remaining personal things .... □

5 Limit your time on social media and TV-watching .... □

6 Get inspiration listening to other people and reading books on "Simple Living" .... □

7 Go from multi-tasking to one-tasking .... □

8 Choose Discrete Colors in your Home .... □

9 Make it a habit to say "Enough is Enough" .... □

10 Take Pauses and have some alone time to manage your stress level (see 1.4) .... □

In conclusion:

"Simple Living" emerges as a symbol of cognitive surplus!

The novel *Pilot-in-the-plane* model of effectuation is illustrated in the vignette. It meets the future as something you can influence by your actions creating your own opportunities. The struggle for personal control is as old as humankind itself—primitive and innate. There is abundant evidence that most people desire security in their lives, and that such strivings for security span history and cultures. However, economic psychology suggests an enormous range of human behaviors too, that relate to striving for stronger self-control in some way and are intrinsically linked to healthy human functioning. For instance, personal control is linked to the development of self-esteem and the reduction of stress, whereas loss of control increases the likelihood of feelings of helplessness and depression. In other words, having a desire for control over your life does not make you a "control freak" although your friends may say so! Instead, it is normal and healthy. Many entrepreneurs instinctively recognize the importance of personal control because they want to be their own boss and choose their own course. Control enables entrepreneurs to work on things they think are important, set their own schedules and work with whom they want. Many entrepreneurs confirm that they feel differently about running a business they own as compared with working for a wage, and that they value being in control. For them, the experience of personal control associates closely with freedom, self-direction and autonomy. The strength of a person's desire for control is an element of his/her identity: `Who you are`. Everyone has some desire for control, but the intensity of that desire varies in accordance with dopamine responsiveness. A strong desire for control may motivate someone to become an entrepreneur, but the experience of working for himself may strengthen the desire even further. Four principles characterize *Pilot-in-a-plane*:

1. When expert entrepreneurs seek to build a new venture, they follow the old saying: `One Bird in hand is better than 10 on the roof`. This symbol the gift of pragmatic dialectic development that plays out in four categories:
    a. Who I am — my traits, tastes, and abilities?
    b. What I know — my education, training, expertise, and experience?
    c. Who I know — my social and professional networks?
    d. What I can – my financial resources

Using a combination of these means, the entrepreneur begins to imagine possibilities and act! Most often, it begins small with the closest means and moves almost directly into implementation without elaborate planning. With each action, possible outcomes are reconfigured. Eventually, certain emerging effects coagulate into clearly achievable and desirable goals—landmarks begin to appear on the blank map. A crucial important precaution in all phases is to maintain the economic realism of the project which means to maintain the ability to survive a worst-case-scenario of stopping the project. Tools for economic management are elaborated in section 1.3.2-5.

2. If you come across sour lemons, make lemonade! The second principle of effectual reasoning is at the heart of entrepreneurial expertise—the ability to turn the unexpected into the profitable. Expert entrepreneurs learn not only to work with surprises but also to take advantage of them. In most contingency plans, surprises are

worst-case scenarios. But because entrepreneurs do not tie their idea to any theorized or preconceived `market`, anything and everything is potentially a surprise that can lead to a valuable opportunity. An entrepreneurial quality testing the positive mindset!

3. The crazy quilt principle of effectual reasoning is the focus on building partnerships rather than beating competitors. Since entrepreneurs tend to start the process without assuming the existence of a predetermined market for their idea, they don't know who their competitors will be, so detailed competitive analyses have little value. Instead, entrepreneurs generally take the product to the nearest potential customer. Some of the people they interact with make a commitment to the venture, committing time and/or money and/or resources and, thus, self-select into the new-venture creation process. The partnership principle entails well with the affordable loss principle to bring the entrepreneur's idea to market with very little cash expenditure. Obtaining pre-commitments from key stakeholders, suppliers or customers helps reduce uncertainty in the early stages of creating an enterprise. Finally, since the entrepreneur is not married to any particular market for his or her idea, the expanding network of strategic partnerships determines, to a great extent, which market or markets the company will eventually end up entering or creating.

4 The entrepreneur's means provide the starting point. The action begins in earnest when the entrepreneur begins interacting with people. Sometimes the starting point is an idea in the format of a provisional goal. Sometimes the interaction is specifically initiated in the terms of "what can we do?" The entrepreneur determines

> possibilities together with partners, regardless, each interaction can terminate without a commitment. That interaction might result in a commitment both to add a stakeholder and his means to the venture and at the same time, new goals also accompany the new commitment. At any time in this cycle, unexpected events, information, and meetings can change the environment the venture is developing. The entrepreneur must survey his economic situation with an option to survive a worst-case-scenario.

The sections 1.3.2-6 present some additional management tools to get your plane airborne!

1.3.2 The Technical Aspect

From the 80s and symbolized by the Internet an unprecedented development and expansion of data-processing machines based on the circular feedback structure is now peaking as artificial intelligence (AI). This fourth phase of the industrial revolution exemplified by Robotics is capable of taking over most physical work and simple service functions in all domains of ordinary human life. See Box 4 with 10 examples of AI.

Box 4. Examples of Artificial Intelligence (AI)

AI-enabled customer assistants servicing online shopping with the status of your order, and helping you in finding a particular product based on your description, among others
1. Personalized shopping experiences. E.g. provides Google online store with information like your location, your browser, device etc, apart from how much time you spend on each page
2. In healthcare AI is already a game-changer, improving every part of the industry. From safeguarding patients' personal records against cybercriminals to assisting in surgeries
3. Collaboration of the finance industry and AI is a perfect match. The financial sector heavily relies on real-time reporting, accuracy, and processing of large volumes of data to make crucial decisions
4. Drones and smart cars (without drivers) are so far the most prominent demonstrations of AI than
5. Travel and Navigation. AI suggests efficient routes to home, make travel arrangements and helps people in taking the big leap. In particular, travel agencies capitalize the usage of smart devices
6. Social Media. Every time you are using social media, your decisions are being influenced by AI
7. Rise of AI has exceptionally solidified the term "smart home". A significant number of smart home devices learn your behavior so that their settings automagical adjust to make your experience as frictionless as possible. These smart home devices are often controlled by smart voice assistants
8. AI-powered technologies inspire new songs. Inputs gathered from millions of newspaper headlines, conversations, and speeches help musicians create themes
9. Security Technologies like facial recognition and voice recognition are getting better each day

A system is commonly defined as a group of interacting units or elements that have a common purpose. The units or elements of a system can be cogs, wires, people, computers, and so on. Systems are generally classified as *open systems* or closed systems and they can take the form of mechanical, biological, or social systems. Open systems refer to systems that interact with other systems or the outside environment, whereas closed systems refer to systems having relatively little interaction with other systems or the outside environment. Living organisms are considered open systems because they take in substances from their environment, such as food and air and return other substances to their environment. Similarly, some organizations consume raw materials in the production of products and emit finished goods and pollution as a result. In contrast, a watch is an example of a closed system that is a relatively self-contained, self-maintaining unit that has little interaction or exchange with its environment.

A closed system perspective views organization as relatively independent of environmental influences and conceives the organization as a system of management, technology, personnel, equipment, and materials. This tends to exclude competitors, suppliers, distributors, and governmental regulators. The closed-system perspective basically views an organization much as a thermostat where limited environmental input outside of changes in temperature is considered for effective operation. Once set, thermostats require little maintenance in their ongoing, self-stabilizing function. Up through the 1960s, managers did not ignore the outside environment such as other organizations, markets, government regulations, and the like, but their strategies and other decision-making processes considered only vaguely the impact these external forces might have on the internal operations of the organization.

Open systems theory originated in the natural sciences as cybernetics and subsequently spread to fields as diverse as computer science, ecology, engineering, management, and psychotherapy. In contrast to closed systems, the open system perspective views an organization as an entity that takes inputs from the environment, transforms them, and releases them as outputs in tandem with reciprocal effects on the organization itself along with the environment in which the organization operates. That is, the organization becomes part and parcel of the environment in which it is situated and initiates feedback mechanisms to the results achieved by the outputs of the organization on the environment. The open systems approach serves as a model of modern business activity, that is, business as a process of transforming inputs to outputs while realizing that inputs are taken from the external environment and outputs are placed into this same environment. Companies use inputs such as labor, funds, equipment, and materials to produce goods or to provide services.

The saying is, that the secret of personal business planning, is to know that `To eat an elephant you have to cut it in proper pieces`. The primary tool for work organization is Time-and-action scheduling. The modern entrepreneur is facilitated by such standard tools as part of electronic phones with contact details as well. All needed, is the personal discipline as Pilot-in-plane to strictly prioritize the schedule and minimize time and costs to unnecessary purposes.

When you have chosen specific materials and services for the product, economics becomes important for optimization of the final product. For simplicity, suppose a physical product for instance a special tea, is produced. More ingredients are needed and each of them requires choosing between all these options considering the economic relationship between effectiveness regarding the final product and the unit price. The relationship factor productivity and price should be as equal as possible for all ingredients otherwise the production costs could be reduced substituting the cheaper production factor with another with a better cost-effectiveness. This raises the principal question of defining the target group. Should it be designed for the low-, medium- or upper economic class of society? The answer is crucial to the technical planning axiom known as Pareto-optimization (Pareto, 1906):

Box 5. Pareto-optimization of Technology

In the beginning of the 20th Century Pareto advanced a mathematical model of `The best of all worlds` which economists term the conditions of optimal social resource allocation. The learning from Pareto optimality is quite online with the pragmatism that the value of a production factor is the relative marginal utility for an end-product. Before that time, philosophers related the value of a product was closely related to the subjective intention to make it e.g. religion. The optimal combination of multiple factors of production e.g. land, labor, capital and enterprise, is that of equal marginal cost per utility unit as specified:

Pareto Optimal Allocation:

$$dX1/P1=\frac{dX1}{P1}=\frac{dX2}{P2}\ldots\frac{dXi}{Pi}\ldots\frac{dXn}{Pn}\text{ =Production Factor Pi=Price of i}$$

...

→Minimal Variable Product Costs (Vc) = ΣXi*Pi

A practical example of application of the Formula is planning of a new electronic device. In that case you have more technical choices about the quality-price-ratio of the different components. Following the model, you firstly clarify the demand of your target group. Does the target group appreciate high quality the engineer chooses components in the best quality and a higher sales price? If the target group primarily looks for a discount price, the engineer chooses cheaper components to be able to sell at a low price which at first glance may have the same function.

Figure 10. Economies of scale

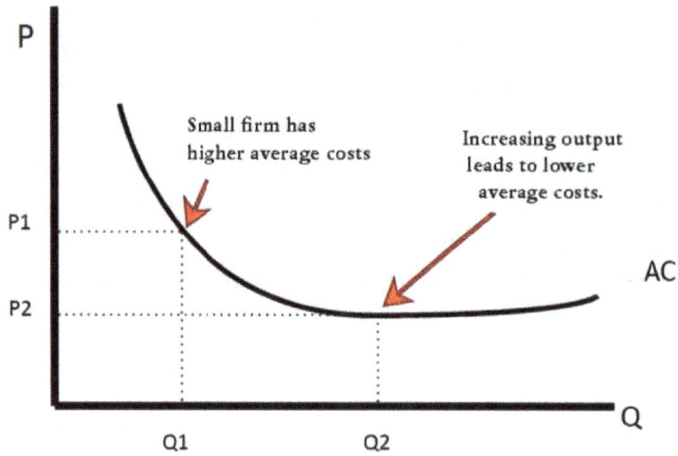

The ongoing AI-revolution takes a high and varied level of individual competence to perform and relatively little capital to implement. At the same time there is little resistance to innovations as everybody understands the practical benefits wherefore penetration time is shorter than earlier. The sharp classical distinction between running the business and research and development (R&D) is eroded as many corporations do have specific R&D functions where the working conditions for some employees resemble a lot those of independent entrepreneurs. In all, this makes the AI-revolution attractive to persons with talent for technological development either as classical independent entrepreneurs or as employees in specialized corporate R&D departments.

1.3.3 The Organization Aspect

Production is not just an aggregate of materials, services and production factors, but an integrated complex of all these elements. The general law of organization of production is typically described by the Cobb-Douglas Function from 1924 where all the production factors in the Pareto Formula are integrated into labor, capital and natural resources.

Economies of scale occur when increased output leads to lower unit costs. (lower average costs). Figure 10 illustrates economies of scale as when firms increase output from Q1 to Q2 and average production costs fall from P1 to P2.

There are many different types and examples of how firms can benefit from economies of scale – including specialization, bulk buying, and the use of assembly lines:

- TECHNICAL - Large capital equipment with high fixed costs
- SPECIALIZATION - More division of labor and specialization within production
- BULK BUYING - Lower average costs for buying large quantities
- MARKETING - National Ad campaigns are more effective due to brand effects
- RISK BEARING - Bigger firms are more able to survive downturns
- CONTAINER PRINCIPLE - Increase in surface redoubles the container volume
- FINANCIAL - Larger firms get better interest rates from the banks
- EXTERNAL - Relative large benefits to large companies when the industry grows as a whole
- LOCALIZATION - Benefits from tax shelters and/or closeness to end-users and/or specialists

Box 6. The Cobb-Douglas Production Function

Q = Total production (the real value of all goods produced in a year)
L = Labor: The physical and mental services of in production, including working hours.
C = Capital: Capital are the durable goods of the economy produced to produce other goods. This definition identifies capital resources as real capital including all the physical resources produced as machines, tools and buildings. However, economists also use the term capital in a special way as in nominal capital, referring to money that is also considered a capital resource.
A = Natural resources: The physical resources in nature, to be used in production in their raw, natural form. Examples include farming land, energy resources for fueling our cars and heating our houses, ores and other minerals, and today even such environmental resources as clean air and drinkable water.

$Q = A\,L\,\beta\,C\,\alpha$
α and β are the output elasticities of capital and labor representing the relative output shares of K and L:
$\alpha + \beta > 1$ shows increasing returns to scale (economies of scale) with rising profit rates as characteristic to globalized markets primarily due to non-technical factors such as ownership, localization and internalizing.
$\alpha + \beta < 1$ shows decreasing returns to scale is the standard case in classical economics

1.3.4 The Marketing Aspect

Having completed the technical and organizational production planning, marketing analysis is relevant. Marketing analysis serves more purposes and is based on the saying that `The customer is always right`. Better preliminary understanding of the customer`s Rewards and Insecurity related to the product. However, even satisfied customers are not loyal, wherefore additional understanding of specific user utilities and insecurities is crucial. Within socioeconomic groups, specifications are useful regarding age, sex, background knowledge, special interests and worries. The Info Box shows guidelines in the development of a marketing strategy.

Box 7. Critical Steps towards a Marketing Plan

I STRATEGIC TENETS
1 Specific Challenges
This point applies only to 1st generation products and not to successive improvements
2 Explain why people should buy this specific Product/Service?
Define a few crystal-clear comparative advantages ("Hooks")!
3 What characterizes the Supplier?
Resources - Competences - Relationships
4 What characterizes the Target Group!
Interview both the primary and secondary target groups focusing:
- Needs, aspirations and interests as living persons
- Demographic and socioeconomic characteristics
- Modern consumers seek information and discover needs on their own

5 Identify and analyze Competitors!
Name and characterize competitors and describe their product
6 What's the Position of the Brand?
What´s interesting to the Target Group and yourself?
What´s your competitors already providing?
7 Identify the primary media to the target group!
Publish a mission statement that clarifies the difference you do:
Values, effects and issues. Tone-of-voice must match position
II PRACTICAL MARKETING ACTIVITIES!
● Choose distribution channels for Adds, Website and Free Exposure
● The major outcome is assessment of a contribution margin (M) that maximizes the net revenue of the project with a realistic on insecurity factors regarding sales forecasts. Marketing costs are included as Fixed Costs.
● Get Feedback on status, development, effect and results

1.3.5 The Financial Aspect

When consumers buy durable goods as a domicile, they need more cash than they may draw from running income. When an entrepreneur aims to start a production of goods or services, extra cash is needed to build production and marketing facilities. When laborers and capitalists earn more than they want to consume, they accumulate savings. The financial system includes banks (public sector or private sector), financial markets, financial instruments, and financial services.

Investors expect to gain a profit as risk-premium for their investment wherefore they demand an interest of loans. The market balance between lending and borrowing is determined by the rate of interest. The role of the rate of interest is illustrated in Figure 11 that compares alternative finance plans that may relate to mortgage in a domicile. In case, you need a relatively short repayment period of 10 years the difference in annual payment for a cheap loan at 3% p.a. and an expensive one of 10% is not extreme. It is 12% and 16%. In case, you can get a long term finance of 30 years, the level of interest becomes very important. The annual payment is 5% and 10.5% or the double. This simple case illustrates the crucial significance of the interest rate for long-termed economic decision-making.

Figure 11. Comparison of alternative finance plans

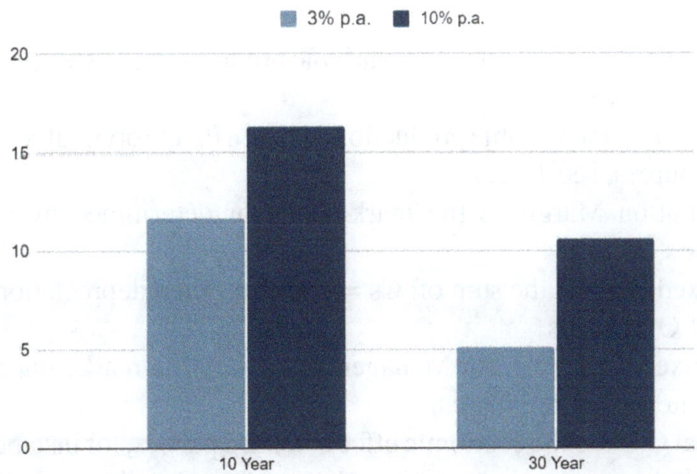

Figure 11 shows the impact of the borrowing rate of interest in the overall assessment of investment projects. The borrowing rate (i) is crucial to private investments in 3 ways:

$\mathbf{C_s}$ = Interest and depreciation of Overheads depend on both rate of interest and lifetime of equipment
+ SAL = Fixed wages for Manager and sales staff
+ Cash = Interest of running capital

The start-up phase of entrepreneurship is paved with many financial traps! The typical success criteria are survival in 5 years. Typically within year 3, the entrepreneur must decide, if the project is viable or not. Modern society offers more public and private types of financial support to aspirants of entrepreneurship in the early phase, where fair deals with normal banks can be difficult. One type of public support guaranteed to the bank is repayment of 75% of the necessary start-up loan to enable finance at a normal rate or interest. The problem of early entrepreneurship is often not finance itself, but the lack of financial maturity to handle it. To plan the capital need properly, an overview of the whole project economy is required. This requires budgeting of all components of production, for instance technology, organization and marketing as summarized in the revenue formula (ROI) often referred to as the `Formula 1 of Economics`.

Formula 1: ROI = Vc(Q)*(M-1) – F(r,Y) ±(SoC)

Q=Optimal Production Scale is the variable production costs with an optimal production size, see 1.3.3

Vc(Q)=ΣCi*Pi is the variable production costs at a Pareto optimal combination of resources, see 1.3.2

M=Contribution Margin is the mark-up factor determined by marketing analysis, see 3.3.4

F(r,Y)=Fixed Costs is the sum of: Cs = Interest (i) and depreciation in years (Y) of Overheads

+SAL = Fixed wages e.g. for Manager, sales staff and marketing costs

+Cash = Interest of running capital

SoC=Social Costs is the economic effects to third parties, for instance effects of global warming due to CO2-emission from fossil energy. SoC must be included in Doughnut Economics, but it cannot be expected that businesses voluntarily do include negative SoC that deteriorate their competetivieness. So, legislation must assure the inclusion of negative SoC. SoC must be positive, too. So, education is supposed to have positive SoC due to spin-off from students to other people.

The best initial ownership structure is often either a sole proprietorship or -- if more than one owner is involved -- a partnership. A sole proprietorship is a one-person business that is not registered with the state like a limited liability company (LLC) or corporations. It takes anything special or file of any papers to set up a sole proprietorship -- you create one just by going into business for yourself. Legally, a sole proprietorship is inseparable from its owner as the business and the owner are one and the same. The owner (s) reports business income and losses on their personal tax return and is personally liable for any business-related obligations, such as debts.

Sole proprietorships and partnerships make sense in a business where personal liability isn't a big worry e.g. a small service business in which you are unlikely to be sued and for which you won't be borrowing much money for inventory or other costs. Advantages and disadvantages of alternative legally established corporations, where external consultancy is recommended, are listed in Table 3.

Table 3. Five alternatives to sole proprietorship/partnership

Legal Form	Advantages	Disadvantages
Limited Partnership	-Option to include partners without losing control	-The limited partner is not liable for debts
Limited Liability Company (LLC)	-Limited liability to debts -Independent legal and tax unity	-Legal costs of establishing -Separate tax unity
Corporation (for-profit)	-Limited liability to debts and legal tax unity -Option to registration at the stock exchange	-Legal costs of establishing -Separate tax unity
Non-profit Corporation	-Solicits tax free public and private grants and donations related to their non-profit purpose	
Cooperative	Check special regulations in your country	

Box 8. B-Lab

Certified B Corporations are businesses that meet the highest standards of verified social and environmental performance, public transparency, and legal accountability to balance profit and purpose. B Corps are accelerating a global culture shift to redefine success in business and build a more inclusive and sustainable economy, see: https://bcorporation.net/ .
Society's most challenging problems cannot be solved by government and nonprofits alone. The B Corp community works toward reduced inequality, lower levels of poverty, a healthier environment, stronger communities, and the creation of more high-quality jobs with dignity and purpose. By harnessing the power of business, B Corps use profits and growth as a means to a greater end: positive impact for their employees, communities, and the environment.
B Corps form a community of leaders and drive a global movement of people using business as a force for good. The values and aspirations of the B Corp community are embedded in the B Corp Declaration of Interdependence.

A new type of corporation is the *B-Corporation* (B-Corp) emerging among businessmen with the purpose of building a more social inclusive and sustainable economy balancing purpose and profit (Rae, 2012). B-Corps are legally required to consider the impact of their decisions on their workers, customers, suppliers, community, and the environment and therefore a prototype of Doughnut corporations. The state of B-Corp 2020 is that +50.000 corporations in 60 different countries and 150 different industries. Some well-established multinational companies go even further and establish a triple bottom line. So, Novo Nordic Ldt. made 2006 a formal agreement with WWF on inclusion of sustainability as a formalized corporate and besides, the B-corp concept is recognized too. This tripartite bottom line is still relatively rare in multinational corporations but leaves no indication that it deteriorates the business effectiveness of the corporation.

1.3.6 The Management Aspect

In the early state of industrialization, the thumb rule was that an appropriate profit margin (Return on invested capital (ROI)) was 20% p.a. presupposing 80% utilization (Levy, 2014). In modern retail trade M covers both the contribution margin in gross and retail distribution with a level about M = 2 (100% contribution margin) is termed the keystone margin and may be considered a minimum for sound businesses. In very specialized production e.g. medico-technology is M far higher e.g. 5. ROI is based on variable production costs as a function of production size ($V_c(Q)$) who is combined with a mark-up factor (M) to determine the supply price that represents a balance between the target of serving customers as good as possible and the need to cover $V_c(Q)$. Knowledge on the economic target group is crucial to calculation of M. At the discount level for standard goods, it is difficult to get a high M due to strong competition. It is far easier to get a high M on luxuries, especially if you are marketing goods or services with original qualities to the upper income class and penetration is usually faster, too. Further, different categories of fixed costs (F(r)) must be covered by M. When changes in the respective P_i, in- or decreasing overall effectiveness, the full gain (loss) is attributed to ROI supposing M is unchanged. When all components are carefully examined, the crucial step in preparation of a business model is to evaluate ROI.

1.4 MODERN ECONOMIC-POLITICAL COLLABORATION

A synopsis of democratic economic-political positions in industrialized economies is illustrated in Figure 18 where Individual entrepreneurial freedom versus central managed economy are counter poles. Within this spectrum more distinct ideologies have developed over time:

Box 9. Heuristic 3 for Business Planning

0 Identification of a business case
A business project begins with either an idea of a new product or a new target group for an existing product or even better, a novel product/service with a novel target group. Having determined the innovative character of the business case, the initial over-all analysis must identify the key challenges and their respective solution with a view on the overall economy. If the initial analysis concludes a GO, the following points guides towards a thorough decision
1 Entrepreneurship is a personal path. Be sure you have the necessary mindset! A true Doughnut Agent has a natural preference for "Simple Living" and entrepreneurial business
(See Template 2 in 1.2 as well as Pilot-in-plane prototype in 1.3.1)
2 Assess your resource combination from as many angles is possible by the `Cracy Quilt`-principle to identify both qualities and limitations
(See Pareto-optimal resource allocation in 1.3.2-3)
3 Clarify both your customers, competitors and insecurities in the market plan remembering the ability to turn a sour citrus into a sweet one
(See crucial elements of the marketing analysis in 1.3.4)
4 Imagine a prototype business day: Who is responsible for what and When?
5 Make a secured budget from the prototype day with the Bird-in-hand principle:
a) Main budget and planned finance for prototype running using ROI
b) Alternative budget for survival in Worst-case scenario
1) Production size (Q), 2) Optimal resources (Vc), 3) Marketing analysis (M) and 4) Fixed cost (F)
ROI = Q(M-1)Vc – F(I,Y) ±(SoC)
(Info Box 8 guides the marketing analysis (M)
6 Set initial benchmarks for your business development for instance 3 years!
7 Be aware of the circular interrelatedness of all above steps (It's not a serial list)!
(Template 2 on "Positivist Dialectics" gives several tips for preparation for this step)

Neoliberalism

Neoliberalism is strong in all industrialized countries and aims simply to minimize governmental economic regulation in favor of development by the `Invisible Market Hand`. This type of society is termed `Minimal State` and centers respect for individual rights as a key standard for assessing state action (Nozick 1974; Rasmussen 1993). The minimal state restricts its activities to protection of the human rights of freedom, internally by the police and system of justice, externally by the military.

Social Liberalism

Social liberalism is mediated towards the center by the social liberalism founded by the Swedish economist Bertil Ohlin who together with the social democrat economist Gunnar Myrdal are considered fathers of the Nordic welfare state. Social liberalism is a variant of liberalism that endorses a sufficient strong state to regulate free markets and correct market-failures. This implicates the expansion of civil and political rights to social welfare. A social welfare policy is expected to address economic and social issues such as 1) poverty, 2) healthcare and 3) education. German social liberalism is termed Ordoliberalism.

Social Democracy

Social democracy started in Northwest and Central Europe to mediate socialism towards the democratic center in the last part of the 19th Century. Modern social democrats represent the stronger political opposition to Neoliberalism in Europe as a democratic evolutionary social alternative to a Marxist Revolution. Social democrats are rooted in labor market unions and positioned center-left in the democratic spectrum. Social democrats accept the market economy and give priority to economic equalization by social welfare policy. The 10 countries in the Organization of Economic and Social Development (OECD) with most years of social democratic governance or social democratic coalitions do all have special sociological conditions to establish a strong social democratic alternative to Neoliberalism. Firstly, small countries have a stronger societal cohesion due more ethnical homogeneity e.g. Netherlands and the small Nordic countries. Secondly, strong modern cultural traumas arising from previous dictatorships in Germany, Spain and Portugal have developed strong social democracies, too.

Socialism

Karl Marx opposed economic liberalism in "Das Kapital" (1867) with response in Communist-oriented labor-segments of society. Communism aims to avoid the private accumulation of profit by collective ownership to the means of production in a central managed economy. This model was on a large scale tried out and failed in Eastern Europe 1917-89.

Socialism has had different faces over time. A modern cybernetic socialist framework for the West focuses on equality by democratic governance and is the socialist model here (Hoffman 2010).

The Chinese Socialist Market Economy (SME) resembles Social Democracy in the sharing of a basic strategy of collaboration between a technologic innovative market sector and a collective welfare sector. A major difference is, that while Western social democracy has grown out of labor unions by participation in democratic elections, the Chinese system is established by violent take-over of political power in a civil war in the vacuum after World War II. The Communist Party of China defeated the Feudal Qing Dynasty and 1949 proclaimed the People's Republic of China which ended hundreds of years of Western colonial dominance in China. The period 1950-1978 was dominated by a cultural revolution led by Mao Zedong aiming control of the entire China by the Chinese Communist Party. Mao's "theory of continuous revolution" viewed the market as an "embodiment of capitalism". Mao preferred a centrally planned economic system, which hindered Chinese firms' market orientation. In the post-Mao Era, after 1978 economic and political reforms, the market track encouraged economic agents to participate in the market although they are still required to fulfill social obligations. In this period, formation of a strong labor organization as base for a Western-like democratization, was effectively counteracted by circular interaction of bureaucratic state measures rather than by direct confrontation (Cheng, 2014).

The cultural root of modern China is even older than Christianity, that of Confucianism originating in the 5th Century B.C. While human equality is an obligation of Christianity, Confucianism respects the social hierarchy and expects everybody to comply with both the rights and the duties entitled to their roles. The Protestant belief in `Treating other people as you wish them to treat you` is in Confucianism modified to: `Don´t do to other people what you don't want them to do to you`. Confucianism means too, that when the top rank does not fulfil their obligations they should be replaced, as when the Chinese Communist Party took over from the Feudal Qing Dynasty.

Other Non-economic Political Ideologies

Another political ideology represented in most democracies is conservatism. Conservatism is a political and social philosophy promoting traditional social institutions in the context of culture and civilization. Conservatives seek to preserve a range of institutions such as monarchy, religion, parliamentary government, and property rights, with the aim of emphasizing social stability and continuity. The economic positioning is either online with Neoliberalism, social liberalism or egalitarian social welfare and consequently ambiguous.

A Post-industrial Economic-Political Spectrum

The relation between the political center and the poles is undergoing substantial political changes as an impact of the rise of the creative class as summarized in Figure 12 (Template 4).

Figure 12. Post-industrial economic-political spectrum
Note: *Extremist ideologies (Communism and Neoliberalism) are either ineffective or threatening. However, already center-oriented ideologies as `Social Liberalism` and `Social Democrats` do have a long history,too.*
PS! *China claims to be a socialist market economy. However, the graph does not apply to China because China is not a representative democracy.*

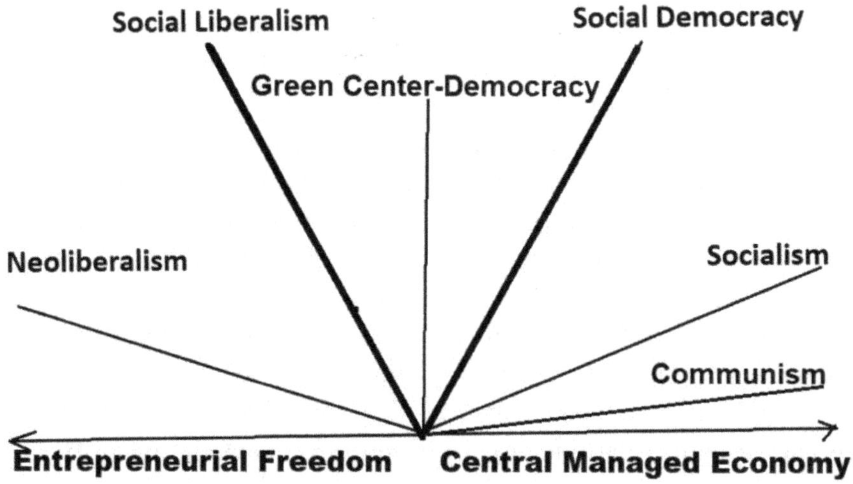

Examples of recognition of the new complementary political spectrum from center-left to center-right are formation of critical infrastructure as the education and healthcare systems that often rely on broad political coalitions. Environmental protection, as focused in Chapter 4, deserves strong support across the political center in the near future. A democratic party with a green profile and a complementary view on the economic-political spectrum, that qualifies as Doughnut party, is `Die Grűne` in Germany.

1.5 SUMMARY ON PLURALIST BEHAVIORAL ECONOMICS: HEURISTICS FOR PRACTICAL PEOPLE

Chapter 1 identifies 4 patterns of behavior to replace the mono-dimensional classical model of rationality by Pluralist Doughnut Economics. All 4 Heuristics have the same vignette of an enlightened Janus head indicating basic qualities of the Open-minded with both passionate *Preferences* and *Ratio* to assess issues from all angles. For practical guidance of development of practical business skills become confident with these mental tools:

Firstly, a Heuristic Profiler ending 1.1 serves end-user training of sensitivity towards the differentiation of economic agents in accordance with their basic risk-willingness.

Secondly, 1.2 identifies “Simple Living” as the most rational lifestyle in the affluent society with low marginal utility of extra consumption. Besides Benefits for health and ecological footprint adoption of Heuristic 2 `Simple Living` implicates savings on the household account that can contribute to eventual entrepreneurial ventures.

Thirdly, 1.3 identifies entrepreneurial ingenuity, as prototyped by the Pilot-in-plane model as the most effective production behavior. Anyway, try out Heuristic 3 for Business Planning on your favorite entrepreneurial project as a project planning experience before you make real decisions.

Fourth and final, the Doughnut Agent must consider more than his/her own bottom line including his social foundation and the ecological ceiling, too. Section 1.4 identifies the classical economic-political ideologies as complementary in a modern political spectrum where Right-wing Neoliberalism and Left-wing Neo Socialism are modified to modern versions focusing respectively liberal entrepreneurial ingenuity and social equalization policies sharing green and social center-oriented policies as means to correct actual market failures due to globalization of markets and global heating. The following Chapters elaborate the scope of specific interventions to strive for the relevant social and ecological goals.

In-all, the integrated application of the above 4 Heuristics constitutes the necessary base for version 2.0 of economic agents practicing Doughnut Economics!

Figure 13. Economic findings figures

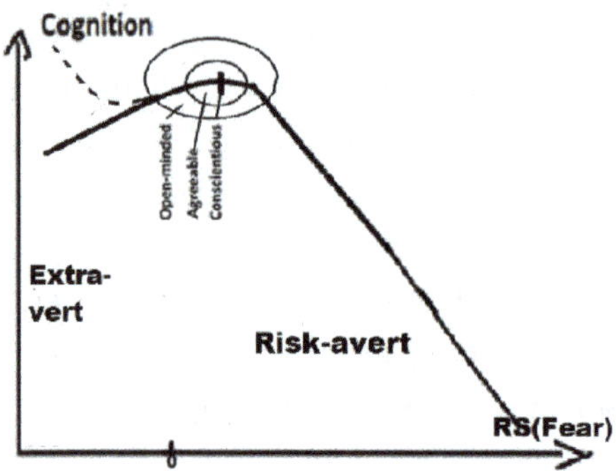

Neuroeconomic Psychology

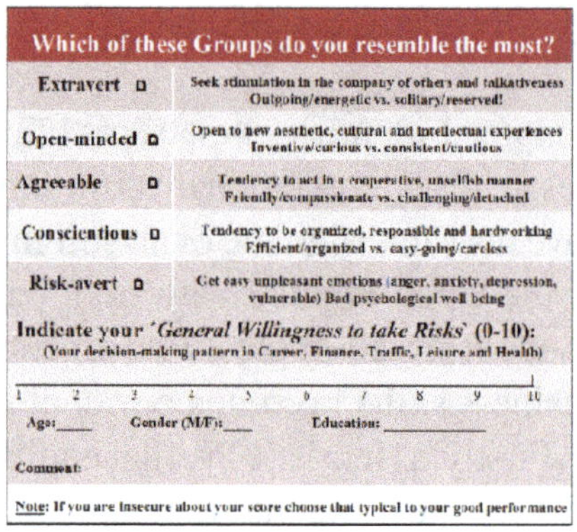

Which of these Groups do you resemble the most?	
Extravert □	Seek stimulation in the company of others and talkativeness Outgoing/energetic vs. solitary/reserved!
Open-minded □	Open to new aesthetic, cultural and intellectual experiences Inventive/curious vs. consistent/cautious
Agreeable □	Tendency to act in a cooperative, unselfish manner Friendly/compassionate vs. challenging/detached
Conscientious □	Tendency to be organized, responsible and hardworking Efficient/organized vs. easy-going/careless
Risk-avert □	Get easy unpleasant emotions (anger, anxiety, depression, vulnerable) Bad psychological well being

Indicate your *'General Willingness to take Risks'* (0-10):
(Your decision-making pattern in Career, Finance, Traffic, Leisure and Health)

1 2 3 4 5 6 7 8 9 10

Age:____ Gender (M/F):____ Education: __________

Comment:

Note: If you are insecure about your score choose that typical to your good performance

Profiler Heuristic

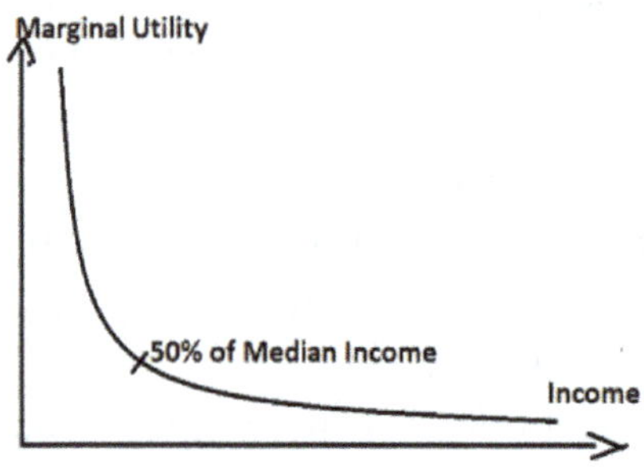

Declining Marginal Utility

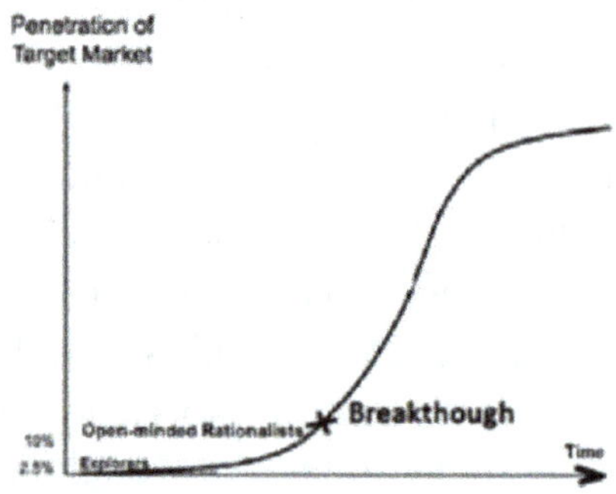

Market Penetration Function

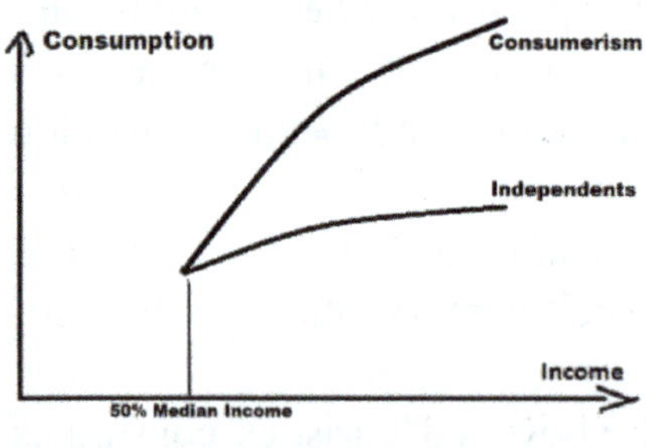

Consumer Profiles

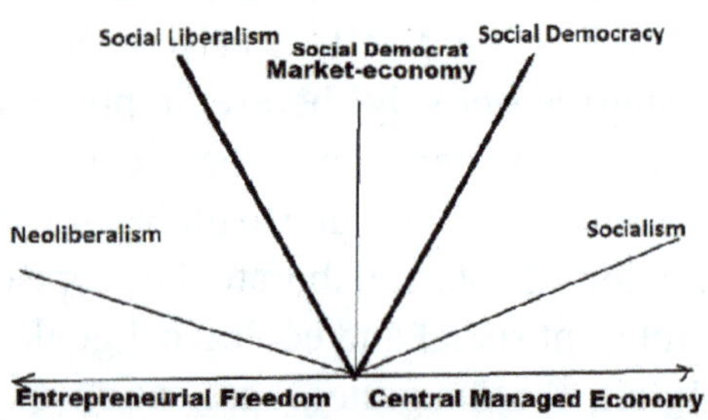

Complementary Economic Ideologies

Figure 14. Five Vignettes Constituting Excellent Entrepreneurship

Review Questions

1 Review Figures explaining the illustrated economic findings*:*

2 What`s the key competences of the Open-minded?
(Reread eventually 1.1)
3 Explain the Cobb-Douglas production function!
(Reread eventually 1.3)
4 Explain the principles of marketing analysis?
(Reread eventually 1.3.4)
5 Explain the determinants of Formula 1 in Economics?
(Reread eventually 1.3.5)
6 Try out for yourself each of the 4 business heuristics:
1 Profiler Heuristic (Review eventually 1.1.1)
2 `Guide to Simple Living` (Reread eventually 1.2)
3 Guide to Business Planning (Reread eventually 1.3)
4 Guide to the Collaborative Democracy (Reread eventually 1.4)

REFERENCES

Andersen, K., & Lorentzen, M. (2005). *The Geography of the Danish Creative Class – A Mapping and Analysis Danish part of "Technology, Talent and Tolerance in European Cities: A comparative analysis"*. CBS.

Becker, A., Deckers, T., & Dohmen, T. (2012). The Relationship Between Economic Preferences and Psychological Personality Measures. *Annual Review of Economics*, *4*, 453–478.

Becker, G. S. (1993). *Human Capital: A Theoretical and Empirical Analysis, with Special Reference to Education* (3rd ed.). University of Chicago Press.

Cheng, X. (2017). *The Circular State – The Symbolic Labor Politics in Transitional China*. Horizon Res. Publ.

Dohmen, T., & Falk, A. (2012). *Individual Risk Attitudes: Measurement, Determinants and Behavioral Consequence*. JEEA.

Florida, R. (2002). *The Rise of the Creative Class: And How it's transforming work, leisure, community and everyday life*. Perseus Book Group.

Goldberg, L. R. (1993). The structure of phenotypic personality traits. *The American Psychologist*, *48*(1), 26–34. PMID:8427480

Gountas, J., & Ciorciari, J. (2010). Inside the Minds of Trendsetters. *Aus Magazine Sci/Tech*, 14-17.

Hoffman, R. (2010). A Cybernetic Approach to Economics. *Hum Know*, *7*(45), 89–97.

Kahneman, D. (2003). Maps of bounded rationality: Psychology for behavioral economics. *The American Economic Review*, *93*(5), 1449–1475.

Kern, M. L., & McCarthy, P. X. (2019). Social media-predicted personality traits and values can help match people to their ideal jobs. *Proceedings of the National Academy of Sciences of the United States of America*. PMID:31843929

Larsen, T. (2017). Homo Neuroeconomicus – a Neuroeconomic Review of Functional Magnetic Resonance Imaging of Economic Choice. *IJUHD*, *7*(1), 44–57.

Larsen, T. (2019). Neuroeconomic Psychology: 3 cognitive modules for end-users. *IJPCE*, *9*(1), 1–22.

Laurie-Martinez, D., & Canessa, N. (2004). Frontopolar Cortex decision-making efficiency: Comparing brain activity of experts with different professional backgrounds during an exploration-exploitation task. *Frontiers in Human Neuroscience*, *7*, 1–10.

Levy, J. (2014). *Accounting for Profit and the History of Capital*. University of Chicago Press.

Luhr, J. (1997). *The Simple Living Guide: A Sourcebook for Less Stressful, More Joyful Living*. Harmony.

Malthus, T. R. (1826). *An Essay on the Principles of Population*. John Murray.

Mazlow, A. (1962). *Toward a Psychology of Being*. Van Nostrand.

Nozick, R. (1974). *Anarchy*. State and Utopia.

Pareto, D. (1906). *Manual of Political Economy*.

Peck, J. (2005). Struggling with the creative class. *Internat. J. pf Urban and Reg. Res.*, *29*(4), 740–770.

Rae, A. (2012). Assessing the Accountability of the Benefit Corporation: Will This New Gray Sector Organization Enhance Corporate Social Responsibility? *Journal of Business Ethics*, *110*(1), 133–150.

Rasmussen, A.F. (1993). *Fra Socialstat til Minimalstat*. Saxo.com.

Rogers, E. (1962). *Diffusion of Innovations*. Free Press of Glencoe.

Saraswathy, S., & Read, S. (2001). *Effectual Entrepreneurship*. Routledge.

Schutt, F. (2003). *The Importance of Human Capital for Economic Growth. IWIM*. Uni. of Bremen.

Schwab, K. (2017). *The Fourth Industrial Revolution*. Penguin Random Books.

Vedel, A. (2016). The Personality of Academic Majors. *American Scientist*.

Vedel, A., & Thomsen, D. K. (2017). The Dark Triad among academic majors. *Personality and Individual Differences*, *116*, 81–105.

von Neuman, J., & Morgenstern, O. (1944). *Theory of Games and Economic Behavior*. Princeton Uni. Press.

APPENDIX 1

Portrait of Martin Thorborg: A Serial Entrepreneur

Introduction

Martin Thorborg is 50 years old (2020). Already, at the age of 23 he became an entrepreneur. Originally, he aimed to be a policeman. However, despite passing the admittance test to the police school he missed the taking up due to administrative bureaucracy. This made him so angry that he took responsibility for his own life becoming an entrepreneur, according to his own words because he couldn't do anything else. His first entrepreneurial venture was in 1993 where he in some kind of desperation formed the company MTH Data that copied shareware plays and sold them to newspapers. This was extremely hard work as all copies were made on his own PC with a speed of up to 4000 in a weekend. In 1994 he opened the game shop CyberCom, which still exists, together with a good friend. That became a good time where they moved to become the best in the street.

In 1995 he sold his share and founded together with some friends cybernet.dk that became the first commercial supplier of Internet in Denmark. Recognizing the difficulties of selling private access to the Internet at that early stage, they also founded Jubii later in 1995. Jubii was a homepage that both served as digital adverb to cybernet.dk and helped Danes to find other fine Danish webpages (search engine function). 1996 they pioneered the introduction of homepage adverbs. 1997 they took in a professional investor and sold cybernet.dk.

In 1999 the Jubii group founded the company AcSys that made advanced search engines for websites. Although the products were fine, they came too early, and AcSys collapsed leaving the founders with a large debt. Martin worked extremely hard in two years, living privately for the salary of his girlfriend, to pay back every penny of his debt.

2001, the search engine Jubii, was so successful that it received more gigantic offers from even larger foreign search engines, and Jubii was sold to Lycos for a large amount of shares in that company.

Since 2001, Martin has been involved in the foundation of about 30 new net-based companies that offer various services often directed towards helping new entrepreneurs.

Martin characterizes himself today as a happy, serial-entrepreneur, lecturer, investor, father, pocket philosopher and director on Dinero. Dinero is an online company offering accounting services to SME and has got a large market share in Denmark in a few years.

The purpose of this special study is to assess how the profile of a real-life entrepreneur as Martin Thorborg relates to the tenets of modern behavioral economics developed above in this Chapter.

Method

Firstly, the personality of Martin Thorborg is assessed by the Heuristic Profiler developed by Neuroeconomic Psychology.

Secondly, the entrepreneurial style of Martin Thorborg is compared with the characteristics of the entrepreneurial prototype identified by Sarawathy (2001) as described above in Section 1.3.1. Each of the four characteristics of entrepreneurs are assessed as:

- Normal (1)
- Good (2)
- Excellent (3).

The data base for both the above aspects is public sources on the Internet (Websites and YouTube videos). The final profile is submitted to and confirmed by Martin Thorborg.

Resulting Profile

According to Neuroeconomic Psychology economic agents divide in five different types. The entrepreneurial response of Martin to his bureaucratic rejection from the Police School clearly demonstrate an Extravert personality. However, his conscientious response to the 1999 bankruptcy demonstrate as clearly a strong conscientiousness in his character. On this background, it is remarkable sure, that due to the bankruptcy, he has developed a center-oriented personality, more precisely that of an Open-minded personality. This development is consolidated by his subsequent business history and is completely online with the theory that the Open-minded has replaced the Conscientious personality as prototype of economic behavior. The preferred slogan of Martin is "To burn with will" which signals an extraordinary belief in own ability to convince other people about his case that arises from strong basal passion disciplined by experience in accordance with the Open-minded personality. This means that although Martin expresses an enormous passion in his public performance as free-lance lecturer in entrepreneurship, he has another side too, that of mental robustness to maintain focus in situations with severe stress as accentuated, in a number of business cases. This adaptability to function with both passion and protection is the core quality of the Open-minded personality.

How does the Open-minded business behavior of Martin comply with the characteristics of the prototype of an entrepreneur?

Firstly, his ability to turn a sour citrus into a sweet lemon is among other cases demonstrated by the 1995 venture of founding Jubii, both to restore poor sales in one (cybernet.dk) and exploiting new options by the Internet.

Secondly, his ability to present "Crazy Quilts" are strongly noticed by his collaborators as indicated by the collaborative norm of waiting until he presents his new idea for the third time until they respond to it. The special characteristic of Martin in this dimension is not thus he chooses "Crazy" partners, but some that allows him to live out his own crazy ideas

Thirdly, his ability to dialectic development is demonstrated by his interviews with other entrepreneurs demonstrating a good ability to dialogue, to listen to others, to pose sensible questions and maintain the line of dialogue.

Fourthly, his matured ability to stick to "Bird-in-hand" rather than birds on the roof is demonstrated by his strong contemporary engagement in improvement of the accounting skills of SME`s.

In summary, the very Open-minded personality Martin Thorborg demonstrates, in an excellent way, the best characteristics of a modern prototype entrepreneur.

Internet References to Martin Thorborg

The following websites shows the data used for the profile and a lot more:

- 600 Videos from M. Thorborg to entrepreneurs: https://www.youtube.com/user/martinthorborg
- Homepage for 100.000 Entrepreneurs: https://www.amino.dk/
- Martin Thorborg på Facebook: https://www.facebook.com/martinthorborg

APPENDIX 2

Simple Living 2020: A Simple Life in a Complicated Time

We live in a time that is difficult to manage. Not only are we facing a health crisis, an economic crisis and a climate crisis at the same time, but the individual also faces an array of choices and opportunities. It can be perceived as a good thing that the availability of products is so great that we are able to shop until we drop online, while simultaneously having a wealth of digital communication platforms and media that we can access 24 hours a day. There has never been as many products to consume; so many things to supply to our homes and so much information available.

It sounds appealing, but it gets complicated in practice. An unmanageable time with too many products to buy (especially the non-essentials) and far too much information results in plenty of people feeling overwhelmed. What should we choose? There is always more to buy, more shows on Netflix to watch, more posts to scroll through on social media, more we can achieve in the 24 hours of the day. It is a screw without an end, and this volume of choices, the constant chase of the next material fix or the next like on Instagram can lead to stress and feeling as though there is not enough time to accomplish everything. It leads to an experience of a loss of meaning; you feel both inadequate and incomplete. These feelings trigger a need for the opposite: calmness, balance, an everyday life that is manageable. In other words, a need to live with less.

Simple Living: A Definition

Simple living is the antidote to the unmanageability of modern life. It is a lifestyle that aids the individual in finding a calmer life, but it has a broader aim. Simple living is a sustainable choice, a way of life in 2020 in which you reduce your consumption and thereby your climate footprint. To live simply is a personal choice, but through this choice you also contribute to a more sustainable future for the global community. The simple living lifestyle can be defined as a voluntary choice to participate in a lifestyle which consists of your choosing to live with the means available to you and be content with what you have, rather than with what you desire to own or wish to achieve. It is about turning your back to the mantra that more equals better. Instead, you find the meaning in the few, but important things. From there, there are several paths to achieve a simple life. For some, it is about living with less, reducing the number of personal belongings, thus moving towards a minimalist lifestyle in which there is time and peace to focus on what is important as well as meaningful. For others, simple living is about becoming self-sufficient, living sustainably and reducing your climate footprint.

There is no book of correct answers for simple living and no matter the path taken, the destination remains the same. It is about rediscovering your peace, being in control and balance in a hitherto troubled life. It is about living a sustainable life in a double sense. Specifically, the simple lifestyle typically manifests itself in the concept of consuming less, living on fewer square metres and rediscovering your connection with the most important things in life.

My Own Path Once Looked Like This Too

In 2014, I quit a steady job to live a slow and simple life instead. Since then, I have spent my time writing books as well as spending more time with my children and we have travelled together as a family. We have few things in our home; we do not have a car and as a 45-year-old, I still have not held a driving license. I travel on my bike or by train whenever I need to travel from place to place. And in this lies a good example of how a simple life involves several sacrifices. With simple living, you sacrifice a few things: kitchen appliances, a cramped closet, physical and digital subscriptions, personal prestige and the opportunity to write boastful updates on LinkedIn. On the other hand, there is a lot you suddenly receive. More time, more experiences, healthier personal finances, a life in harmony with nature and a compass to distinguish between the essential and the insignificant in life.

It is a relationship based on sacrifices I like to take on, and in a time where more people are affected by stress, simple living is an attractive alternative to the complicated, modern lifestyle. Stress is not only sad and problematic for the individual; it also has societal consequences. The healthcare system falls under pressure, and companies lose skilled employees to sick leave. On its own, simple living does not solve this problem; however, it can contribute to its solution. A simple, balanced life is a great antidote to stress. In this way, the sustainable aspect of simple living does not only become a question of reducing your climate footprint, but it also becomes a way to contribute to a more sustainable working and personal life for the individual.

Simple Living is Not New

While simple living is highly topical and relevant in 2020, it is not a suddenly emerging fashion phenomenon – a trend in the first decades of the 21st century. By engaging in simple living, you put yourself on the shoulders of some of the greatest thinkers in the world's history, in the same way as the central religions of the world all emphasize the importance of the simple life, offering room for reflection and contemplation. Jesus spent 40 days in the desert; Buddha sat under a tree, and the Prophet Muhammad ate on the floor and patched his sandals himself.

Modern people may not choose to stay more than a month in a scorching desert, but those who choose to live simply will know that their way of life adheres to a long tradition. From the stoics of antiquity to the Enlightenment's Jean-Jacques Rousseau and the 19th century's Henry David Thoreau to the writers of our time such as Joshua Becker, Ryan Nicodemus and Joshua Fields Milburn (the latter two are also known as the popular The Minimalists), philosophers and thinkers have embraced the simple life as a way to achieve peace and balance.

It is as the British medieval monk, William of Occam, known for Occam's Razor (an epistemological principle of cutting the unnecessary from an explanation), put it:

It is vain to do with more what can be done with less.

- William of Occam.

In 2020, a life with simple living is to rediscover the joy of the simpler things in life. The scent of a cup of coffee first thing in the morning, the foliage on the trees in a forest one day in October, the deep conversations shared with a good friend on a walk along the beach one bright evening in June. Those are just a few of the things that the manic society obsessed with consumption and materialism makes us forget. We do not believe that we have the time to experience this. We do not feel as though it pays off immediately: it is not a material object we can put in our windowsill like a kind of trophy. To simplify life reminds us of what is profoundly important and significant in life. It is rarely the latest electronic gadget, produced under unsustainable and climate-damaging conditions. It is rather the positive relationship shared in a community, the experiences that make us wiser and expand our horizons, the magic of the little things that open our world to something bigger.

How Simple Living Stands in 2020

There are several paradoxes associated with the simple living movement as it stands on the threshold of a new decade. On one hand, in recent years, there has been a broad interest in the simple life, which has manifested itself in an array of popular book releases, frequently visited blogs and high-profile TV shows on streaming services such as Netflix. On the other hand, there are strong commercial and political interests that are attempting to stimulate the desire to buy and consume. On one hand, the Japanese Marie Kondo's book 'The Life-changing Magic of Tidying Up' became an international best-seller; on the other hand, the sales figures for Black Friday break records every year. Marie Kondo is just one of several exponents of a lifestyle that focuses on the simple and manageable who has garnered a lot of attention. Another example is the Tiny House-movement in which you settle your debt, sell your non-essential items, and move from many to fewer square metres (as shown in the popular TV show, Tiny House Nation). Here, as with Marie Kondo, it is not solely about decorating your home in a manageable way that lets you be surrounded by the things that evoke joy, but an economic aspect with two perspectives is added as well. Firstly, it provides more sustainable personal finances for those who choose to live small. Secondly, by living on a few square metres, which does not require much in terms of heating and electricity, your climate footprint is much smaller than in large homes. In the long run, it will lead to a healthier and more sustainable global economy.

A third movement that in recent years has gained a lot of traction is minimalism, which, among others, was depicted in the film Minimalism: A Documentary. This movement is about living with as few things as possible to feel more satisfied with life. A fourth tendency, embraced by the principles of simple living, is seen in diets as the choice falls upon the simple and natural over the complicated and processed. In recent years, there has been an increasing focus on food produced locally and on eating seasonal foods. The Danish restaurant located in Copenhagen, Norma, which has been awarded the title world's best restaurant four times, is an extreme exponent of this way of thinking. This has, in return, left its mark on a wide range of consumers. As such, the tendencies are there, the interest is there and the centuries old principles regarding a simple but meaningful existence thrive. This interest will continue; perhaps with less of Marie Kondo and more of a focus on a simple, climate-friendly lifestyle for years to come. These are not the only tendencies, though. An increase in online commerce, a political desire to stimulate private consumption in the wake of COVID-19 and skilled marketers who know how to sell the idea of the next material item being the road to happiness and satisfaction are stumbling blocks in the years to come which is likely to complicate the otherwise good intentions of the simple life movement. We are going to experience people who succeed in making a simple and sustainable life a reality; people for whom simple living remains an intention, and people who will continue to consume and complicate their lives in the same way they always have. The cautious and hopeful anticipation is that the crowd of people who see the positive double aspect in simple living – that you, as an individual, will experience a calmer and more balanced everyday life while this lifestyle simultaneously contributes to a more sustainable future for the planet – will grow.

The First Steps to a Simple Life

If you wish to experience a simple life, there are several paths for you to take. Contrary to what some lifestyle blogs and YouTube channels claim, there is no one-size-fits-all recipe to achieve a simple life. People are different and so is the path to achieving a simple life. Thoreau's way differed from Rousseau's, who, in return, achieved it in a different way than one of the world's most famous personalities, Mahatma Gandhi. Simple living is a personal choice, thus meaning that the road to simple living will not be the same for everyone. However, there are tendencies that characterise the shift from the complicated life to the simple life. Typically, it is a process that involves the following points:

- Reflection on life and what is important in life
- Getting rid of physical belongings and learning to live for less
- Developing new, sustainable habits – physically as well as digitally
- Spending time on what is perceived as meaningful and valuable

That being said, how you reflect upon your life and what conclusions you may reach, is highly individual. Which physical belongings you decide to get rid of and how much less you live for can vary from individual to individual. The new habits you establish are typically also different depending on the person. Along the same lines, what you perceive as meaningful is a personal matter. For some, it may be to develop professionally. For others, it is to spend more time with your loved ones. Some may prefer to unfold their potential creatively or to spend their time helping others. These things cannot be plotted into a formula, but the process itself will remain recognizable to those who have worked towards a simpler life.

A Personal Choice with Global Perspectives

Ultimately, simple living is a personal choice. It is a choice that only the individual is capable of making. Thereby, it may quickly sound like a selfish self-realisation project. However, simple living is much more than that. It is a chance to regain balance and reach a peace of mind, allowing you to feel in control and have the energy to be something to someone else. To help where help is needed and to develop innovative ideas and thoughts that add value to your community – thoughts that may not reach the surface in a complicated and unmanageable time in which your head is occupied by the pursuit of the next material fix. At the same time, a simple life is a life with less consumption, less impact on the climate and less pressure on the planet's resources. As such, simple living is a life for an individual, but also contributes with positive consequences for the global community.

Chapter 2
From Local to Globalized Markets

ABSTRACT

The classical market function is a self-stabilizing mechanism approaching an optimal allocation of resources as previewed by Pareto. However, the overwhelming technological progress by market economy, due to extreme economies of scale at the level of globalized technology, has turned the classical assumptions upside-down. In the globalized economy, production costs are continuously declining, and due branding effects demand slightly increase with quantities sold. This results in enormous monopolist revenues, far beyond what is justified by business incentives. An economic-statistical outlook on the most important global super economies and their stated policies on protection of the Ecosystem is presented. It leads to a pension investment guide. Finally, a SWOT-analysis of liberalist market growth ends the chapter.

2.1 THE CLASSICAL MARKET

Adam Smith launched 1776 the concept of the `Invisible Market hand` (IMH) to explain how the market delivers growth. However, it took 100 years and a series of economists including Ricardo and Marshall to develop the model of the market that automatically balances demand and supply. As demand increases the price rises and supply raises, too. Inversely, supply declines when the price declines as the less effective producers no longer get a profit. So, an equilibrium (E) is established. In the short-term, adaptation is affected

DOI: 10.4018/978-1-7998-6424-0.ch002

by fluctuations in stocks and prices. In the long-term both price and stocks become stabilized. This simple, non-bureaucratic stabilization mechanism worked for local agricultural products in early industrialism in the UK.

Figure 1. Classical local market

Note: *The Invisible Market Hand (IMH) offers a non-bureaucratic alternative to centralized public regulation. If the Demand of a specific good exceeds Supply, producers expand production in the next period. If Supply exceeds Demand, the firm lowers the price to find E.*

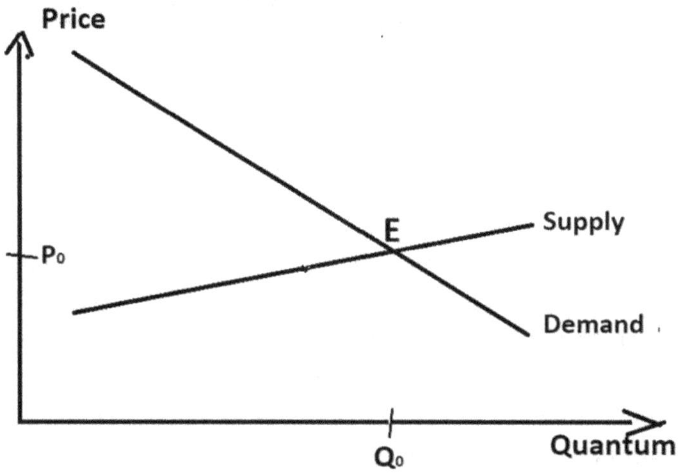

Figure 1 applies to the classical capital market, too. Extraordinary profit is only temporary as markets with extraordinary profit attract entrepreneurs which increase all aspects of competition, also that of normalizing extraordinary profit.

A recognized shortcoming of the classical market is termed *monopolistic competition*. It emerges when only one company produces a given good e.g. telecommunication facilities. A monopolist supplier can improve profit, increasing price beyond E as illustrated in Figure 2. The reasoning of the monopolist is that he/her must consider both the price elasticity and the marginal production costs to find the optimal size of the prize increase and the derived reduction of turnover from Q_0 to Q`.

Figure 2. Monopolistic competition

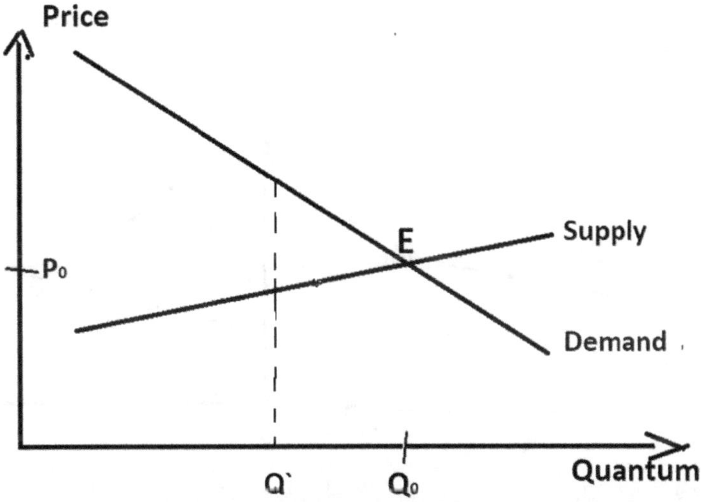

For instance, monopolistic profit occurs when more construction companies in advance agree on their offers in a public invitation to submit tenders, so that one company bids on one project while another bids on the next. The more complex the production becomes the more options for organized supply behaviors appear. This type of business manipulation is illegal since the Sherman Act 1890 outlawed "every contract or conspiracy in restraint of trade" including "monopolization" and treated violations as crimes. So far supplier exploitation of monopolistic markets has been considered as exceptions to regulate by legislation rather than the main business case.

If trade was determined bilaterally instead of by anonymous market processes, enterprises could demand a maximum price from each customer, reflecting the marginal utility for this consumer. Other consumers with a lower marginal utility would have to pay a little less and so forth. Figure 2 shows how the benefit by the IMH, the shaded area, mainly flows to the consumer. Due competition between the enterprises, they are forced to supply goods to P_E corresponding to the consumer with the lowest marginal utility. This means that the accumulated difference between the maximum and the market price represents a consumer surplus by IMH compared to the situation of bilateral trading.

Figure 3. Consumer benefit from competitive market
Note: *The benefits of IMH flows to the consumer by anonymous trading on a competitive market (A). Any public business restriction, for instance taxes, reduces the total consumer benefit (B). So, Neoliberalists prefer the `Minimal State`.*

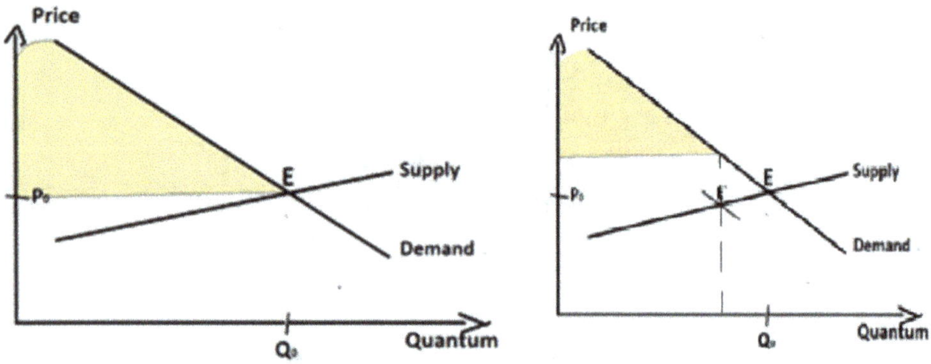

Figure 3 illustrates the disadvantage to social welfare of tax on personal income. A proportional tax on personal income reduces by the income effect the market equilibrium E to E` with a lowered total social benefit. So, Neoliberalism prefers "The Minimal State" with minimal regulation of private enterprise. The most crucial triumph for IMH appeared in the 70s far away from the liberalist market place when leading members of the Chinese Communist Party recognized that to get strong economic growth in China they had to abandon the central managed economy of the allied USSR and adopt IMH forming a new type of economic system that of `Socialist Market Economy`. 10 years later the `Iron Wall` fall apart and IMH has been cherished in far the larger part of the global economy.

2.2 ECONOMIES OF SCALE AND GLOBALIZATION

2.2.1 Characteristics of Globalized Markets

World War I practically suspended Antitrust legislation (Sherman Act 1890 as extended by the Clayton Antitrust Act 1914) until a renewed focus was raised by the rapid growth of multinational companies (MNC) from the 80es. The new market reality is that monopolist profit is no longer an outlawed exception to perfect competition, but a lawful normality based on economies of scale turning IMH upside down. The modern root of dominance of MNC in globalized markets is explained in Figure 3 where both the demand of for instance electronic products correlates slightly positively with price due branding-effects and even more important, the Cobb-Douglas production function has increasing returns to scale. The intersection between supply and demand is no longer a self-sustaining classical equilibrium, but the point of monopolistic gains (M) with reinforcing surplus of revenue compared to costs.

Figure 4. Globalized market

Note: *In globalized markets dominated by economies of scale production costs continuously decline in contrast to the classical assumption in Figure 1. Further Demand does not decline by rising prices but is mildly rising due to branding effects. So, the intersection of Supply and Demand is no longer a self-stabilizing equilibrium but break-even for monopolist ROIt (M)*

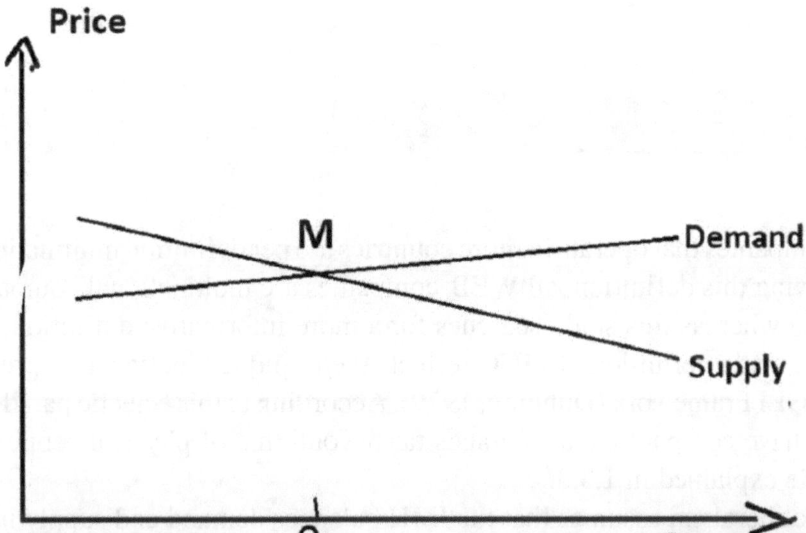

Box 1. Special Advantages of Multinational Companies

(1) Ownership advantages encompass the development and ownership of proprietary technology or widely recognized brands that competitors cannot use. MNC are often technological leaders that invest heavily in developing new products, processes and brands, which are kept confidential and protected by intellectual property rights.
(2) Localization advantages refer to benefits from locating near the final buyers or closer to more abundant and cheaper production factors, such as expert engineering, raw materials or tax shelter.
(3) Finally, multinationals internalize benefits from owning a technology, brand, expertise, or patent that is risky or unprofitable to rent or license to another corporation due difficulties enforcing international contracts.
Source: Dunning 1979.

Figure 5. Organization of knowledge-based management
Source: *With permission from B. Teiling, 2018.*
Note: *The brand is crucial to MNC wherefore local market presence is crucial. Head Center staff (HC Hub) is minimized to financial experts. Specialists in R&D move to the actual place of relevance with internal networks and contacts to local VIP`s*

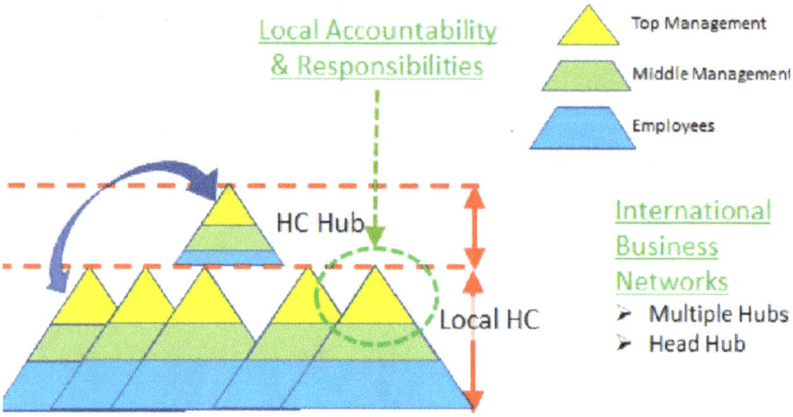

Companies that operate in more countries are per definition multinational. Following this definition, all WEB-companies are multinational companies (MNC) whereas this study searches for a more informative definition. The paradigmatic definition of MNC reflects their unique function as expressed in the OLI Framework (Dunning, 1979). According to this eclectic paradigm, MNC have comparative advantages far beyond that of physical economies of scale explained in 1.3.3.

Neoliberalism assumes that the IMH balances demand and supply in the way that high prices increase supply while low prices increase demand, see Figure 1. This stabilization mechanism worked for local agricultural products in the early days of industrialism. The root of MNC dominance in globalized markets is explained in Figure 3. The modern market reality is firstly that the demand, for instance of electronic products correlates mildly positively with price due to branding-effects. Secondly, average production costs decline due to economies of scale including lower taxes. In these conditions, the intersection point between supply and demand is not a self-sustaining equilibrium. In Figure 4 the critical point is that of monopolistic gains (M) with reinforcing net revenues.

Figure 6. Super MNC combining finance and production

Note on the Hegemony of MNC 2010:
-Accounts for 48% of US Foreigh Trade
-Accounts for 40% of capital expenditures with only 20% of workers
-Accounts for 73% R&D Expenses
-Top 100 MNC increased since 2008 net capital with 12% p.a.
Source: *Bloomberg & PWC Annual Report*

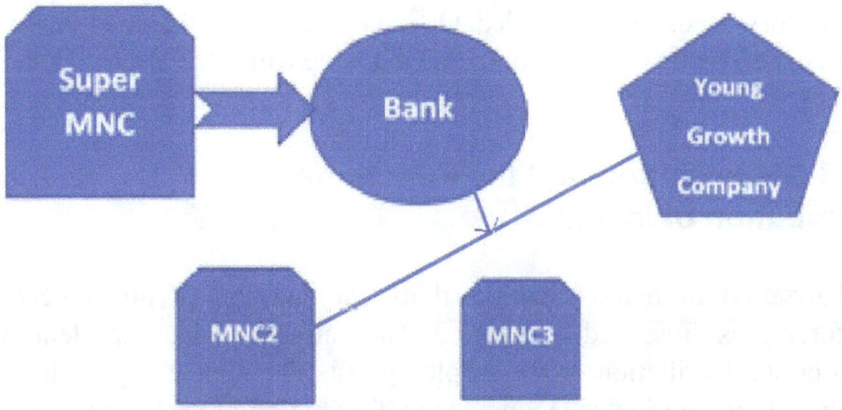

2.2.2 Organization of Multinational Companies (MNC)

Figure 5 illustrates the modern organization of MNC as based on experiences with organizational development in more MNC (Teiling, 2018). MNC perceives itself as a *knowledge-based integrated hierarchy* of Top-management, Middle-management, and Employees. The core of modern business development is networking between a variety of focused specialists and as good communication as possible with representatives of the local society of employees, customers, and politicians. This reflects that the core of modern management is knowledge-based coordination of specialists. Knowledge-based management is in this way far away from the classical military organization where loyalty to management is the basic quality.

To optimize organizational flexibility, local competence, accountability, and responsibility of the specialist functions in Global Headquarters (HC Hub) are maximally decentralized into national holistic corporations (LHC) with both intensive local and international networking. The only remaining functions in the HC Hub are general finance (Relations with shareholders and banks). However, the hegemony of MNC has another side too, as illustrated in Figure 6 as the case of a `Super MNC`that owns a bank besides production, R&D and marketing facilities.

When the `Super MNC` in Figure 6 aims a takeover of a young growth company by the associated MNC2, it requires extra capital. So, the `Super MNC` advises informally its own bank to enable a takeover by MNC2 although MNC3 may have a better offer (thin lines). This is of course exploitation of a monopolistic situation, that disrupts any ideal about Pareto-optimal allocation of social resources, but hard to prove in the real world as no formal proof of such a story needs to be provided. Officially, the bank can claim that it has advised the `Young Growth Company` to merge with MNC2 due to business reasons.

2.2.3 Globalization and the Functional Distribution of Income

Globalization of markets means that accumulation of profit becomes reinforcing, is illustrated in Figure 3. This raises a societal problem of an appropriate distribution of the surplus profit. The simple approach to the functional distribution of income is the distribution of profit to the owners and wages to the employees. Profit is in classical economics a useful risk-premium that intensifies creative entrepreneurship in expanding branches with promising returns on investments and a development serving the common good by better/cheaper goods and services.

Until 1970, economic growth was distributed in a relatively stable way between ROI and wages due the formation of social democratic parties rooted in strong labor unions. Since 1970, the rise of multinational companies (MNC) has changed this trend in favor of ROI (Francese & Mulas-Granados, 2015). This study by the International Monetary Fund (IMF) shows that the key driver in this new development trend is not directly MNC, but rather an associated formation of a new class of international super-managers with extreme high salaries/benefits. This class is known as the "Top 1%" in the income hierarchy possessing about half of global income and wealth . The formation Top 1% is a market failure that needs to be corrected by democratic measures. The Top 1% in the USA had 2019 a mean income of half a million USD and an average net wealth of 10 million USD.

Figure 7. Lorenz curve on the distribution of personal income

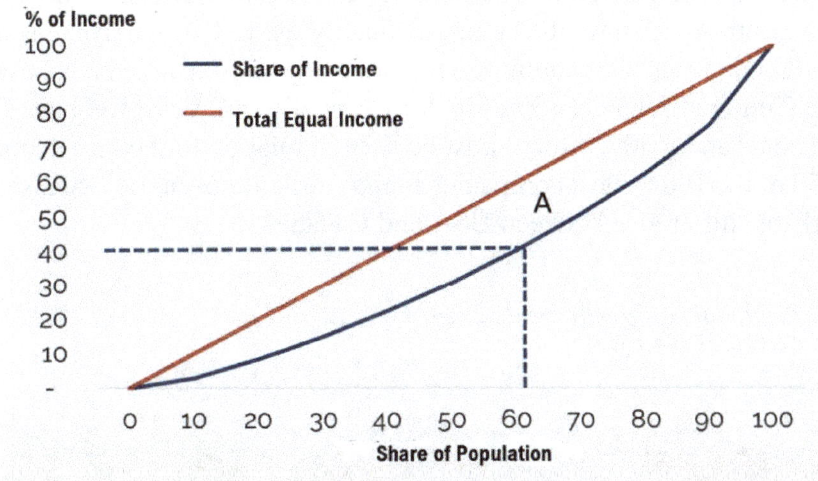

The distribution of income is often described by the Lorentz Curve shown in Figure 7. In the Lorentz Curve, persons (taxpayers) are ranked according to their personal income. Those with the lowest income are in the bottom and those with the highest income in the top. Ordering persons by income means that the shape of the accumulated curve indicates the degree of inequality. In a population, where all have the same income, is the Lorentz Curve a straight line. The functional distribution is determined as a struggle between the top and the bottom income levels (Jantzen & Volpert, 2016).

The Lorenz Curve is not the only way describing inequality in income. Another way is to calculate the relationship between the aggregated income of the top 20% of the population with the bottom 20%. The Gini-coefficient indicates the share of total income to redistribute from incomes over the average to those below the average to reach complete equity. A complete equity is not feasible. Firstly, a lower job-frequency of women compared to men conditions some inequality. Secondly, younger persons in education have a lower factor productivity / income than more experienced workers. Thirdly, elder persons who are retired from the working life have a lower income than those in work. Fourthly, it is a privilege of managers to give extra financial rewards to very productive employees. Fifthly, it is to the benefit of all to accept that successful entrepreneurs earn a special ROI due risk-taking. In all, the factors mean that a dynamic society requires a Gini-coefficient of at least 25%.

Figure 8 shows Global Gini-coefficients 2019. The group of emerging growth economies Brazil in Southern America, China and India in Asia as well as South Africa have the largest inequality with a Gini-coefficient about 50%. EU-countries in Scandinavia and Germany and Japan in Asia have the lowest Gini-coefficients (<30%) in the World. The USA and UK have Gini-coefficients about 40% which must be seen in relation to the fact that more than 50 of the 100 richest companies in the world are from the USA, see the remarkable difference between USA and Canada.

Figure 8. Global Gini-coefficients 2019
Source: *World Bank Database*

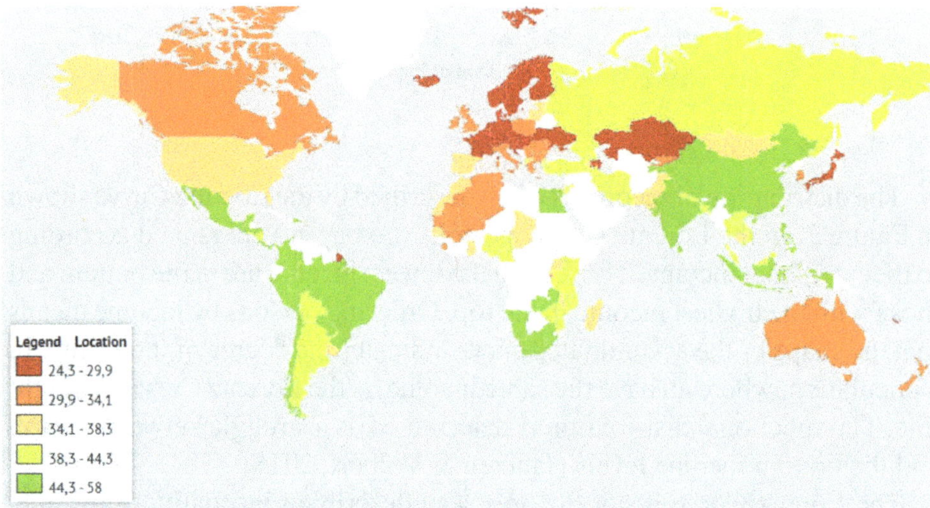

Despite the central role of profit maximization in the microeconomic growth model, it was not the original argument for the onset of industrialization. The original driver was admiration for entrepreneurial ingenuity in the Manchester School of Economics. The calculation of profit is a later invention. The concept of profit emerged during the 19th Century with the administrative technique of double-entry accounting (both the material and pecuniary side of an economic transaction).

In the first half of the 20th Century, profit was one among more social business goals. Profit became the long-term goal to encourage financial development of enterprises about 1970 as shareholders declared profit maximization as the top priority for corporate management. A study of the Lorenz Curve identifies the best fitting model to data on the personal distribution of US income as one describing the relative political strength of bottom respective the top of the economic Lorenz hierarchy (Jantzen & Volpert, 2015). This finding is online with the overall economic-political impression of the global distribution of national Gini-coefficients where industrialized countries with a strong social democratic tradition have less excessive inequality. The rising global inequality reflects the hegemony of MNC compared with democratic governments or in figures, the dominance of the upper income class compared to the middle class. This new world order is investigated below.

2.3 OUTLOOK ON THE NEW ECONOMIC WORLD ORDER

2.3.1 International Economic Statistics

The critical question of economic strength in a global perspective is framed by the Tables 1 that shows key figures for selected economies, other important global regions and Top 100 Companies:

1. The Front column (1) lists important countries/regions in the world economy. Their economic impact is indicated by the product of population size Column (2) and GDP per capita (Column 3) that is indicated both in USD by exchange rates and Power Purchasing Parities (PPP). PPP compares the overall consumer purchasing power across countries by a correction factor calculated as the relative total costs of a 'standard basket of consumer goods'. Two currencies are in equilibrium or at par when a standard basket of goods accounted for by the exchange rate is priced the same in both countries. To make a comparison of prices across countries a wide range of goods and services must be considered. As some governments aim to keep under-valued exchange rates to support their international economic competitiveness, PPP provides a more realistic indicator of economic capacity than the exchange rates.

A simple, easy, fast, and less accurate alternative to PPP, to check if national exchange rates express national productivity, is the "Big Mac-test". Check if the local price of a Big Mac Meal, converted to USD, is higher or lower than the US-price. If the local price is lower, the local currency is undervalued.

2. Columns 4-6 characterizes the social economic structure. The Gini-coefficient (4) indicates the inequality in distribution of income. The

amount of data that must be collected and the complexity of comparisons makes this comparison difficult. The theory predicts that rising inequality in GDP per capita is negative in rich countries but positive in poor countries. A study by the World Economic Forum confirms that on average in relative rich countries, a 1 percentage point increase in the Gini coefficient reduces GDP per capita by around 1.1% over a five-year period. The long-run (cumulative) effect is larger amounting to about -4.5%.

Further (5) complements (4) with calculation of the relative poverty rate as the share of population with <50% of national median income. Finally (6) shows national public net debt as share of GDP.

3. Columns 7-8 presents key indicators of macroeconomic bio-ecological outcomes:

    a. CO_2-emission per Capita as indicator of the state of transition to carbon neutrality
    b. Life expectancy as the broadest possible indicator of the national quality of life (The ideal indicator is Health-adjusted Life-expectancy (HALE). However, complete global HALE statistics is not yet available

In Column 1 the horizontal order of global economic strength finds the G7-group on top, followed by China and other emerging economies. Finally, averages follow for important global regions.

4. Table 2 by key figures on the Hegemony of Top 100 Companies. They are characterized by National origin (2-3), Market capital (4) and Gains (Return-of-investment) (4-5) and Market Value (6).

International trade is regulated by the World Trade Organization (WTO) that replaced the General Agreement on Trade and Tariffs in 1994. In 2019, international trade aggregated according to WTO to 25 Trillion USD or about 30% of the world economy. Goods account for 80% of world trade with China as the largest agent and clothing as the largest item. The residual 20% of world trade is services with the USA as the largest agent and computer services as the largest item. Since the financial crisis 2008 world production and world trade has been growing with the same speed.

Table 1a. Indicators on global economies 2020

Country 1	Population (Millions) 2	GDP/Capita (1000 (1000 USD) PPP) 3a 3b	GINI-Coefficient % 4	Relative Poverty (2014-17) 5	Public Net Debt/ GDP % 6	CO_2/ Capita (Metric t.) 7	Life Expectancy (Years) 8
G7*: (44% of GGP)	**772**	**48**	**39%**	**15%**	**91%**	**12** (24% of Wd)	**82**
Canada*	37	49 100%	32%	12%	35%	19	83
France*	66	44 110%	29%	8%	88%	4	83
Germany*	83	50 110%	30%	10%	60%	10	82
Italy*	59	35 120%	32%	14%	135%	5	84
Japan*	130	42 110%	38%	16%	220%	10	84
UK*	67	42 110%	32%	11%	80%	5	81
USA* (25% of GWP)	**330**	**65 100%**	**47%**	**18%**	**105%**	**16** (14% of Wd)	**80**
EU[8]	450	33 120%	31%	21%	85%	6	81
China (15% of GWP)	**1.420**	9[9] 210%	**40%**	**No data**	50%	**8** (30% of Wd)	**77**
India	1.370	2 400%	35%	-	70%	2	69
Russia	145	11 260%	41%	-	15%	12	70
Brazil	215	10 180%	49%	-	90%	3	75
South Africa	57	6 220%	59%	-	65%	7	58
Other Latin America	445	7 -	-	-	-	3	76
Other South Asia	535	2 -	-	-	-	2	71
Other Africa	1.260	2 -	-	-	-	1	62
World	**7.715**	**11**	**38%**	**N/D**	**N/D**	**5**	**72**

Note: Col 2: EU after Brexit; Col 3,4,7: World Bank; Col 5: OECD 2014-17: 50% of Median; Col 6: IMF Col 8: WHO.

G7, accounting for 44% of global GDP, has dominated the international economy since the 70es, although accounting for only 10% of the World Population. G7 was originally founded 1973, in reply to the Oil crisis, as a Forum between the seven largest economies in the International Monetary Fund (IMF). Within G7, the USA represents more than half of the economy which gives US natural leadership. The dominance of the USA is even stronger when the impact of the Top 100 companies is included in the analysis

Table 1b. Global impact of top 100 companies 2017

Country 1	Number 2	Market Value 2017 (Billion USD) 3	Gains 2016-17 (Billion USD) 4	Gains 2009-17 (Billion USD) 5	Market Value 2009 (Billion USD) 6
USA	55	10.928 (**65%**)	1.389 (15%)	7.123 (187%)	3.805
China	10	1.801 (**10%**)	245 (16%)	740 (70%)	1.061
Other G7	19	2.254 (**13%**)	285 (14%)	352 (19%)	1.902
Rest of World	16	2.055 (**12%**)	-51 (2%)	423 (26%)	1.632
Total	100	17.438 (**100%**)	1.868 (12%)	9.038 (108%)	8.400

Source: Bloomberg/PWC Analysis 2018[8]. The total market capital of Top 100 companies is 20% of global GDP.

Box 2. International Trade Agreements

The core principles of WTO are: 1) Most favored Nation and 2) Mutuality
Point 1 means that no other nations could be favored more than those within WTO.
This may be suspended for groups of countries already having established a Free Trade Agreement or Tariff Union e.g. the North American Agreement on Free Trade (NAFTA).
Point 2 means that the countries within WTO are favored at least as much as any other country.
Today, three levels of international trade are in action:

- A Free Trade Area is an agreement between two or more countries to remove tariffs and other restrictions to trade (e.g. restrictions on transport) and respect points 1-2 but maintaining such restrictions towards third countries. An existing example if NAFTA in North America
- A Customs Union is a group of countries that has removed all internal restrictions to trade as tariffs and other quantitative restrictions and has established a common set of tariffs towards non-member countries. An example is the customs union between the European Union (EU) and Turkey from 1996. Even customs unions are sub-optimal distorting import away from efficient suppliers in developing countries
- A Single Market is an even more expanded economic cooperation than a customs union which allows free internal movement of capital, labor and services, too. The leading example of an internal market is the EU which seeks to guarantee free internal movement of all four types of mobile economic resources goods, services, capital and labor. EU developed from a tariff union towards a single market 1993 to keep up with the growth rates of the rest of the world. It was recognized that a single market requires a single currency, too. The Maastricht Agreement 1993 established the Eurozone as a voluntary currency option to members. The Eurozone has divided the EU in two levels of cooperation. At the establishing 2002,19 out of 28 member-countries joined the Eurozone while countries like the UK, Sweden and Denmark did not. After Brexit the Eurozone comprises 82% of the EU-population.

Notes on official statistical sources of international economic activity:
1 United Nations (UN): A single entry point to economics and social indicators is unstats.un.org/ . For statistics on population size and composition, births, deaths, marriage and divorce, see Demographic Yearbook system
Special UN-organisation have open access to their databases: Food and Agriculture (FAO) has databases at: www.fao.org/. World Health Organization (WHO) has databases at: www.who.int/
Intergovernmental Panel on Climate Change (IPCC): UN body for assessing the science related to climate change. Provides policymakers with regular scientific assessments on climate change, see www.ipcc.ch/

2 World Bank (WB): It claims to pursue two targets, to end extreme poverty and promote shared prosperity in a sustainable way. Free and open access to global development data at data.worldbank.org/

3 International Monetary Fund (IMF): It works to foster global monetary cooperation, secure financial stability, facilitate international trade, promote high employment and sustainable economic growth, an reduce poverty around the world. See IMF-databases: www.imf.org/
4 Organization of Economic and Co-operative Development (OECD): Where you find, compare and share the latest OECD data: charts, maps, tables and related publications, see www.oecd.org/
5 World Trade Organization (WTO): WTO provides quantitative information in relation to economic and trade policy.
Give access to data on trade flows, tariffs, non-tariff measures (NTMs) and trade in value added, se www.wto.org/ .

where 65% of the total market capital is from the USA. Extreme American dominance has consolidated since the global financial crisis 2008 as US Top 100 companies have accumulated market capital with redoubled growth rates compared to the rest of the world.

A theory says that the future is dominated by super economies rather than superpowers (Bahl, 2013). This means that economic interests are becoming more important to citizens than political security interests. Ideological political differences between the West and China are supposed to have a declining impact compared to the rising impact of economic ecology and trade interests.

A closer scrutiny of the figures in Table 1a is based on comparison of the GDP of the super economies by PPP rather than by nominal exchange rates. This changes the order of the super economies in favor of China who also has a higher rate of growth than the USA. India has rank 3 in PPP and an actual rate of growth at the level of China. Further, it must be noted that the USA is not a coordinated entity regarding environmental policy where each of the Federal States are quite sovereign.

On this background, it seems relevant to look for te Chinese development strategy as the dominant factor in economic development in the decades to come. A development that seems accelerated by the official step down from several lines of international leadership of the US during the Trump administration although this line is reversed by the new Biden-Harris administration.

2.3.2 Chinese Economic Policy

The "Belt and Road"-initiative

The actual Chinese rate of growth (and other emerging economies) are much larger than those of G7. Further, the general financial stability of China is more solid than within G7 for instance as indicated by national debt rates! The world economic center is simply moving from Europe/North America to Asia as manifested in the "Belt and Road"-initiative 2013-47, see Figure 9. The Chinese

governmental development strategy towards 2050 involves infrastructure and investments in 152 countries and international organizations in all Continents, but North and South America. "Belt" refers to the over land and by rail transportation (Silk Road Economic Belt) and "Road" to the sea routes (21th Century Maritime Silk Road). The Chinese government calls the initiative "A bid to enhance regional connectivity and embrace a brighter future". Others see it as a Chinese push for dominance in global affairs 2050.

Figure 9. Chinese "belt and road" initiative 2013-47

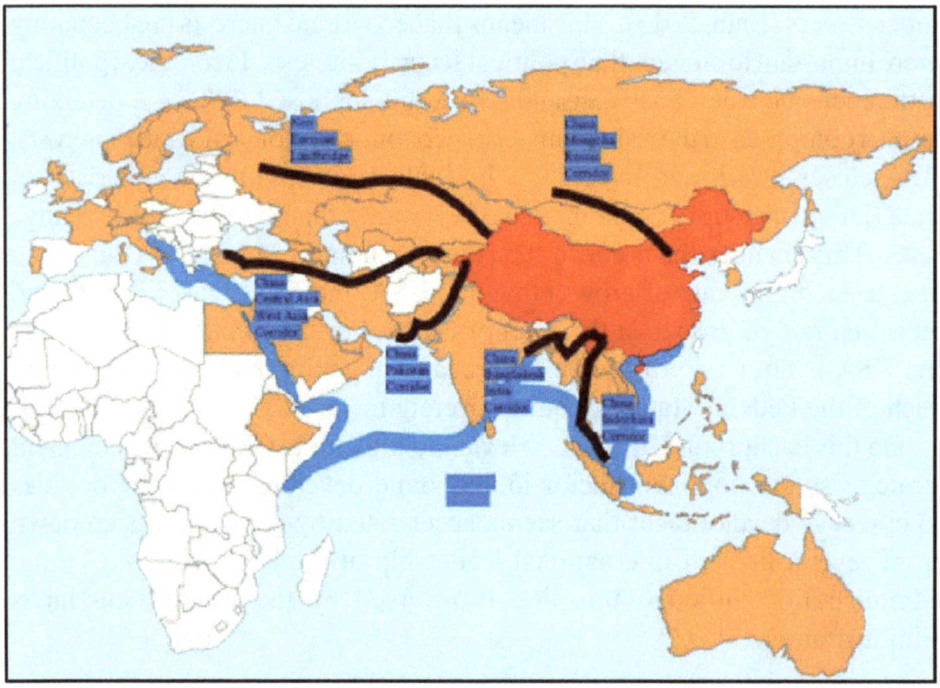

The economic policy of modern China is a complementary view on government and market which by the Chinese government is termed `Socialist Market Economy`. The comparative effectiveness of the market **r**egarding development of technological progress means that great entrepreneurs are recognized as social heroes. The government focuses long-term development of good infrastructure and selective subsidies to relevant infant industries within a relatively solid fiscal policy with only moderate public deficits (50% of GDP).

The operational concept of Chinese political economy is termed Demand Side Management (DSM) leaving market forces to provide the productive supplies that society wants. The Chinese One-Party System (Communist Party) sanctions by governmental power individuals and corporations, that deviate from the party line. A simple, fast and direct governmental method compared to that of Western democracies.

The total Chinese public debt amounts according to official figures to 50% of GDP in 2017 compared to 91% in G7 (Xinhua News, 2017). The budgeted net public deficit is 2.9% of GDP or just within the limits of what is considered healthy fiscal policy in the EU. This confirms the general impression of an over-all solidity of Chinese economic policy. China is today the only world economic key player with substantial financial freedom for long-term investments. The socialist Chinese market economy states the following priorities of public finance:

1. `Winning the critical battle to forestall and defuse major risks`
   This priority faces clean-up of unofficial debts of local governments
2. `Winning the critical battle against poverty through targeted alleviation`
   This priority addresses absolute poverty in certain rural regions e.g. Tibet. However, the central government support to this priority amounts only to about 0.5% of total public expenses
3. `Winning the critical battle to prevent and control pollution`
   This priority faces salient environmental problems e.g. air pollution and will promote an overall improvement in ecosystems. The central government support to this priority is as small as 0.1%

The comparative advantage of Chinese economic policy as compared with non-Asian members of G7 is a national discipline that in the long-term historical perspective points back to the Confucian heritage of belief in the natural hierarchy. So, China has implemented a national surveillance system based on linking a national identity card to modern GPS-technology enabling the mapping of the timeline of all citizens. So, both technical and cultural factors explain the effective Chinese handling of the CORONA Pandemic.

Regarding long-term economic policy, the national discipline firstly helps to maintain low inflation in combination with underpricing of the non-convertible Chinese currency (Yuan). This policy is further strengthened by gigantic state subsidies to Chinese export industries e.g. by exemption to the added-value tax. In all, this creates a stable long-term trade surplus, especially towards the USA. The Chinese growth rate has for a longer period been 2-digit. The last few years, however, it is nearly halved although still far higher than G7.

The Chinese 2050 High Renewable Energy Penetration Scenario

China is the largest economy of the world and the world leader regarding CO_2-emission. Already 2002, the Communist Party Congress agreed on a plan for sustainable development that promotes a circular *economy*. Circular economy is implemented in corporate (*micro*), inter-firm (*meso*) and societal levels (*macro*).

Corporate implementation refers to initiatives related to the Eco-design of manufacturing plants for instanced cleaner production and Environmental Management Systems (EMS) that are meant to reduce the production of harmful by-products.

Inter-firm initiatives at the meso level implement Eco-industry parks (EIPs), where industrial plants are constructed in close proximity and capitalize on the trading of industrial by-products, ultimately reducing waste.

Societal level initiatives refer to development of Eco-cities and Eco-provinces, which address the social concern on both production and consumption that pollute.

Measures of the performance of the circular economy in regional and industrial park areas are implemented, too. Circular economy is based on the 3R principle (Reduce, Re-use, Recycle).

The Chinese 2050 Scenario has a unique planning quality that can inspire societal long-term planning all over the world. It is both technically and economically feasible for renewable energy to satisfy over 60 percent of China's primary energy consumption and 85 percent of electricity consumption by 2050 {10(. The main goal for the 2050 Scenario is to build a common vision among China's key stakeholders for an energy sector centered on renewables. The 2050 Scenario develops a roadmap of actions that must be taken to move towards a high renewable energy future where the Chinese CO2-emission is reduced to their 1980-level before the onset of modern industrialization. Key targets for core agents are specified respectively for government, power industry and executive industries. Specific Chinese incentives for wind, solar and nuclear energy are actually tested in more Chinese pilot-studies before large-scale implementation and are online with the climate policy of other member-countries in the Paris Agreement. Further, China has invested a huge capital in the development of prototypes of electric cars to become forerunner in the large-scale production of electric cars.

From a technical point of view of Western energy planning, notice the Chinese social economic 2050-vision that exclusively focuses on the aggregate macroeconomic strength (GDP by PPP) without any particular view on the distribution of income. The state of distribution of income 2020 is that Chinese with a Gini-coefficient of 50% is one of the most unequal societies in the world.

2.3.3. Summary on the Economic World Order

The implementation of human equality in the format of representative democracy has challenged the Feudal hierarchical order since the Renaissance. Today, the hegemony of MNC by globalization of markets challenges democratic government in the format of the Fourth Industrial Revolution promoting digital technology even as artificial intelligence. A statistical outlook on global economics (Table 1) shows that 2020 the market value of Top 100 MNC accounts for about 25% of the global GDP and the annual growth rate of MNC is 3-fold higher than global GDP. The growing Hegemony of MNC means that all nations have to consider MNC responses to their economic policy. For example has the average level of corporate income tax been reduced significantly since the financial crisis 2008 as nations follow an individual path towards attracting MNC.

At the level of global politics, the hegemony of MNC seems to imply a basic change in national security policy away from power-oriented formation of blocks of countries as it peaked during the `Cold War` characterized by 2 security blocks centering respectively USA and USSR. Table 1a shows that already China has surpassed the US as the largest economy indicated by PPP and the Chinese rate of economic growth is more fold higher. Other global economies are such as the EU and India. Further, it is important that the Chinese foreign policy is more sophisticated than that of the USSR. Chinese foreign policy is profiled by the `Belt and Road` - initiative as illustrated in Figure 9. This means that the advancement of international trade relations (centering China) is the leading Chinese driver. So, the dominant target in future foreign policy appears as advancement of trade relations. This implies too, that for instance Western countries should downsize the propagation of `Foreign Humanist Value Policy` and recognize there are more paths to human development for instance Confucianism as alternative to Christianity.

Another important aspect of the Fourth Industrial Revolution for ordinary people is the rise of social media that raises social communication and the dissemination of human knowledge to new all time highs. A researcher assesses this aspect so important that globalization makes the world flat (Friedman, 2005). One of the new broad economic options by social media is easier and better access to self-pension investments. This option is elaborated in 3.4.

Whatever the hegemony of MNC, the broad access to social media or something else are the most important aspect of globalization that`s investigated in 2.4 SWOT-analysis of Market Economy. However, before switching to this global level of analysis, an individual pension investment guide is presented with a view to the new economic conditions in the globalized economy.

2.3.4 Pension Investment Guide

Introduction

In the industrialized economies about half of the households own some shares and the share of households with shares increases over time. This development is in accordance with the declining marginal utility of consumption and the growing span between `Consumerism` and `Simple Living` identified in Chapter 1.2. Further the incentive to private investment in shares is stimulated by the low or even negative interest on deposits in commercial banks since 2015. Chapter 1.3 develops Formula 1, summarizing the business conditions determining `Return of Investment (ROI)` as a function of production volume, variable and fixed costs and contribution margin.

An obvious motive for private households to invest arises from the fact that most modern people must assure full or partial finance of their lifestyle about 25 years after retirement from the labor market. The largest capital transaction in most households is the eventual investment in a private dwelling, however, financial pension investment in shares is a clean test of the households understanding of the market forces. Already, the Introduction outlined the market laws of *marginalism, real-value* and *opportunity costs* as core axioms of market economics. Below, the broad principles for financial economics are outlined with focus on self-pension investment.

Figure 10. US growth and S&P 500 since 1947
Source: *S&P Statistics*

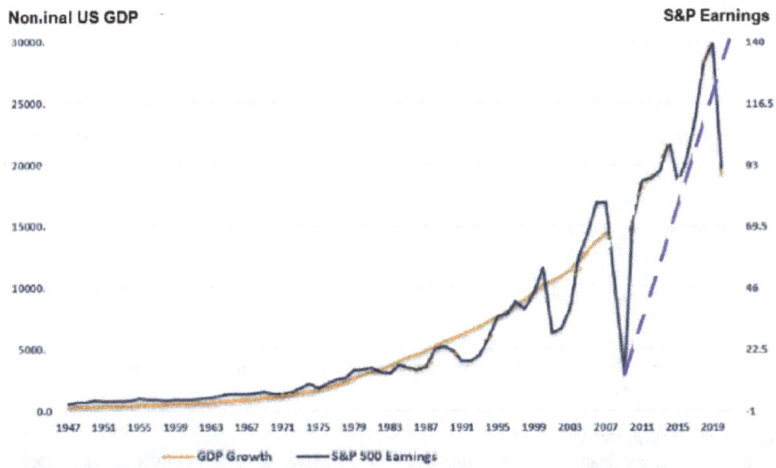

Broad Guidelines on Financial Investment

1 Have a long-Term Horizon

The most sure finding about stock share prices is that they move both up and down in cycles that are unpredictable to most people. The good news are, that so far the average stock market index has a long term tendency to rise. In this context, the best assurance for a positive long-term outcome is clear and simple: an investment horizon of at least 5 years expecting a moderate average outcome of 5-10% pro annum. Further, private investors must realize that they have to spend some time following their investment wherefore opening investments of 20.000 USD is lower limit.

More adventurous investors may be tempted to go for larger, short-term outcomes for instance as day-traders. However, newcomer investors are strongly warned against this type of ventures and stick to a less ambitious, but also less stressful investment strategy!

2 Give Priority to Global Growth Sectors

The big investment question is what type of shares to look for? The broadest reply is to go for shares in companies that operate in growth sectors as sector growth probably disseminates to other companies in the sector, too. Chapter

2.2 explains how globalization is closely related to extraordinary economies of scale that has constituted the hegemony of multinational companies (MNC). Figure 10 illustrates the relative development in the US since 1947 of ROI (S&P 500 Earnings) and Nominal GDP.

Box 3. Green Horizon Summit by WEF 2020: The Pivotal Role of Finance

● Green finance is any structured financial activity that has been created to ensure a better environmental outcome.
● -The value of green bonds traded is expected to hit $2.36 trillion 2023.
● -The European Central Bank is getting heavily involved in green finance.
● -The top three green bond issuers are the US, China and France.
● -The World Economic Forum focuses on how green finance can help in the recovery from
● COVID-19.
● At its simplest, green finance is any structured financial activity – a product or service – that's been created to ensure a better environmental outcome. It includes an array of loans, debt mechanisms and investments that are used to encourage the development of green projects or minimize the impact on the climate of more regular projects. Or a combination.

Funding sustainable development

For the United Nations, green financing plays an important role in delivering several of its Sustainable Development Goals. Its Environment team is already working with public and private sector organizations in an attempt to align international financial systems to the sustainable development agenda.

Some of the activities UN Environment is involved in include helping countries re-engineer their regulatory frameworks – so that green borrowing becomes compliant, for example – and helping steer public sector planning in a more environmentally friendly direction.

Clean sources of energy can be brought to fruition through the right combination of planning consent, strategic priorities and availability of capital. Such projects could be given preferential treatment to make them a more attractive option than, for example, fossil-fuel derived energy infrastructure. Typical projects, that fall under the green finance umbrella, include:

● Renewable energy and energy efficiency
● Prevention and control of pollution
● Conservation of biodiversity
● Initiatives towards circular economy
● Sustainable use of natural resources and land

Figure 10 shows that from 1947 until the financial crisis 2008 the US growth in ROI (S&P Earnings) is closely proportional to the nominal growth in GDP. Since 2009, the growth in S&P is quite faster than that of GDP (Stapled blue line). This is operated in an investment strategy giving priority to pension investment in HighTec-MNC:

1. Chapter 3.1 identifies digitalization as the core of the ongoing 4th Industrial Revolution. GAFA (Google, Apple, Facebook and Amazon) are impressive examples of this type of MNC. However, a primeval forest of new companies in artificial intelligence (AI) appears these years, too.
2. As further elaborated in Chapter 4, the energy sector is in fast transition towards carbon neutrality. This deep technological change requires huge

investments in new alternatives to fossil energy. Investments in green technology rise fast with good ROI as outlined in the Info Box below.

4. Pharmaceuticals is an important element of the modern welfare state too whereof healthcare is a key component as developed in Chapter . The pharmaceutical industry has for many years exhibited high rates of growth in both turnover and ROI. A number of these companies are also involved in the actual development of Covid-19 vaccines.
5. Related to the pharmaceuticals is the development of new healthcare technologies e.g. scanners, blood tests and training equipment. A sub-sector of healthcare with a record of high outcomes for investors, too.
6. A classic sector for profitable investments is the real estate sector that is expected to continue growth in the future, too.

The priorities outlined above are in no way exclusive. Good investors must always be aware of surprising new options.

3 Diversify Investments

Minimize your risk by diversification! The most important security complement to the investment horizon is diversification spreading the portfolio to more sectors as outlined above.

The most obvious way to spread the investment risk seems to be delegation of the investment responsibility to investment associations who are supposed to include professional investment know-how, too. However, there is no evidence that investment associations provide a better outcome to investors than laymen`s investments. This is largely due to direct and indirect transaction costs imposed by banks to associated investment companies. However, investment companies that are independent of banks do exist, too. A major risk for investment in this type of company is that the internal power becomes centralized to a few key persons that are capable of providing special benefits to themselves.

Due to the shortcomings of spreading the risk by special investment companies, more and more persons get motivated to invest their idle capital themselves. A way to increase the outcome of private investment, and at the same time increase both the earning options and diversify the risk, is to gear investment by bank loans at a lower rate of interest than the expected earnings from shares. Such geared investments implicate a special risk beyond losing your private capital, that of bankruptcy, if the stock market crashes. On this background, it is recommended that private gearing of investments should maximally implicate foreign loans corresponding to 50% of total assets, as well as presupposing that the investor have had good results at least 3 years, before he/her starts gearing.

To exemplify the security value of diversification, pharmaceuticals and the energy sector have different risk profiles. Pharmaceuticals are not so sensitive to demand recessions but depend very much on knowledge-intensive development of new products or new markets. The demand for energy depends on the other hand very much on broad economic growth and far less of specific game-changing technological breakthroughs. They are good investment complements!

4 Key Business Indicators

A series of key indicators serve to identify good investment shares:

4.1 Technical Analysis (TA)

Investment decisions must depart from updated information. An overview of price fluctuations during the last 5 years / 6 months is a first glance indicator as the tendency may continue. Is the share rising or falling or stagnating? However, it is unwise to put too much emphasis on a short-term momentum with a pension horizon on investments. Tendencies are indicated with arrows.

4.2-4 Price–Earnings Ratio (P/E)

A simple crucial indicator of the price level for a specific share is the P/E which indicates the price for an annual ROI corresponding to the latest ROI. The simple P/E is for most public shares refined both with a forwarded value and the relation to the growth rate for Earnings (PEG).

P/E must be considered in relation to the borrowing rate (i). Ultrashort the primary criteria for choosing between active (Shares) and passive (Bonds) financial investments is specified in Formula:

Formula 2: $P/E < 1/i$

Suppose for instance that the borrowing rate is 5%. So, $P/E < 20$ is an attractive buying price. However, when the borrowing rate of interest is halved to 2,5%, P/E up to 40 is an attractive buying price.

After the financial collapse 2008, the international level of interest declined markedly from a normal about 5% to close to zero today. Figure 6 shows that the level of low interest coincides with an extraordinary rise in share prices (S&P). The expectancy is that the level of extreme low interest remains in the 2020s due to the large surpluses in multinational companies.

4.5 Inner Value (Market Price Compared to Accounted (Booked) Value (P/B))

A simple defensive indicator is P/B. P/B<1 indicates that the accumulated sales value of assets is larger than the market value of the whole company. High P/B indicates high branding value.

4.6 External Value Compared with Turnover (EV/T)

A high EV/T indicates that intellectual capital, for instance Patents, is an especially important part of the total value of the company.

4.7 Other Business Indicators

Several other sorts of information may affect the share price, for example:

- Specific company news regards management, innovations, insecurities, etc
- News on company performance or that of competitors
- Investor sentiments
- Macroeconomic indicators: 1) Interest rate, 2) Inflation. 3) GDP and 4) Unemployment

5 Information Sources

In order, to get the required information for informed investment decisions, a variety of free information sources are available on the Internet. This includes for example:

- Investopedia.com explains relevant key terms and analytical methods
- Websites from national shareholder associations publish a lot of inspiring analyses
- Websites from the different stock exchanges contain most relevant data for trading decisions

- A variety of private websites with information on shares e.g. media as Bloomberg

Select your favorite Stock Exchange, for instance your national, select 25 favorite shares to follow and become familiar with them, for instance the *NasdaqOMXnordic*. See decision-making example in Table 2 comparing 5 selections ultimo 2020. Select the best investment option:

Table 2. Key statistics for stock share investment comparisons

Company	TA 1	P/E 1	For w•P/E 3	PEG 4	P/B 5	EV/T 6	Other Info 7
Ørsted	↑↑	13	+100%	1.3	3.4	4.3	**ROI peaked 17&18**
Vestas	↑↑	28	-25%	4.0	5.4	1.5	
Chr H Hold	↑↓	37	-10%	4.0	12	8.7	
Rockwool	↑↑	17	ND	ND	2.3	1.5	ND= no data
Novo Nordic	→→	24	-10%	2.9	1.7	7.5	

Warning on Complacency

In case you are having success with your pension investments you may be tempted to expand further and faster than you planned from the beginning. This temptation is well-known among gamblers. The best prevention of such error is to develop your competence in Positivist Dialectics as guided in Chapter 5.2. Especially the training of judgement in accordance with the principles of Long-Term Memorization is important.

2.4 SWOT-ANALYSIS OF LIBERALIST MARKET GROWTH

2.4.1. Definitions

This growth model originated by the First Industrial Revolution in the UK in the midst of the 18th Century. 1917-89 market growth was challenged by the central managed economy in Eastern Europe (Communism). The co-existence of these two basically opposite growth models in Europe represents a gigantic social experiment involving more hundreds of million people in the period from 1945 until the Fall of the `Iron Curtain`, 1989.

A comprehensive system assessment tool applied in the business world is the SWOT Analysis (Strength, Weakness, Opportunity and Threat). SWOT assesses the system all beneficial and harmful aspects of the system from both the Internal and the External side and in both helpful and harmful, see Table 3 (Andrews 1979; Gurel & Tat 2017). Typically 2-3 issues of each of the four dimensions are enough to describe the situation.

Table 3. SWOT analysis

	Beneficial	Harmful
Internal	**S** Strengths	**W** Weaknesses
External	**O** Options	**T** Threats

Below, a SWOT-analysis is done of liberal market growth compared with that of central managed economies in Eastern Europe in order to identify eventual market failures. Part 2 APPLIED DOUGHNUT ECONOMICS reviews appropriate interventions towards market failures.

2.4.2 Strength: A 15-fold Rise in GDP per Capita with better Quality of Life

How sure is it, that the 15-fold growth in GDP per capita in G7 is due to IMH? The opposite to IMH – central managed economy – has been tried out in Eastern Europe in the period from the Russian Revolution 1917 to the "Fall of the Iron Wall 1989". This large-scale social experiment with hundreds of millions of people during >70 years provides a unique option for comparison with IMH. Key figures on relative economic growth are summarized in Table 4 (Maddison, 2003). It shows that the centrally planned economy in Russia had a good initial growth in the Stalinist period up to World War II. This path of growth continued until the mid 70es, where it decayed in the period where liberalist globalization by IMH gave pace to market economies. The history of Eastern Europe – dominated by USSR 1950-89 – is very parallel to that of USSR with the amendment that after the decline of USSR, Eastern Europe benefits from inclusion in the EU where it is the fastest growing region.- an extra argument of special growth capacity of IMH.

Table 4. GDP growth rates per capita across economic systems (%)

Country	1928-40	1950-59	1959-76	1976-91	1991-98	2000-2017
USSR/Russia	3.8	2.9	3.2	0	-7.5	1.7[1]
Eastern Europe	N/D	3.2	3.5	-0.8	1.8	4[2]
China	N/D	5.2	1.2	5.6	7.0	9.4
G7				3.0		1.7

Source: Maddison A (2003) (11): The World Economy: Historical Statistics, OECD: Data 1928-98.
World Bank Database: Data 2000- and G7 1976-91.
Notes: 2000-08 Russian economy grow by 8% p.a. which recovered the loss of productivity in the first Decennium after the collapse of USSR Since the financial crisis and the low price of crude oil the
Russian growth has been at the level of G7. Countries in Eastern Europe joined the EU per 1.5.2004.

Further, Table 4 shows the surprising finding, that while private capitalism (IMH) is superior to socialism (USSR), the growth capacity of the Chinese state capitalism seems to be superior to that of private capitalism. In 50 years from the mid 70es Chinese economy has accomplished the same 15-fold growth that took 200 years in the private capitalist world.

2.4.3 Weakness: Reinforcing concentration of Income/Wealth

Until 1970, economic growth was distributed in a relatively stable way between ROI and wages due the formation of social democratic parties rooted in strong labor unions. Since 1970, the rise of multinational companies (MNC) due extraordinary economies of scale by globalization, has changed this trend in favor of ROI (Francese & Mulas-Granados, 2015) . This change arises essentially from clear comparative advantages of MNC that count for much more than the simple physical size of factories. Firstly, the demand of e.g. electronic products due branding-effects is only weakly related to price wherefore the inclination of the Demand curve typically is slightly positive rather than negative. Secondly, the marginal production costs – determining Supply - decline due economies of scale which represents the most radical break with classical economics. In the changed conditions, the intersection point between supply and demand is not a self-sustaining equilibrium, but the point of reinforcing monopolistic gains (M).

The hegemony of MNC is directly illustrated by the development of the tax on corporate profit. In this area, the hegemony of multinational companies is manifested by an average decline in corporate tax rates within the EU on 10 percent points since 1990 from about 35% to 25%. This expresses the competition among nations to attract multinational companies. Only a stronger international cooperation of economic policy, for instance a minimal rate of corporate tax, has a chance to match the ongoing pressures from multinational corporations.

2.4.4 Opportunity: Elimination of Relative Poverty by Welfare Economy

Table 1a illustrates how market-based economic growth enables elimination of poverty. The absolute level of poverty is estimated to be 5 USD/day by the World Bank 2015. 10% of the world population lives in absolute poverty which represents a dramatic progress compared to 1980 where 50% lived in absolute poverty. In the industrialized world, the discussion focuses on relative poverty, which beyond basal physical survival enables an acceptable social living. Relative poverty is often defined by economists as 50% of the median income. 2017, the median personal income in the USA was 32.000 USD indicating 16.000 USD as the relative poverty threshold. This is 8 times more income than absolute poverty (16.000/(5*365)) USD. Chapter 3 reviews existing knowledge on how relative poverty can be eliminated.

2.4.5 Threat: A Climate Catastrophe by

Since the 70s the economic growth has been a growing challenge according to the Ecosystem (Meadows et al., 1972). Currently the International Panel on Climate Change (IPCC) reports on the global state of the climate. The calculation models of IPCC show that global heating up to 1,5°C has moderate effects on the climate while global heating beyond 2°C disrupts the existing balance and turns global heating reinforcing with disastrous consequences as rising sea levels, extreme periods of drought, extreme periods of rain and flooding, other extreme weather conditions and reduced biodiversity. The actual prospects of climate change summarize as follows (IPCC, 2019):

"Human activities are estimated to have caused 1.0°C of global warming above pre-industrial levels around 1750. Global warming is likely to reach 1.5°C between 2030 and 2050 if it continues to increase at the current rate".

4.4.6 Conclusion of SWOT-Analysis

A Neoliberalist response to the conclusions of the SWOT-analysis is advanced by the statistician Bjorn Lomborg. A cost-effectiveness analysis (CEA) – analogue to evaluation of healthcare interventions – calculates the price of saving life years by alternative measures to reduce CO2-emission. This type of calculation indicates that it is better business to gain extra living years by a simple prophylactic measure such as smoking cessation. However, such a reductionist approach overlooks that the Ecosystem is a complex integrated with unique internal dynamics. An economic intervention counteracting the "Green-house effect" must respect the internal climatic dynamics as clarified by the meteorological research! Within healthcare a smoking cessation intervention is not supposed to have that strong impact on general healthcare.

Conclusions of the SWOT-analysis restructure macroeconomics in Part 2. DOUGHNUT ECONOMICS:

Chapter 3 reviews findings on the New_Welfare Economy.

Chapter 4 reviews `Economic Ecology` towards the "Green-house effect".

Review Questions

1. Explain the learnings from each of the Figures

Figure 11.

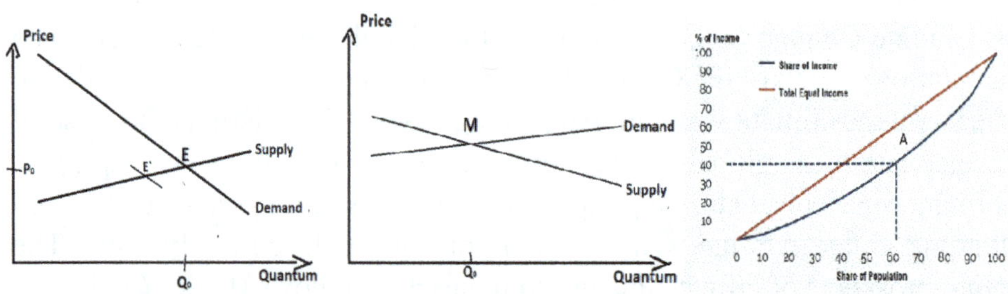

Competitive Market (Reread eventually 2.1) ***Monopolistic Market*** (Reread eventually 2.2) ***Lorenz Distribution*** (Reread eventually 2.2)

2) Explain each of the 5 basic laws of liberal market economy: (Reread eventually the Introduction)
   - Individual Choices by Opportunity Costs
   - Marginal Decision-Making

- Principle of Diminishing Returns
- Principle of Voluntary Returns
- Comparisons based on real rather than nominal values

3) What's the difference between `Monopolistic Competition` and `Hegemony of MNC`? (Reread eventually 2.2)
4) What's the difference in the world orders of `Cold War between Superpowers` respective `Economic Competition between Super Economies`? (Reread eventually 2.3)
5) What`s the Crucial Parameters of International Economic Strength? (Reread eventually Table 2 in 2.3)
6) Explain the parameters of Formula 2 (Reread eventually 2.3.3))
7) What's the SWOT-conclusions on liberal market economy? (Reread eventually 2.4)
    - ***Strength?***
    - ***Weakness?***
    - ***Opportunity?***
    - ***Threat?***

REFERENCES

Andrews, R. K. (1975). *The Concept of Corporate Strategy*. McGraw Hill.

Bahl, R. (2013). *Supereconomies. China and the Future of the World*. Allen Lane.

Chinese 2050 High Renewable Energy Penetration Scenario. (2015). Chinese Nat. Renew. Energy Centre.

Clayton Antitrust Act (1914). United States Congress.

Dunning, J. H. (1979). Toward an Eclectic Theory of International Production: Some Empirical Tests. *Journal of International Business Studies, 11*(1), 9–31. doi:10.1057/palgrave.jibs.8490593

Francese, M., & Mulas-Granados, C. (2015). *Functional Income Distribution and Its Role in Explaining Inequality*. IMF. doi:10.5089/9781513549828.001

Friedman, T. L. (2005). *The World is Flat. A Brief History of the Twenty-First Century*. Picador.

Global Top 100 Companies by market capitalization. (2017). PWC: www.pwc.com/top100

Gurel, E., & Tat, M. (2017). SWOT analysis: A theoretical review. *J Internat Soc Res, 10*(51), 1–23. doi:10.17719/jisr.2017.1832

Intergovernmental Panel on Climate Change (IPCC). (2019). *Summary Report*. https://www.ipcc.ch/2019/

Jantzen, R. T., & Volpert, K. (2013). *On the Mathematics of Income Inequality: Splitting the Gini Index in Two*. Mathematical Association of America.

Maddison, A. (2003). The World Economy: Historical Statistics. In *OECD: Data 1928-98*. OECD.

Meadows, D. H., Meadows, D. L., Randers, J., & Behrens, W. W. I. I. I. (1972). *Limits to Growth*. Rom-klubben.

Petty, T. (2014). *Capital in the Twenty-First Century*. Belknap/Harvard University Press.

Report on the Execution of the Central and Local Budgets for 2017 and the Draft of Central and Local Budgets for 2018. (n.d.). Chinese Ministry of Finance/Xinhua News Agency.

Smith, A. (1776). *Inquiry into the Nature and Causes of the Wealth of Nations*. doi:10.1093/oseo/instance.00043218

Teiling, B. (2018). Accountability of MNCs in Societal Transformation. In *Proc 19. Symposium on Sustainable Development*. International Institute of Advanced Studies (IIAS).

Section 2
Doughnut Economics

Chapter 3
New Welfare Economy

ABSTRACT

A review of the welfare economy finds that seven Nobel Laureates recommend a tax system with negative income. The size, entitlement to, meeting out, and finance of universal basic income (UBI) are concluded in accordance with other social security legislation. Further, New Public Management 2.0 is outlined. It also includes national accountancy with multinational companies. The final section presents a COVID-19-based index on social vulnerability that reveals serious limitations to deal with the climate threat in a majority of G7 countries in contrast to the excellent coping with COVID-19 of the larger Asian economies.

INTRODUCTION

Figure 1. Illustration by H. Schinzel

DOI: 10.4018/978-1-7998-6424-0.ch003

Mainstream concepts are challenged in more ways by the globalization of markets. Classical income distribution is directly disrupted, and monopolist behaviors are no longer an exception but the standard case. Further, the expansion of collective services makes effectiveness of public services a key challenge, too. Chapter 3 `New Welfare Economy` is based on the latest research.

The rapid rising global threat from global heating related to economic growth gives today economic top priority to environmental protection. Chapter 4 on Economic Ecology focuses on this challenge based on surveys of the state of the Ecosystem as well as the state of energy alternatives to fossil energy sources.

3.1 STABILIZATION POLICY

The cybernetic client-server-integrator model structures macroeconomics in Households (Client), Business (Server) and Government (Integrator). The circular cash-flow between consumers, enterprises and public institutions constitutes the national economic system where consumer expenses are identical to the factor income of someone. However, the national economy is today more or less an open system strongly affected by export to and import from other countries, too. Table 1 defines major components of an open macroeconomy (Keynes, 1936). Keynes showed that classical self-stabilization of employment is blocked due to inherent inertia. National fiscal policy must support a high level of aggregate employment increasing public expenses to assure a high level of employment in periods of business recession. The masterpiece of Keynes was the "New Deal" of Roosevelt 1932 which became pathbreaking to recover from "The Great Depression 1929". Keynes fiscal strategy applies not to recession due to poor international competitiveness. This explains why Germany was reluctant to support expansive fiscal policies in some countries in Southern Europe after the breakdown of the international financial crisis 2009.

Recovery from recurrent demand-based business recessions is the short-term target for Doughnut Economics. Major components of modern fiscal and monetary policies are explained in Table 1.

Table 1. Components of macroeconomics

Component	Firms (B)		Households (H)		Government (G)		National Income	
	Out	In	Out	In	Out	In	Out	In
A. Goods and Services	(W)	(C_H) C_G	C_B	(W)	C_G -	- -	$\underline{Y}$(Emp)	C_H C_G
B. Saving-Investment	S_B	I_B	S_H	S_B	S_G	I_G	S_{B+H+G}	I_{B+G}
C. Public Transfers	T_B	Sub_B	T_H	Sub_H	Sub_{B+H}	T_{B+H}		
D. Foreign Trade	Im_B	X	Im_H				Im_{B+H}	X

Note 1: W is wages. **C** is Consumer expenses at the level of "Goods and Services".
The aggregated level of "Savings (**S**) and Investments (**I**)" depends on the level of interest (i).
"Public Transfers" or cash payments (**T**) are specified to Firms ($\mathbf{T_B}$) respective Households ($\mathbf{T_H}$).
"Foreign Trade" (Exports and Imports) reflects the international level of competitiveness.
Note 2: Beyond components specified in $Y_{(Emp)}$, macroeconomics include *non-priced voluntary community work (Commons)* e.g. Sports clubs, Cultural associations, Housing associations, social care and healthcare and environmental protection. Every third adult participates in voluntary community work at least once a year contributing with about 10% of normal work hours. Voluntary community work, although not accounted for in national production statistics, is an important social factor for the well-being of the population. Further, non-governmental organizations (NGO) based on extensive use of voluntary work play an important role in long-term macroeconomic development policy, for instance welfare and healthcare as well as modern Environmental protection.

A modern Keynes Macro model understands national economic dynamics as the interaction between Firms (B) serving Households (H) as regulated by governmental (G) by fiscal and monetary policy components as specified in Table 1. The aggregated economic activity generated by these players is totaled in the national income account. The national aggregate of the components determines the level of employment as illustrated in the macroeconomic equation (Formula 3):

Formula 3: $Y_{Emp} = C_B + C_H + S_{B+H+G} - I_{B+G} + Ex - Im_{B+H}$

National economic policy aims to have both a high level of employment (Y_{Emp}) to make use of available resources as well as low inflation (**r**) to protect the international competitiveness ensuring balance in Foreign Trade. So, core targets for economic politics, is to identify appropriate interventions in the macroeconomic conditions for the macroeconomic players, so that the overall target is fulfilled as good as possible in the long-term.

In order, to design effective macroeconomic interventions, it is crucial to understand the reinforcement aspect of such interventions which is termed *multiplicator effects* in macroeconomics. For example, a fiscal measure intervention to improve employment can be tax reductions leaving firms and households with a larger disposable income to use for extra private consumption creating more jobs. More jobs mean even extra income wherefore the multiplicator effect of the tax cut means it is even larger than originally planned. However, recent research shows that the expansive effect of tax cuts mostly benefits very rich people more fold due to derived capitalization by rising stock market prizes. This means that expansive fiscal policy by investment in necessary green technology has a far broader utility effect in the years to come.

Besides fiscal policies, monetary policy is important as expansionary macroeconomic stabilization, too. Monetary policies stimulate private investments easing borrowing either by direct lowering of the borrowing rate or by expanding the total amount of credit from the national bank increasing the total level of credit from the banking sector.

It must be recognized that the expansive fiscal and monetary policies are not the solution to all cases of excessive unemployment. In some cases, excessive unemployment is rooted in poor international competitiveness of a country. For example, have some EU-countries in Southern Europe, for instance Greece and Italy, given that beneficial general pension schemes to their citizens that the supply of labor become reduced and rapid wage-driven inflation coexists with high unemployment rates. This situation requires "structural economic reforms'' that reduces government over-spending, which of course is perceived by ordinary citizens in these countries, as very tough times.

Further, the present Pluralist Doughnut Economics modifies the view on stabilization policy in the way the Top priorities of *GreenTec and Redistribution of income* must be reflected in the design of expansive policies, for instance after Covid-19. Especially, it is warned to give tax income reductions as this stimulus effect mostly relies on many fold benefits to the high-income segment in the format of demand pushed increases in stock exchange equities.

A special long-term risk of Keynes-like expansionary fiscal and monetary policy is the rapid increases in the public debt indicated as share of GDP. A study of the World Bank concludes that when the `Public Debt` exceeds 70% of GDP, it becomes reinforcing as it weakens the national growth rate. Table 1a in 2.3 shows that already before Covid-19, Public Debt exceeded 70% in all G7 buty Germany and Canada. After Covid-19, public debt has increased a lot in all countries. Budget discipline is an important issue in the polarization between Right and Left political wings. In order to improve the long flexibility in all democratic countries, not at least within G7, it is recommended especially to the `Left Wing`, that aims to be leading in the heavy social reforms recommended by the SWOT Analysis in 2.5, to show more modesty in the pressures for other public expenses the reforms of Top priority. This recommendation is especially relevant to the US where changing administrations since that of Reagan continuously have had large budget deficits. Republicans defend erroneously budget deficits due to tax reductions aiming to increase employment and Democrats defend public deficits with a social conscience that appears as short-termed.

3.2 SOCIAL WELFARE POLICY BEYOND THE MINIMAL STATE

3.2.1 Social Welfare Expenses in OECD

The Organization for Economic Co-operation and Development (OECD) administers a huge database on economic and social life in the member states which forms the base for this section. OECD includes 35 member-countries whereof 25 are from Europe. Out of the large economies the most significant non-members of OECD are the group of emerging economies (China, India, Russia, Brazil and South Africa).

Post-industrial living requires many goods and services that involve other persons (collective goods) wherefore the outcome is a group utility rather besides the individual value. General government, including defense, security and judicial services, are termed Minimal State. Other domains of collective services are social security, healthcare, pensions and education. Regarding these sectors the optimal political organization regarding public versus private responsibility is disputed. The aggregate costs of the minimal and extended services are termed welfare costs. To identify welfare reforms opted to increase the common satisfaction, Table 2 shows key figures on total welfare costs in OECD. The sub-sections comprise G7 and the Nordic countries (Denmark, Finland, Norway and Sweden). Total gross social expenses are the larger welfare target and covers expenses to organize public or private social services for the assistance of disadvantaged groups e.g. spending on a range of things, such as looked-after children and long-term care for the elderly, the sick and disabled. Also, social welfare expenses comprise temporary, permanent, and additional incomes. Gross means that some social cash payments count as taxable income. Total public and private welfare expenses account for 43% of GDP in OECD ranging from 42% in Canada to 60% in France and USA. The relative high level of welfare expenses in the USA is due to relatively large private shares of social expenses and healthcare. A third welfare target is pensions for the elderly where the public coverage varies the most (from

5% in Canada to 16% in Italy). Across G7, three countries spend more than 50% of GDP on welfare. These countries, France, Italy and USA also have the most threatening public debt (90-120% of GDP) compared to the internal criteria in the EU for solid public finances, £60%.

As public and private collective welfare (exclusive Pensions) consumes from 40 through 50% of GDP within G7, the organization of welfare services is by distance the most important economic-political issue. Despite significant differences in the private-public finance regarding the tertiary level of education, no important differences are detected regarding the total costs. The costs of healthcare are quite homogeneous, too, except for the liberalist US healthcare system which costs the double of other G7 and covers a lower population share. The privatized US Healthcare system is both extremely and offers a low coverage of the population as 15% has no coverage at all.

Table 2. Welfare costs in selected OECD countries (% of GDP 2018)

Welfare	Nordic	Canada	France	Germany	Italy	UK	USA	Japan	G7	OECD
Social[1] (Incl. Cash)	31% (6%)	23% (5%)	35% (3%)	28% (4%)	30% (4%)	28% (4%)	31% (2%)	25% (2%)		24% (4%)
Health[2]	7%	7%	9%	8%	7%	8%	16%[2]	8%		6%
Education[3]	6%	7%[5]	6%	4%	4%	7%[5]	7%[5]	4%		5%
Total	**44%**	**39%**	**46%**	**40%**	**41%**	**43%**	**53%**	**37%**	**45%**	**35%**
Pension[4]	11%	5%	14%	10%	16%	6%	7%	9%		8%
Life-expectancy		**83**	**83**	**82**	**84**	**81**	**80**	**84**	**82**	

Notes: Primary source of data is OECD database 2018 which has comparative data for 1960, too.
[1]Gross social expenses including private expenses but are exclusive social cash payments.
[2]Public expenses. Expenses for the USA includes private insurance expenses with 7% of GDP.
[3]Public expenses for primary, secondary and tertiary education.
[4]Public cash pensions for old age and veterans. Information on private pension investments is not available.
[5]Includes private expenses aggregating to about 2% of GDP.

The focus for improvement of welfare policies is definite social care. The new neuroeconomic psychology presented in 1.4 has already changed the political economy. Regarding welfare policy, the social aspect must recognize that security rather than classical economic rationality dominates the bottom of society addressed by social welfare policy. 2019 WHO Europe has launched a Report that demands more income stability in the bottom of society for reasons of social medicine (3). The reasons are that the strong social inequality in health can be moderated by better social security in the bottom of society.

Further an economic approach to social welfare policy must include the tax system as personal taxes directly affect the social distribution of income. So, an introduction to tax systems is necessary before the new social welfare aspect can be addressed.

3.2.2 Principles of Personal Tax Systems

A problematic issue in modern welfare policy is the organization of social security. The subsistence of all adult citizens in post-industrial economies is in various degrees secured by numerous specific legislations related to different life events such as unemployment, sickness and recovery, disability and aging. Besides, the finance of all these social security subsidies is achieved by an even larger number of special taxes and exemptions. Typically, a post-industrial state has >1000 tax laws and specific legislations on employment comprise 25.000 pages. This level of complexity makes it impossible for ordinary citizens to overview legislations wherefore the bureaucratic aspect of social security weakens the good intentions behind it. The options of a drastic simplification of social security legislations in combination with a more effective redistribution effect is investigated below, as the key issue of public welfare, departing from basic principles of personal taxing.

The most important source of government revenue is tax. A tax is a compulsory payment from individuals and companies to the government based on certain rules or criteria such as income earned, property owned, capital gains made, or expenditure incurred (money spent) on domestic and imported articles. Already Adam Smith stated principles of taxation, that still are valid. Based on international comparison, the most important demands on modern tax systems are:

1 Allocation Neutrality

A tax system should be designed to be neutral in the sense that it should disturb the market forces as little as possible, unless there is a good reason to the contrary. For example, the government may impose tax on polluting activities, e.g. CO_2-emission, to discourage firms to pollute the environment. Likewise, a tax on cigarettes will serve a two-fold purpose: raising revenue and discouraging consumption of this harmful item. In both cases, the market is disturbed but in a desirable way. An example of an allocation neutral tax is a value-added tax on all goods and services supposing the revenue is used for public purposes with at least the same marginal utility as private goods.

A threat to allocation neutrality is a combination of tax rates, special tax deductions and individual subsidies that suspend the income incentive to work. People typically respond strongly to incentives, that lack of a work inventive is destructive both to the individual and society. A large economic sector where public regulation in many countries blocks for a Pareto-optimal allocation is the housing sector. From an economic point of view, society is better off with a flexible housing sector where the cost of a domicile corresponds to the user-value. However, politicians aim to protect special groups of voters with specific regulations that block market function.

2 Horizontal Equity

Horizontal equity is when equally situated individuals are taxed equal and persons of equal income pay identical amounts in taxes. There is hardly any controversy about the principle but it is difficult to fulfil in practice as two families with the same income can be very different. What if one family has eight children and the other has none? What if one family has unusually high medical expenses, while the other has none? To minimize horizontal inequality due to differences in household structure special tax rules apply to married couples.

3 Vertical Equity (Ability-to-Pay)

If equals are to be treated equally, un-equals should be treated unequally. This precept is known as vertical equity. This concept has been translated into the *ability-to-pay* principle, according to which those most able to pay should pay the most taxes. Broadly, the principle suggests that the fairest tax is one based on one's financial ability to support governmental activities through.

Simple fairness demands equal sacrifice by both rich and poor. A rich man must pay more money in taxes than a poor man for each to bear the same burden in supporting governmental services. Table 2 summarizes the analysis of the redistribution effect of alternative systems of personal income tax in a post-industrial economy. The proportional income tax represents the USA while the progressive income tax may represent social democrat welfare states e.g. the Nordic Countries. In the comparison of proportional and progressive income tax an individual annual income of 12.000 Euro represents the relative poverty boundary. An annual individual income of 35.000 Euro represents the mean income. An annual income of 100.000 Euro is a high income. In both systems the actual personal tax has some tax-free bottom levels with proliferations which for simplification are set to equal the relative poverty boundary.

Table 3. Proportional and progressive tax systems with/without basic income

Income (1000 Euro)	Personal Tax System			Tax Payment (Euro)		
	Proportional	Progressive	Progressive + Basic Income	Proportional	Progressive	Progressive + Basic Income
12.000	0	0	25%-12.000	0	0	-9.000
12.000 - 35.000	25%	25%	25%-12.000	5.750	5.750	**-3.250**
35.000 -100.000	25%	40%	40%-12.000	22.000	31.750	22.750
Set Off + Proliferation						+9.000
Tax Revenue				**22.000**	**31.750**	**31.750**

The comparison also presents an alternative income tax system, where progressive income tax is combined with a universal subsidy instead of bottom income deductions. Besides ensuring social security, the universal subsidy benefits average taxpayers as they are not paying any income tax at all but receive net 3.250 Euro from the Government per year. At first glance, the dark side of benefit appears to be a drastic reduction of the total tax revenue, however, set offs in existing cash subsidies and cancellation of tax deduction proliferations can cover the most of this gap.

3.2.3 Universal Basic Income

Benefits from Universal Basic Income (UBI)

A series of Nobel Prize Laureates (Milton, Meade, Samuelson, Simon, Solow, Tinbergen and Tobin) recommend negative income tax for redistribution of income in accordance with Table 3 (Gentilini et al., 2020). All taxpayers below a certain income level receive a subsidy from the Government to ensure a minimum income. In some versions the subsidy covers only the difference between the actual income and the bottom level. In the general version termed Universal Basic Income (UBI), the subsidy is equal to the baseline of relative poverty and independent of all other personal income, wealth, and relations to the labor market. UBI is the version of negative income tax with the strongest redistribution effect extending the classical social contract between individuals and social authorities (Rousseau) to include economic rights. Further, UBI is also as already mentioned recommended for reasons of social medicine, see Info Box 1 (HAGH, 2018).

Box 1. Health Impact of basic income

Individual Level:
Mental health, Supporting Intrinsic motivation, sense of Security/control, empowerment as demonstrated e.g. in the Finnish UBI sample test9
Systemic Society Level:
Generating a foundation for comprehensive economic security system, senses of belonging, security in society, inclusion and social participation, and accountability, build/rebuild universal welfare state. Field Experiment with Guaranteed Annual Income in Canada demonstrates 8.5% decline in the hospitalization rate between 1974-1978 where mental health is a major component
Policy Level:
Lowering public sector costs linked with poverty/insecurity to the health sector, supporting preventative health interventions, impact more direct but not confined to the lower part of the gradient only (proportional and universal effect)9
Limitations:
These effects are conditional on other change in the policy environment (fiscal capability/political preferences, economic policy)

However, to mainstream economists the benefits of UBI are not so simple, because a free income to all citizens is expected to reduce work motivation, consecutively the labor supply and finally economic growth. So, in the long-term society may be worse off with UBI. The contra-argument by neuroeconomic psychology is, that the insecurity of income among low-income on top of the restriction of consumption weakens general health in a way that turns inequality in health a serious social problem. To assess which of these alternatives fit best to the real world, sample-based pilot-studies of the dynamic effects of UBI are conducted in recent years. Finnish sample included about 2000 participants among social clients in the age span 23-59 years. A statistical control group comprised 5.000 other social clients. The participants received a free, monthly subsidy of 650 USD in two years. The total budget of the project is 20 million EUR. The preliminary results based on the first 12 months participation was published in 2019.

The Finnish UBI-sample shows no effect on labor supply (5). This finding is online with an extensive review from the International Monetary Fund (IMF). A special case where a small reduction in work hours is found by UBI is for single mothers with small children. Another study of a trial with cash transfers in the Islamic Republic of Iran, a small reduction of work hours among 20-29 years old workers was found, however, to the workforce as a whole no such effect was seen. The over-all conclusion from UBI-studies of labor supply is that of no effect in a 12-month time horizon.

Table 4. Qualitative effects of Finnish UBI sample (%)

QUESTION	Experimental Group		Control Group		TOTALS	
	Strongly Agree	Somewhat Agree	Strongly Agree	Somewhat Agree	Experiment	Control
UBI make more financial sense to accept a job offer?	68*	21	42	34	89	76
UBI makes it easier to start your own business?	51*	22	39	24	73	63
Your state of health is good?	15	41	10	36	73	46
Your ability to influence social matters is poor?	16	19	25	23	35*	48

Notes: The Experimental Group comprised 2.000 persons while the Control Group comprised 5.000 (5). Kela and the Ministry of Social Affairs and Health. (2019, Aug. 2.) Press Release.
*Indicates a significant difference (5% Significance).

Box 2. Entitlement of Universal Basic Income (UBI)

1. UBI is assigned to adults (>17 years) which typically represents 75% of the total population.
2. UBI applies exclusively to inhabitants with national Citizenship to prevent international “shopping”.
The international statistics are not very good as some countries like the USA with many illegal immigrants. Other countries, like the UK, have had liberal access to Citizenship from colonial times. Countries like Denmark with relative restrictive access for foreigners do have relevant figures on the share of inhabitants without Citizenship. An estimate on Danish data is that 90% of all adult inhabitants are entitled to UBI.
3. UBI must be differentiated by age in accordance with normal social legislation. Citizens >17 years are entitled to UBI, because youngsters often move away from home to seek professional education at that age. Thus, UBI from the onset of professional education, encourages as many as possible to have the best possible education as a positive spin-off for society. Youngsters 18-25 years are on that background entitled to 50% of the full UBI while persons ≥65 are entitled 70% of the full UBI in accordance with normal pension schemes. Due to differentiation by age – typical 12% youngsters and 20% elderly - the weighted average due to differentiation by age is 88% of a full UBI.
4. Following social welfare legislation, UBI should be differentiated according to size of household. The average household size in industrialized countries is 2-3 persons. The first member of the household receives 100% UBI and the following members receive 50%. The presupposed household of 2.5 loads 70%.
In all, UBI are designed to load: 0.75*0.9*0.87*0.7 corresponding to 41% of the total population.
Supposing UBI corresponds to 50% of median income in accordance with the international norm of relative poverty. With Gini-coefficient, UBI is 33% and 70% of the mean. So, UBI costs 0.5*0.41*0.7 = 14% of GDP

The Finnish UBI-sample examines emotional effects, too, as summarized in Table 3. No negative effect was found on the supply of labor as expected by Neoliberalist economists. In contrast, a significant improvement in the quality of life including the incentive to work. Another UBI-project in Ontario has the same level of subsidy target group as the Finnish. Interviews with a series of participants lead to preliminary conclusions parallel to the Finnish UBI-project.

Entitlement and Finance

Entitlement to and finance of UBI in accordance with social legislation are shown below:

The annual political negotiations of the Fiscal Budget in democracies have typically a range that is less than 1% of GDP. On this background is the introduction of UBI with a gross budget of 14% of GDP a huge reform of public finances that requires careful preplanning and stepwise implementation. In order to approach such a strategy. Before starting such project, a survey of possible sources of finance is required, see Info Box 3

Box 3. Finance of UBI

1. Already large groups of citizens receive cash payments in elder pension, social pensions, disablement pensions, income replacement subsidies, etc. UBI must be set-off in all existing public cash payments to individual citizens. In Table 12 cash payments to individuals amount to 15% of GDP across OECD). 50% or 7.5% of GDP are in this way supposed to be financed by direct set-off in existing public cash payments.
2. Most countries have a bottom line for personal income tax which varies a lot. In the USA, the Federal bottom line is as high as 24.000 USD in 2019. In some countries - like Germany – the bottom deduction is about 10.000 USD but complemented by extra bottom deductions for persons in the workforce (Proliferations). It is expected that the bottom deductions including relevant proliferations aggregate to 100% of UBI (1.000 Euro/Month). A bottom level tax of 25% is justified by the broad finding that even a Minimal State requires about 25% of GDP. A bottom level personal tax of 25% provides 25% the gross UBI budget of 14% corresponding to 3.5% of GDP.
3. More public counseling and training programs are mandatory to receivers of cash payments in social care. By unconditioned UBI, a share of clients is supposed to reject these activities, which saves 1% of GDP.
4. The residual finance of 2% of GDP can be provided by two new tax measures contributing to modification of serious and growing market failures associated with the globalization of markets:

- A tax at the root of CO_2-emission sources (ETS) would contribute significantly to acceleration of the transition to a carbon neutral economy as further analyzed in Chapter 4.
- A "Digital Turn-over Tariff" (DTT) is justified by the comparative advantage of virtual to physical retail businesses e.g. regarding costs of marketing, personal service and housing. DTT should be imposed on the total gross turnover of digital businesses including financial transactions.
- A special income tax on Top 1% incomes to counteract monopolistic revenues by globalization.

The major part of both ETS and DTT are probably handed over to digital customers, but at the same time serious market be financed failures are counteracted.

In all, UBI can be introduced in the most advanced social welfare states without any rise of general income tax tariffs. In liberal welfare states as the USA and UK general income tax tariffs may have to rise a few percent, but in that case they represent a shortcut to advanced social welfare, too. In emerging economies e.g. China and India more UBI- experiments are running e.g. with UBI only at the level of absolute poverty.

Universal Basic Income in a Historical Perspective

The target of UBI summarizes this background as a historical synthesis of democratic politics, welfare economy and social medicine as surveyed in Table 4. The historical root of welfare policy is identified as the charity work performed by religious organizations. After the Great Depression 1929, Truman's New Deal helped a broad share of the population to recover economically. Subsequently and especially after World War II, it gave rise to a broad basket of welfare legislation, especially in countries with well organized labor unions. In the Scandinavian social welfare states that implicated too nearly a fast redoubling of the total tax load from about 25% in 1960 to 45% in the mid 70es. As documented in Table 2, the social welfare state did deliver to citizens as the total private and public expenses to social security, healthcare and education require a lower share of total income than the USA as a prototype of liberal welfare.

Table 5. Neuroeconomic welfare model

Target	Modality		
	Goods/Services	Privileges	Cash Transfers
1. Needs-based solidarity (<1930)	Charity work by religious organizations		
2. Middle-Class economies of scale (1930-2000)	Broad services in healthcare and social care; Active fiscal recovery policy	Proliferations in tax exemptions and Targeted subsidies	Pensions for elderly and disabled; Compensation for unemployment
3. Cognitive solidarity (<2000)			**UBI**

Firstly, UBI appears in the historical context as a synthesis of more aspects as listed in Table 4.

Secondly, it represents a mediation of the classical political animosity in the direction of the center-oriented long-term collaboration advanced by the rise of the creative class as explained in 1.1. As a broad segment of the modern creative class belongs to the economic middle class, this segment is the one that can expect a net gain from UBI, too. The bottom income group gets less net gains than the middle class due to the set-off in existing public social cash payments.

Thirdly, UBI integrates welfare economy and social medicine in the way that long-term income stability from research in social medicine is expected to improve general health across a wide spectrum of sufferings (Haagh & Rohregger, 2019). Further, the near future is expected to increase job-related stress in the bottom of society as artificial intelligence (AI) e.g. by Robotics that replaces a large segment of low-skill jobs. On this background leading global entrepreneurs in AI as Bill Gates and Mark Zuckerberg are now recommending UBI, too.

Box 4. BIEN - Basic Income Earth Network (https://basicincome.org)

Basic income (BI) is defined by BIEN as a periodic cash payment unconditionally delivered to all on an individual basis, without means-test or work requirement:

1. Periodic: it is paid at regular intervals (for example every month), not as a one-off grant.
2. Cash payment: it is paid in an appropriate medium of exchange, allowing those who receive it to decide what they spend it on. It is not, therefore, paid either in kind (such as food or services) or in vouchers dedicated to a specific use.
3. Individual: it is paid on an individual basis—and not, for instance, to households.
4. Universal: it is paid to all, without means test.
5. Unconditional: it is paid without a requirement to work or to demonstrate willingness-to-work.

A wide variety of BI proposals are circulating today. They differ along many other dimensions, including in the amounts of the BI, the source of funding, the nature and size of reductions in other transfers that might accompany it, and so on. BIEN is a charitable organization dedicated to taking an educational role, and therefore, it cannot endorse any particular proposal; it is open to people and affiliates who favor very different proposals or who take information roles themselves.

A BI that is stable in size and frequency and high enough to be, in combination with other social services, part of a policy strategy to eliminate material poverty and enable the social and cultural participation of every individual is often called a "full BI," and a lower one is often called a "partial BI." Both the definitions of "full" and "partial" are controversial, and BIEN has not attempted to define them officially.

Some short-term proposals currently focus on the so-called "partial BI." Such a scheme would not be a full substitute for other redistributive measures but would provide a low – and slowly increasing – basis to which other incomes, including the remaining social security benefits and means-tested guaranteed income supplements, could be added. Some supporters see this as a path toward a full BI; others prefer the strategy of pushing for a full Basic Income from the start; and perhaps some favor only a partial BI.

Many reasons have all been invoked in BI's favor, including liberty and equality, efficiency and community, common ownership of the Earth and equal sharing in the benefits of technical progress, the flexibility of the labor market and the dignity of the poor, the fight against inhumane working conditions, against the desertification of the countryside and against interregional inequalities, the viability of cooperatives and the promotion of adult education, autonomy from bosses, husbands and bureaucrats.

The inability to tackle unemployment with conventional means has, in the last decade or so, become a major reason for the idea being taken seriously throughout Europe by a growing number of scholars and organizations. Social policy and economic policy can no longer be conceived separately, and BI is increasingly viewed as the only viable way of reconciling two of their respective central objectives: poverty relief and full employment. Grassroots activism for BI has increased greatly since 2010. In addition, many prominent European social scientists have now come out in favor of it – among them several Nobel laureates in economics. In a few countries some major politicians, including from parties in government, are also beginning to stick their necks out in support of it. At the same time, the relevant literature – on the economic, ethical, political and legal aspects – is gradually expanding and those promoting the idea, or just interested in it, in various European countries and across the world have started organizing into active networks. Yet, the proposal also receives strong political resistance in most countries.

The homepage gives valuable information on "HISTORY OF BASIC INCOME" as well as "FAQ on BI".

Fourthly, UBI is an option to simplify and rationalize social welfare legislation that in advanced social welfare democracies appears as a patchwork without internal structure due to changing political regimes over time. In more liberalist economies e.g., the USA represents UBI, a potential quantum leap for social welfare.

Fifthly, a recent survey by Gallup and Northeastern University finds a slight majority of Americans opposed to a universal basic income (UBI) as means to support workers displaced by AI adoption. Conversely, about three-fourths of residents in the U.K. and Canada favor the idea. This indicates that UBI very soon can become a hot political issue in democratic welfare countries.

3.3 NEW PUBLIC MANAGEMENT 2.0

3.3.1 Market-like Effectiveness in Public Welfare Services?

Modern welfare policy begins with New Deal 1933 towards the Great Depression and continues with large welfare reforms in the 70es in the Nordic countries and some Continental economies. In Germany the welfare model is known as Ordoliberalism. Social democratic welfare threatened in the 80s public welfare by over-expansion due to inflationary pressures in the private sector. This raises the question of the meaning of effectiveness in public services?

The most market-like method to choose between alternative public welfare projects is to take inspiration from Figure 1 in the Introduction and ask people about what they are willing-to-pay (WTP). The WTP method is widely used for private marketing tests, for instance by publishers having to price a book. There has been some research in pricing public services by WTP, too. However, the WTP research reveals a lot of insecurity in private preferences due to 1) State of the economy, 2) Trendlines/In-season, 3) Individual differences and 4) Circumstances (for instance geography) and 5) Quality.

Due to the insecurity of WTP considering the expectation of some long-term stability in the provision of public services another market-like approach departs from the market effectiveness rather than individual preferences. A broad European approach along this line is termed New Public Management (NPM) (Hood, 1991). NPM is based on principles of private strategic management, transforming stiff detailed budgets to management by goals and data-based supervision. This implicates:

- Outsourcing of services from public in institutions to private companies
- Privatization of public services

- Competition between private and public service suppliers
- Monitoring of the quality of contracted services by statistical indicators

NPM is implemented in more countries and evaluated, for instance in the UK and Denmark. The Thatcher Government implemented NPM in 1990 in healthcare in the UK with paradoxical consequences as public costs rose due to outsourcing costs without public savings and with more complaints (Hood & Dixon, 2015). In Denmark, the Schluter Government launched NPM in 1993. A systematic assessment of overall public service effectiveness in Denmark from 2000-2015 finds ():

- 2000-2005 effectiveness rose 10-15%
- 2005-2010 effectiveness rose 5-7%
- 2010-2015 effectiveness rose 2-3%

In the same period the guaranteed maximum waiting time for elective hospital treatment declined from 3 to 1 months. On the negative side, a qualitative assessment by interviews with civil servants concludes an increase in distrust, conflicts and bureaucracy (Andersen et al., 2016). In reply to the criticism of NPM in Denmark, the strategy of 2% p.a. gain in effectiveness in public services are cancelled (considered implemented) and the pressure on employees eases e.g. by welfare technology and extra staff. The crucial Danish learning is that a market-like efficiency dogma is effective but can stress the staff beyond the limits of healthy work conditions, too. To avoid undue pressures on staff and clients, NPM 2.0 requires that *minimal public staffing standards* must be identified as part of the professionalism it pursues.

Healthcare is more complicated than local municipal social services due to medical specialization. Even local hospitals require an even larger local district than a municipality to establish medical specialization in an economic way. The university level of hospital specialization requires a base of 1 million inhabitants and close cooperation with local hospitals as well. An appropriate frontline of healthcare is municipal general practitioners serving as "Gate-keepers" to specialized healthcare at hospitals or practicing generalists. General practitioners and hospitals should be financed partly by "Per capita fee" and partly by "Fee-for-service" in search of a balance between over-expansion of services due to "Fee for service" and bureaucratic stagnation due to "Per capita fee". Follow up rehabilitation to the growing number of elder patients with chronic diseases requires an elaborated collaboration between hospitals and municipal services by integrated care teams (Larsen, 2011). CEA is a central tool for economic management in healthcare.

Box 5. Example of Cost-Benefit Analysis (CBA)

Suppose politicians want to introduce a new screening program for a specific health risk and face Alternatives A and B with key figures as specified below.

	Program A	Program B
Cost of full program	$1.5 mil.	$2.0 mil.
Number of persons screened	10,000	10,000
Number of drug addicts correctly identified by screening	120	200
Number of identified drug addicts "cured" by therapy segment of program	40	50

From a pragmatic economic point of view the key figures are costs respective outcomes (utility units) of the alternatives. Alternative A costs 37.500 USD per "cured" (outcome) while that of Alternative B is 40.000 USD. In that case Alternative A is preferable and the relative effectiveness arises from the finding that 33% of the identified target population is "cured" while that`s only 25% in Alternative B.

3.3.2 Cost-Effectiveness Analysis (CEA) in Healthcare

The principle is that a common outcome (utility unit) must be identified and priced to compare alternatives which is difficult to apply due to insecurity about the pricing of the utility unit. A weaker format recognizing the insecurity of WTP is the *Cost-effectiveness Analysis* (CEA) where alternative costs of an outcome in natural units are compared. CEA applies only to alternatives within the same welfare sector as the outcome varies between welfare sectors. Within tertiary education, the broadest possible outcome is *Human Resource Development (HRD)* for as many as possible. Within healthcare, the broadest outcome is *QALY* a combined measure of added living years and their quality of life (Drummnond et al., 2009). Within social care, the broadest possible outcome is *Revalidation of the work ability*. Having determined the outcome of different welfare sectors, it is definite healthcare that is best prepared for CEA as there is extensive medical research on the effectiveness of a broad spectrum of healthcare interventions. The relative unit costs of the alternatives must be calculated, see Info Box 5

Cost-effectiveness analysis (CEA) is a tool used to aid decisions about which medical care should be offered. It differs from CBA in the way that the outcome measure is not a broad measure of utility, but a specific health measure that compares the cost and effectiveness of two or more alternatives. Such comparisons are useful when one of the alternatives being considered is standard care, as this allows the decision maker to consider whether an innovation is better than the status quo. The following guidelines of CEA facilitates the comparison of different interventions in healthcare:

- Costs should be estimated from society's perspective. The effects of an intervention on all costs should be considered, not only the direct cost of the intervention, but its effect on healthcare expenditures, and costs incurred by patients.
- Costs and benefits should be discounted at a 3% annual rate, to reflect the lower economic value of an expense that is delayed and the higher value of a benefit that is realized sooner.
- When the effect of the intervention on costs and benefits is not fully realized during the study period, modeling should be used to estimate the costs and benefits over the patient's lifetime.
- The task force also described methods of estimating the statistical significance of cost-effectiveness findings. Note that when cost-effectiveness is a primary study hypothesis, variance in costs and outcomes, and their covariance will affect the sample size.

CEA is not uniformly applied in the healthcare system. Decision makers often adopt new treatments without knowing if they are cost-effective. Even when CEA has been studied, decision makers may not be able to interpret the data, or they may not agree with the results. Despite this limitation, cost-effectiveness is increasingly used to inform healthcare decision makers.

When the choice is between an innovation and standard care, the analyst first applies the principle of strong dominance. Either the innovation or standard care may be preferred using this principal. Strong dominance favors a strategy that is both more effective and less costly. Strong dominance occurs only when the innovation is especially good (it works better and saves cost) or bad (it works worse and costs more).

When the more effective innovation is also more costly, strong dominance provides no guidance. The decision maker must decide if the greater effectiveness justifies the cost of achieving it. For this reason, it is recommended that cost-effectiveness studies use the Quality-Adjusted Life Year (QALY) as the outcome measure. The QALY reflects both the quantity and the quality of life and are now calculated for the most standard treatments. It is the most widespread method of measuring the value of providing a healthcare intervention. In the real world, it represents a quantum leap for economic analysis in healthcare, because it enables economic analysis in healthcare without ex ante agreement on a specific prize for an added living year.

Quality of life adjustments are based on patient or societal ratings of the quality of life associated with different health states. The ratings, also known as "preferences" or "utilities," are on a scale of zero (representing death) to one (representing perfect health). There are several methods for obtaining these ratings. The Time-Trade-Off method asks the individual doing the rating how much healthy life they are willing to give up, to be cured of the condition. The Standard Gamble method asks them how much of a risk of death they are willing to incur to be cured of the condition. The Health Utilities Index (HUI) and EuroQoL are instruments to gather information on quality of life.

When the more effective innovation is also the more costly, the decision maker must decide if the greater effectiveness justifies the cost of achieving it. This is done by calculating an incremental cost-effectiveness ratio. This is the difference in costs divided by the difference in outcomes. The ratio is the most useful when outcomes are expressed in Quality Adjusted Life Years (QALYs).

Due to the Top priority in healthcare of saving life, there is no standard of what constitutes a cost-effective intervention, that is, how low the cost-effectiveness ratio must be for an intervention to be adopted. The ratio of cost-effectiveness varies a lot across medical specialties. For example, is the cost-effectiveness ratio for cancer treatment, amounting to more hundred thousand of USD, 100 fold higher than for simple prophylactic interventions such as smoking cessation, physical fitness and weight control where the costs per extra QALY is a few thousand USD. This mirrors more clearly than elsewhere in society, the huge impact of fear rather than rationality in the population priorities. This constitutes a strong social-medical argument for the UBI elaborated in 3.3. On this background, the application of a systemic approach as CEA is limited to intra-specialty domains where the physicians and economists can agree to use it. From a broader perspective, knowledge of the incremental cost-effectiveness of interventions that have been approved can be helpful and it has been observed that treatments adopted by the U.S. healthcare system cost less than $50,000 per quality-adjusted life year. The criteria for judging cost-effectiveness are different in different healthcare systems and in different countries.

Table 6 gives cost in dollars and outcomes in QALYs for standard care and 5 innovations, listed in order of effectiveness. Firstly, Intervention A is ruled out as strongly dominated by intervention B, which costs less and yields better outcomes. Next, B is seen to dominate standard care as it redoubles QALY without extra costs.

Finally, it is now up to the decision maker to choose among the interventions. However, the subjective value of a QALY may be decisive. If an added QALY is worth at least the $11,000 paid for Intervention E, it can be adopted even if the cost-effectiveness-ratio is best for Intervention B.

Table 6. Example of CEA

Alternative	Cost	QALY`s	Cost-Effectiveness Ratio
E	$55.000	5	11.000
D	$35.000	4	8.750
C	$25.000	3	8.333
B	$10.000	2	**5.000**
A	$12.000	1.5	8.000
Standard	($10,000)	(1)	(10.000)

Limitation of CEA

Compared to quality clinical standards in modern healthcare a strict economic analysis by CEA can be too limited to assess the full range of effects of healthcare intervention. Interventions in healthcare may affect the subjective state of both patients and carers, too. Also, methods of studying the subjective state are developed, in the format of qualitative interviews. So, a complete assessment of interventions that has subjective consequences must include qualitative interviews, too. The format of this type of holistic assessment addressing both the material (economic) and subjective side of healthcare is known as Health Technology Assessment (HTA) (WHO, 2020). At the broadest level, experience with NPM shows that a combination of quantitative and qualitative measures are necessary to get a realistic assessment of economic effectiveness in accordance with the neuroeconomic psychology replacing classical behavioral economics in this approach.

Is CEA Relevant to the Planning of the Education Sector, too?

The education sector resembles the two other big welfare sectors regarding asymmetry of knowledge between client and server which is a strong argument to organize education as part of public welfare. A major difference between education and social care/healthcare is that education is an independent growth factor termed Human Capital (Schutt, 2003). Human capital is the stock of knowledge, habits, social and personality attributes, including creativity, embodied in the ability to perform labor so as to produce economic value. Human capital theory is closely associated with the study of human resources management as found in the practice of business administration and macroeconomics. The original idea of human capital can be traced back at least to Adam Smith in the 18th century. The modern theory has been popularized by Becker since the 60es. Including Human Capital in econometric models feeds the conclusion that it contributes to economic growth as an investment factor online with physical capital. Empirics indicate that Human Capital rather contributes to economic growth by improved dissemination of existing Know-How rather than by direct innovation. The primary role of Human Capital theory is to guide the overall planning of the educational system towards the best possible servicing of human resource development in the economic production life for mutual benefit of the population in their roles as individual providers as well as citizens. In combination, the arguments of asymmetric knowledge and human capital are strong arguments to include education within the scope of welfare services. Further, education expenses as the aggregate of public and private expenses vary much less as a share of GDP than the total public welfare expenses. Education amounts typical to 6-7% of GDP which indicates that the distribution of public-private finance does not affect the size of total education expenditures.

Education for human resource development (HRD) or self-actualization is a completely different approach to education. The bottom line in education is the degree of synergy between pupils/students, their teachers/advisers and both the public and private sectors to accomplish the best educational outcome. The HRD-approach means that the individual choice of education at both secondary and tertiary levels of education are crucial from both the individual and the societal perspectives. Recognition of this point means that counseling and mentoring services to students' choice of education must be as good as possible instead of as cheap as possible. Labor market prognoses have identified two types of imbalances in most developed countries with the free educational choice of:

Table 7. Pros and cons of MNC

PROs	CONs
● Economies of scale in more dimensions with better private effectiveness and lower prices, see Formula 2 p. xx ● More research and development improving products with local technology spillovers e.g. in digitalized HiTec ● Creates jobs and wealth around the world	● Scope for tax avoidance in general ● White laundering by the banking sector ● Monopoly power raises consumer prices and lowers wages ● Often negative impact on the environment

- In secondary education, too many people choose colleges that prepare for tertiary academic education and too few choose manual-based education e.g. for craftsmen
- the prestige which historically has been associated with academic education. The actual focus of the rising creative class on self-actualization rather than social status can improve more respect of those knowing that they have good manual abilities and a practical orientation
- In tertiary education, too many persons choose the Humanities and too few chooses education in the natural sciences. This dilemma has a historical explanation as the Humanities are considered to deal with what true humanity is about. However, modern positivist science arising from the British Empiricism is now developed enough to falsify the substance of any humanist theory. So, to choose impartial between the historical variety of approaches to humanity, it is necessary to have a basic understanding of the essence of modern positivist scientific methodology

3.3.3 National Accountancy of Multinational Companies

The original anti-trust acts (Sherman Act 1890) outlawed "every contract, combination or conspiracy in restraint of trade" including "monopolization" and treated violations as crimes. Monopolistic exploitation of the market was considered an exception rather than the rule. With the actual hegemony of MNC, the classical deterrence strategy is outdated. A new public strategy must account MNC on a regular basis instead of as an exception. Table 6 lists Pros and Cons.

A contemporary public strategy towards MNC must recognize that MNC have far better options to manipulate corporate tax laws than ordinary taxpayers. The new strategy of tax authorities aims on this background to establish *collaborative corporate compliance*. A slogan for the new strategy has been `Certainty for corporations in exchange of transparency for tax authorities`. There is no universal cooperative compliance model, however, three common features include:

- Risk assessment: More sophisticated risk assessment procedures allow for the identiðcation of taxpayers requiring closer monitoring by the tax authority and those who can be trusted to be compliant and/or have more simple business operations and warrant less close monitoring
- Real–time working: Cooperative compliance models generally facilitate real-time working and avoid waiting for tax returns to be ðled followed by an audit/examination, protracted information requests and dispute resolution. Corporate taxpayers bring tax issues to the attention of the tax authority as they are happening, in advance of ðling.
- Mutual understanding: Tax authorities with cooperative compliance models generally commit resources to upskilling tax ofðcials so that they are better equipped to understand the complexities and context of large corporate taxpayers and have frequent engagement with them. In return for increased certainty about the tax, taxpayers are expected to be transparent about their activities

Taxes targeted by MNC must be at the source without the same options of manipulation as complex corporate surplus taxes. Digitalization services by the Internet is a core domain of MNC that is growing exponentially. Virtual internet-based commerce benefits in more ways from physical shops:

- They have huge economies of scale in marketing
- They take advantage of that their target group can inspect the products freely in physical shops before deciding to buy
- They save a lot of investments in a physical shop

A simple Digital Turnover Tax (DTT) – for example 5% - is an obvious target to improve a fair competition between Internet-commerce and physical shops, although it is expected to be passed on to the customers. The DTT doesn`t depend on a distinction between business and private customers, as VAT, wherefore the collection is far simpler than for VAT.

Further, a specific tax on the Wealth of Top 1% personal incomes must be considered to counteract monopolistic gains of MNC. However, this type of measures must be internationally coordinated to prevent unprecedented migration of the target group. Specifically this type of tax is opted to finance international programs to fight poverty and global warming in the poorest regions of the world. It is obvious to anchor such a program in the venue of the UN.

More cases of MNCs harming the environment is known in all branches. The public concern is to discover new forms of pollution and exhaustion before the harm becomes too severe. However, product scandals in one country may destroy consumer confidence to MNC all over the world, wherefore many MNC these years become early movers regarding environmental protection.

Besides the important learnings about social vulnerability to viruses, the CORUNA crisis gives valuable information for improvement of societal evaluation. This new knowledge is going to be included in the assessment of the ability to deal with global warming in Chapter 4.

3.4 Covid-19 and Social Vulnerability

The fact that the modern world according to the SWOT Analysis in 2.5 faces severe threats, means that societies must consider their vulnerability, too. A Report from UNDP recommends development of a social vulnerability index adding a few other variables, e.g. literacy, to welfare indicators (Kalic, 2017). However, the first 6 months of 2020, presents an unexpected opportunity to study the social vulnerability in relation to the Covid-19 pandemic.

- Covid-19 is definite a health threat as a share of infected dies as no vaccine is available primo 2020
- The medical prevention strategy is clear and simple. People must discipline behavior to:
    - Respect a distance of at least 1.5 meter to other people to prevent dissemination by air
    - Be careful with the hygiene of hands to avoid direct contact with the same surfaces as other people
- As the prevention procedure is well-known by the medical profession all over the world, the coordinated national responses primarily reflect the quality of social organization and only secondarily the quality of healthcare

- WHO provides on a daily base free public quality data on the state of the Covid-19 Pandemic in all member-countries, e.g. the number of deaths, as freely accessible on www.worldometers.info

Public deficit budgeting is definitely tempting to politicians as means to boost public services and consecutive private business and societal employment without increasing taxes. Further, modern Keynesian fiscal policy has justified public deficits to recover from demand-based recessions. The World Bank has studied the boundaries of public debt and finds that public debt beyond 75% of GDP makes a nation especially vulnerable to small backslashes in macroeconomic activity. For emerging economies, the backslash starts already at 65%. Creditors first start to worry whether the country will default on the interest payments. This becomes a self-fulfilling prophecy because, as fears rise, so does the amount of interest a country must promise to pay to float new bonds. Countries must borrow at ever-more expensive rates to pay off the older, cheaper debt. If this cycle continues, the nation may be forced to default on its debt altogether. Debt crises have occurred for centuries, as a result of wars or recessions. In the 1980s, a wave of defaults occurred in East Europe, Africa, and Latin America as the result of a boom in bank lending in the 1970s.

Table 8 shows the relationship between the Corona vulnerability index (Covid-19 Deaths per 1.000 1.9.2020 after 1. Wave of infections) and 3 outcome measures "Public Debt as Share of GDP (%)", "GDP per Capita" and "National Life-Expectancy" ordered after the size of the Covid Index in G20. It is immediately seen that "Life Expectancy" varies too little to become a significant indicator. GDP per Capita in USPPP shows no correlation with the Covid Index. However, "Public Debt" is a much better explanation of social vulnerability as indicated by the Covid Index as the 5 countries with the largest vulnerability are also G7-countries with a risky public debt (>70%). Correlation analysis of this hypothesis confirms a significant difference between countries with "Public Debt >70%" and Other G7 regarding Covid vulnerability:

Difference is 574-156 = 418 Death per million inhabitants (STD_{Comb}=163 w/D.G.=17):

The difference in Covid vulnerability between indebted and Other G20 has >95% Confidence

Table 8. Correlates of social vulnerability in G20 per 1.9.2020

G20[1]	Population (Mill.)	CORONA Deaths Index (per M 1.9-2020)	Public Debt 2019 (% of GDP)	GDP per Capita (1000 USPPP)	Life Expectancy (Years)
Singapore	6	5	0[2]	103	84
China	1.400	4	51	20	77
South Korea	53	6	37	45	282
Indonesia		6	30	14	71
Japan	270	10	220	46	84
India	1.315	50	70	8	70
South Africa	60	220	63	14	64
Saudi Arabia	35	100	20	56	75
Russia	150	150	15	30	72
Mexico	130	550	46	21	75
Canada	40	250	35	51	82
Germany	85	240	62	54	81
Switzerland	9	230	41	66	83
Netherlands	18	360	53	58	82
United States	330	550	110√	65	77
Spain	50	620	95√	42	83
France	70	480	100√	47	82
Italy	60	600	135√	40	83
UK	70	620	81√	47	81
Total/Average	**4.151**	**Avg Debt>70%: 574* Avg 13 OTH: 156***	**Debt>70%: √**	**43**	**78**

Notes: G20 consists of EU and 19 individual countries accounting for 90% of Global GDP, 75% of world trade (Excluding EU intra-trade), two-thirds of the world population and approximately half of the world land area.
1 EU as an aggregate is excluded as G20-member due to the internal heterogeneity.
2 Official Debt at 110% is corrected to 0 as it is a gross figure that`s more than covered by investment assets.
* Significant difference with 95% confidence.

3.5 SUMMARY ON NEW WELFARE ECONOMY

Doughnut Economics recommends the following Welfare Policy beyond that of the minimal state:

Figure 2.

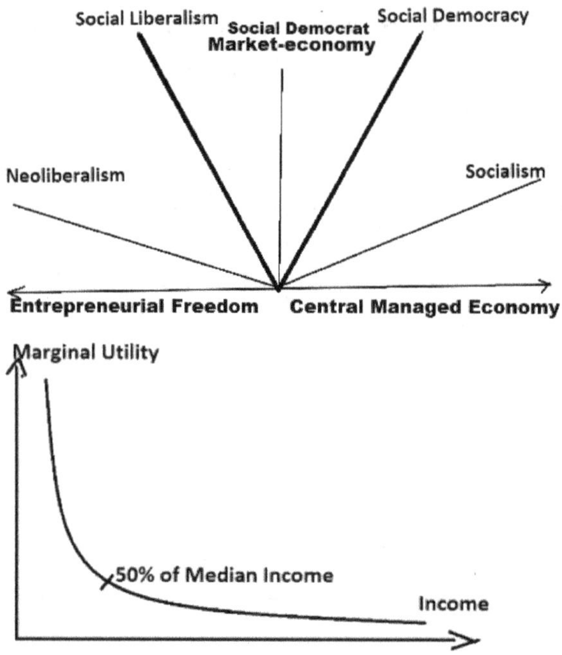

- Public finance of collective needs regarding healthcare, social security and education is more effective than private finance as indicated by analysis of the total private and public costs as share of GDP in OECD. This is especially relevant to healthcare where the strongly asymmetric knowledge between physician and patient become exploited in a liberalist market setting.
- To ensure a market-like effectiveness of public financed collective services some point-wise outsourcing, privatization and internal management incentives are useful in accordance with the principles of New Public Management 2.0. However, the role of service management is as well to protect the clients wherefore the management goal is to identify an appropriate level of minimal staffing norms rather than simply minimizing costs. In healthcare, elaborated Cost-Effective Analysis (CEA) is required for intra-specialty priorities, too.
- Further, NPM 2.0 must today include national accounting of Multinational Companies (MNC) too. The modern standard market case is the hegemony of MNC in the globalized economy. 150 years

ago, exploitation of monopolistic markets were special cases as expressed in the Sherman Act 1890.

- The most effective means of equalization of income is the version of negative income tax termed Universal Basic Income (UBI) at a level covering the relative poverty boundary which typically is defined as 50% of the median income. Calculation examples and sample studies of dynamic effects confirm that UBI can be financed in post-industrial economies without reducing the supply of labor
- A broader societal learning from Covid-19 is derived from the variability of deaths during the 1. Wave in 2020. Covid-19 deaths form an index of societal vulnerability that points forward to strong variability among nations to adapt to oncoming challenges, for instance Global Heating.

REVIEW QUESTIONS

1 Explain the Learning from core Figures of New Welfare Economy (from Chapter 1):

2 Explain the components of Formula 3 (Reread eventually 3.1)
3 What type of tax do economists recommend to equalize income? (Reread eventually 3.2.2)
4 What is Cost-Effectiveness Analysis (CEA)? (Reread eventually 3.3.2)
5 What share of GDP is in play to eliminate relative poverty by UBI? (Reread eventually 3.2)
6 Explain the important means of NPM 2.0? (Reread eventually 3.3.1)
7 Is the effect of NPM 2.0 best in the beginning or in the end? (Reread eventually 3.3.2)
8 Mention both Pros and Cons regarding MNC? (Reread eventually 3.3.3)
9 What type of special taxes should be introduced towards MNC? (Reread eventually 3.3.3)
10 What is the most important strategic learning from COVID-19? (Reread eventually 3.4)

REFERENCES

Andersen, L.B., Bjoernholt, B., Bro, L.B., & Holm-Petersen, C. (2016). Leadership and motivation: a qualitative study of transformational leadership and public service motivation. *Review of Administrative Sciences.*

Drummond, M., & Brixner, D. (2009). Toward a Consensus on the QALY. *Value in Health, 12*(1), 1–5. doi:10.1016/j.jval.2017.01.008 PMID:19250129

Gentilini, U., Grosh, M., & Rigolini, J. (Eds.). (2020). Exploring Universal Basic Income A Guide to Navigating, Concepts, Evidence, and Practices. WB Group.

Haagh, L., & Rohregger, B. (2019). *Universal basic income policies and their potential for addressing health inequities. Transformative approaches to a healthy, prosperous life for all. WHO Reg.* Office for Europe.

Hood, C. (1991). Public Management for All Seasons. *Public Administration, 69*(6), 3–19. doi:10.1111/j.1467-9299.1991.tb00779.x

Hood, C., & Dixon, R. (2015). What We Have to Show for 30 Years of New Public Management: Higher Costs, More Complaints. *Governance: An International Journal of Policy, Administration and Institutions, 28*(3), 265–267. doi:10.1111/gove.12150

Kalic, K. (2017). *Social Vulnerability Assessment Tools for Climate Change and DRR Programming*. UNDP.

Kela and the Ministry of Social Affairs and Health. (2019, Aug. 2). Press Release.

Keynes, J. M. (1936). *The General Theory of Employment, Interest and Money*. Palgrave MacMillan.

Larsen, T. (2011). Clinical Continuity by Integrated Care. In Healthcare Delivery Reform and New Technologies: Organizational Initiatives. IGI. doi:10.4018/978-1-60960-183-6.ch014

Petersen, O. H., Hjelmar, U., & Vrangbæk, K. (2015). Is contracting out of public services still the great panacea? A systematic review of international studies from 2000-2014. *Proceedings NormaCare Meeting.*

Rasnussen, A.F. (1993). *The Minimal State*. Academic Press.

Schutt, F. (2003). *The Importance of Human Capital for Economic Growth. IWIM*. University of Bremen.

WHO. (2020). *Health Technology Assessment*. https://www.who.int/medical_devices/assessment

Chapter 4
Economic Ecology

ABSTRACT

The approach to economic ecology is based on a survey of the state of the ecosystem that departs from the state of global warming as summarized by the Intergovernmental Panel on Climate Change (IPCC). The state of alternatives to fossil energy is reviewed, too. Review of measures to establish a circular economy forms the base of a strategy for transition to carbon neutral economy. The most effective economic intervention towards global heating is identified as a Pigovian Tax on CO2-emission (ET). Evidence on the effectiveness and the state of implementation of ET 2020 is reviewed. For complementary evidence, the ET-calculation model of the Danish Climate Law 2020 is described by representatives of the Danish Climate Council in Appendix by Bendtsen and Stewart.

4.1 THE ECOLOGICAL CEILING

4.1.1 The State of the Ecosystem

Since the Industrial Revolution, humans have emitted more than 2,000 gigatons of carbon dioxide into the atmosphere. (A gigaton is 1 billion metric tons). This thickening blanket of heat-trapping greenhouse gases is the cause of the global warming we are experiencing today as illustrated in Figure 1 showing the development of the global mean temperature since 1850.

DOI: 10.4018/978-1-7998-6424-0.ch004

Figure 1. Global mean temperature since 1850
Source: *Intergovernmental Panel on Climate Change (IPCC).*

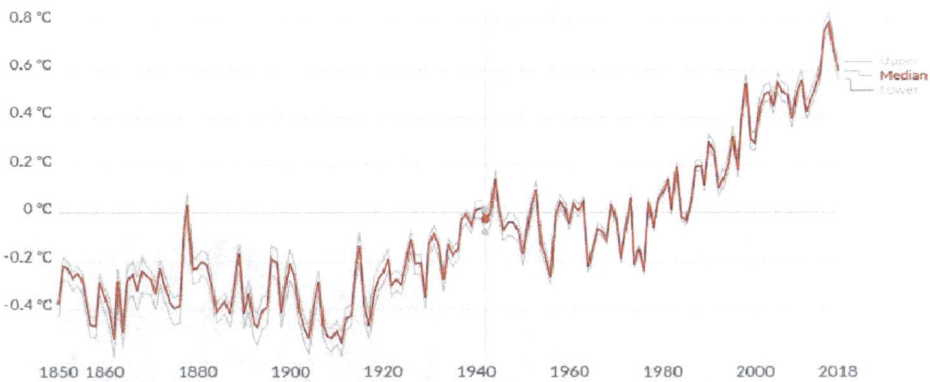

The world temperature fluctuated about a stationary level in the last half of the 19th Century. From about 1900 the global temperature shows a rising trend until today. As the rising global temperature coincides with the accelerated industrialization, an obvious hypothesis is that rising CO2-emission to the atmosphere due to use of fossil energy explains the rising global temperature. The UN-body, International Panel on Climate Change (IPCC), reports currently on the global state of the climate. The climate is a complex balance between heating from sun light and reflection back to the space in the format of ultrared radiation. The concentration of CO_2 in the atmosphere is measured in parts per million (ppm). Midst 18th Century the concentration of atmospheric CO_2 was about 280 mol which represented a rather stable level with very moderate changes related to very long-term changes in the interstellar formations. So far, it has raised from 340 mol in 1980 to 415 mol in 2019 and raises actual 3 mol per year (Zhong & Haugh, 2013). Figure 2 illustrates the relationship between the concentration of CO2 and global heating. With an actual level of 415 mol a critical level of 450 mol is expected already 2030. It represents the border to an expected temperature increase of 2°C which elicits the first of more possible catastrophe-scenarios (AA) with reinforcing rises in the global temperature due to tipping points). Tipping points are points of no return in complex, non-integrated systems as the climate. Important tipping points are recently revealed by climate research in and around the IPCC:

Figure 2. Tipping points by global heating
Source: Intergovernmental Panel for Climate Change (IPCC)
Note: Ecological 'Tipping Points' are the level where Global Heating becomes reinforcing, for instance by release of Methane when the Russion Tundra melts

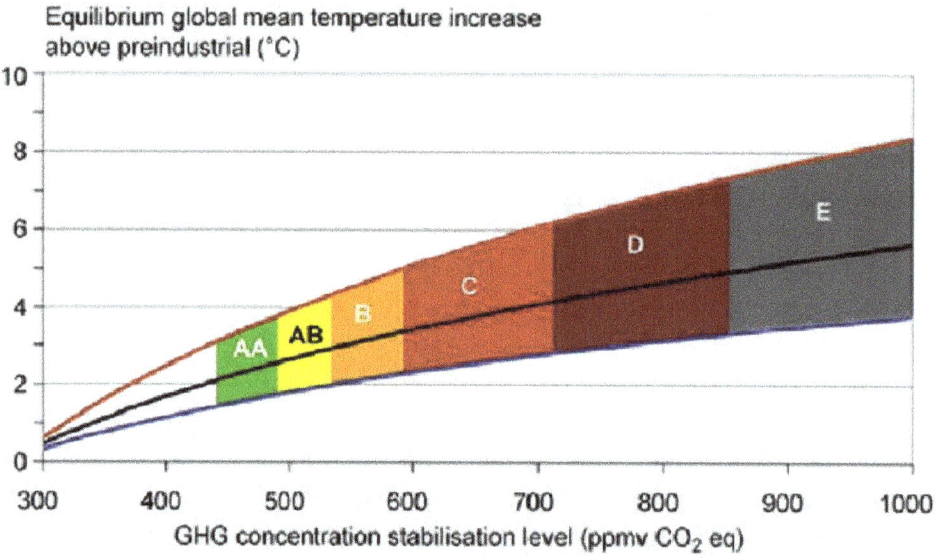

In summary, IPCC concludes that global heating up to 1,5°C has moderate effects on the climate while global heating beyond 2°C disrupts the existing balance and turns global heating reinforcing (Scenarios A-E) with disastrous consequences as rising sea levels, extreme periods of drought, rain and flooding, other extreme weather conditions and reduced biodiversity. At the end, this catastrophe-scenario implicates a complete saturation of the atmosphere with CO2 at a level of 6 *°C* global heating compared to the preindustrial level. It must be noted that the specific border of 450 mol is based on complex calculation implicating a certain tolerance. However, the basic physical principles of the model are solid physical science.

The global emission of CO_2-equivalents amounts to 37 billion ton in 2018 which represents a 2.7% rise compared to 2017. The distribution by economic sector is illustrated in Figure 3. The largest emission sector is that of Electricity, Buildings, Heating and Waste with 41%. Industry emits 21%. Together these sectors account for 62% of CO2 eq and both are relatively easily replaced by non-fossil energy sources. Both Agriculture and Transport have less obvious energy alternatives.

Figure 3. Global emission of CO_2 equivalents by sector
SOURCE*: Reworked Data from International Energy Agency (IEA) 2017.*
DEFINITIONS*:*
Electricity, Buildings, Heat Production and Waste: *Burning of coal, natural gas and oil for electricity is the largest energy source*
Industry: *Fossil fuels burned on site from chemical, metallurgical and mineral transformation processes*
Agriculture, Forestry and Other land Use: *Emissions from cultivation of crops and livestock and deforestation. Does not include CO2-emission that Ecosystems remove from the atmosphere sequestering carbon*
Transportation: *Fossil fuels for road, rail, air and marine transport*

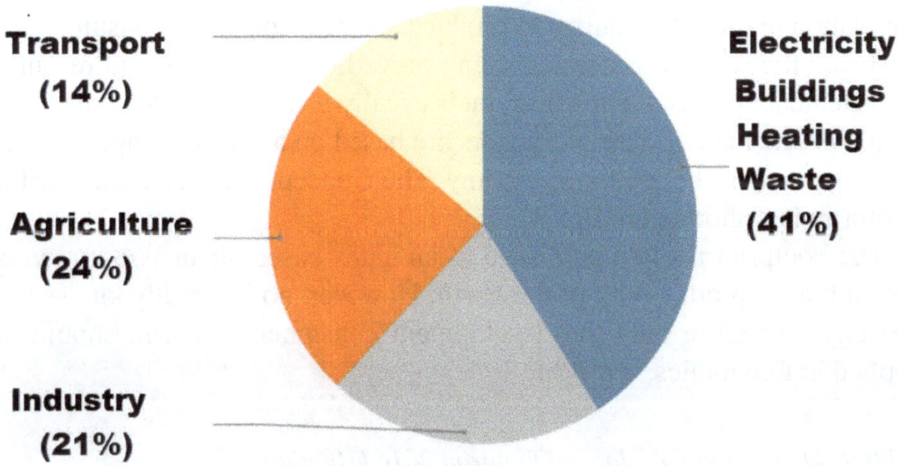

How sure is it that the registered global warming is due to the rising intra-terrestrial CO2-emission? The sun is by distance the most important determinant of the terrestrial climate and minor changes in the activity at the surface of the sun could significantly change the terrestrial climate. The theory of sunspots as an alternative explanation of actual global warming is supported by the astronomical finding that the icecap at the Martian South pole shrunk 20% 1975-98 followed by a period of almost complete stabilization. A study of historical astronomical observations has examined this issue (Schmutz, 2017). For the first time, model calculations show a plausible way that fluctuations in solar activity could have a tangible impact on the climate. The Swiss study expects human-induced global warming to tail off slightly over the next few decades. A weaker sun could reduce temperatures by half a degree. This reduction in temperature is significant, even though it will do little to compensate for human-induced climate change: "We could win valuable time if solar activity declines and slows down the pace of global warming a little. That might help us to deal with the consequences of climate change". But this will be no more than borrowed time since the next minimum will inevitably be followed by a maximum.

4.1.2 Circular Economy as Model of Sustainable Development

An ecological index of sustainability is the Footprint which indicates the balance between biologically productive land and water an individual, population or activity requires to produce all the resources it consumes and to absorb the waste it generates, using prevailing technology and resource management practices. The Footprint is usually measured in global hectares (gha) and the load of different factors are based on a series of Input-Output investigations of the modern economy. The Concept and calculation of the Footprint is elaborated in Box 1.

The Footprint is often published as an index based on an assumption of the biological productivity of the Earth. However, no one really knows this capacity wherefore only the development consumer Footprint should be applied in Economics, see Table 1

Table 1. Man`s global ecological footprint 2016 (10^9 gha)

Year (Population)	Built-Up Land	Carbon Emission	Cropland	Fishing Ground	Forest Production	Grazing Land	Total
1961 (3.1 Bill)	0.1	3.1	1.5	0.3	1.3	0.8	7.1
2016 (7.3 Bill)	0.5	12.3	4.0	0.7	2.0	1.0	20.5

Source: Global Footprint Network – Advancing the Science of Sustainability

Table 1 shows that the Footprint nearly has tribled from 7.1 gha in 1961 through 20.5 gha in 2016. Analysis of this timeline shows that Carbon emission (CO_2) per capita has grown from 3.1 to 12.3 gha which is the dominant factor in the rise of the Global Footprint. Even worse, the carbon footprint is close to being reinforced by ecological science, due to Tipping Points for instance melting the Tundra. Major findings of the Input-Output investigations are summarized in Table 2.

Table 2. Over-all ecological indicators 2019

Sub-system	Parameter	Tolerance	Value and Trend
Climate	Atmospheric carbon dioxide (Parts Per Mill.)	≤350 PPM	420 PPM (+3 PPM per year; Worsening)
Ozone Layer	Atmospheric Ozone (Dobson Units, DU)	≤275 DU	283 DU (Improving)
Agriculture	Nitrogen applies as fertilizer (Mill. Tons)	≤62 Mill. Tons	Around 160 Mill. Tons (Worsening)
	Phosphorus applies as fertilizer (Mill. Tons)	≤6.2 Mill. Tons	Around 14 Mill. Tons (Worsening)
Freshwater	Blue water consumption	≤4.000 m^3	+2.600 m^3/Year (Rising)
Forested Land	Forest-covered land / Prior to Industrialization	≥75%[1]	62% (Declining)
Pollution	No global supervision parameter neither for ● air pollution ● chemical pollution	-Evidence on correlation between local air pollution and Mortality -Evidence on correlation between many different specific forms of chemical pollution and mortality with specific tolerance limits -The overall state of pollution varies between countries	
Biodiversity PBES Rep2019	Proportion since 1900 of threatened species compared to all species	Abundance of native species in major land-based habitats has fallen ≥20% since 1900. The numbers of invasive alien species have risen by about 70% since 1970.	

Source: Rework and update based on Steffen et al. 2015

Note: 1 The tolerance for Forested Land depends closely on the level of CO_2 in the atmosphere.

Figure 4. The global distribution of the human footprint

Source.: *Reworked Data from the Footprint Network*

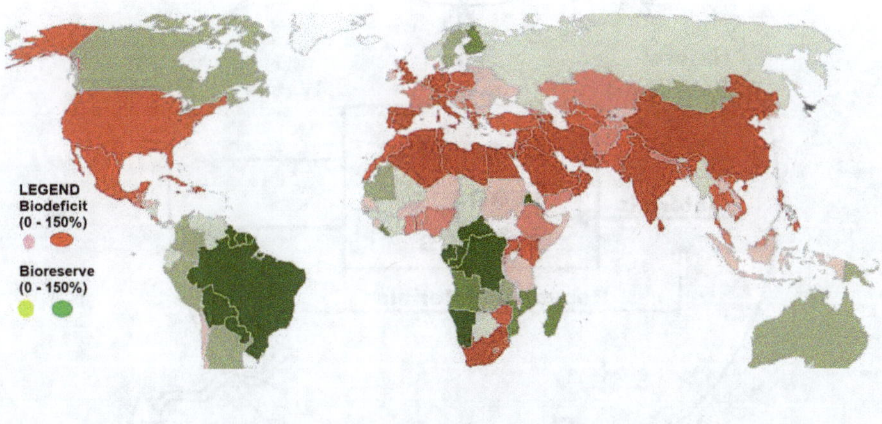

The international differences in Footprint is illustrated in Figure 4. The red color shades indicate the degree of overload. Extreme overload is located in the USA on the American Continent. EU and UK in Europe. The oil states in Arabia and Northern Africa. China and India in Asia. In this group of rich countries, Canada and France have markedly lower Footprints than countries with a comparable socioeconomic structure. In contrast, far the most countries with Bio Reserves are pre-industrial countries except for Canada and the Scandinavian countries (except Denmark).

Environmental quality cannot be maintained by continued liberal economic growth! Improved environmental quality requires political intervention to improve *circular economy minimizing waste and pollution* by the 3R`s (Reduction, Recirculation and Reuse). Figure 5 illustrates `Economic Ecology` where economic transactions are considered embedded between our brain and the Ecosystem. Further, it shows the imbalance of heating as the inflow arrow of sun energy is thicker than the reflection back to the universe. Also, it shows the need to reinforce recirculation of materials minimizing waste.

Figure 5. Model of circular economy
Definition of Circular Economy by World Economic Forum
A circular economy is an industrial system that is restorative or regenerative by intention and design. It replaces the end-of-life concept with restoration, shifts towards the use of renewable energy, eliminate the use of toxic chemicals, which impair reuse and return to the biosphere. It eliminates waste through design of materials, products, systems, and business models

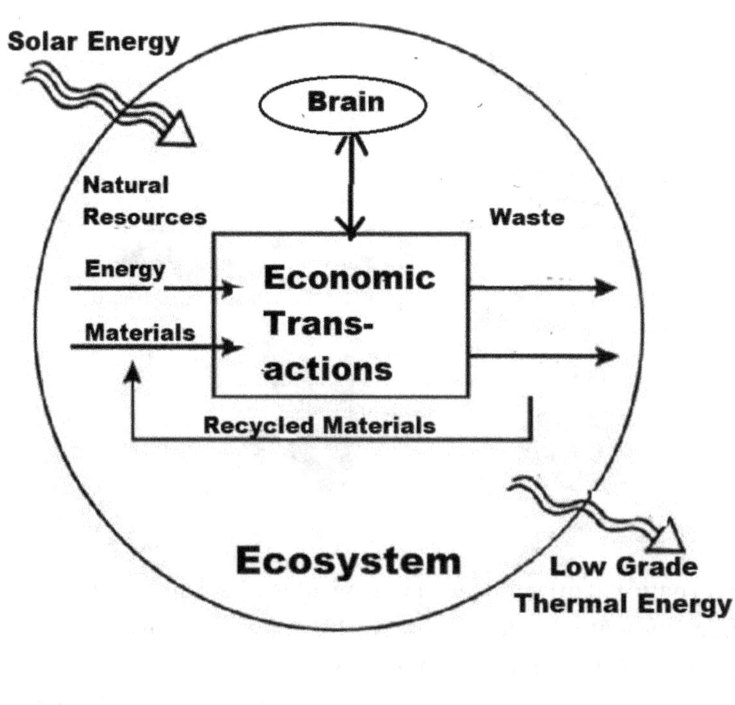

Box 1. The Ecological Footprint

Ecological Footprint: A measure of how much area of biologically productive land and water an individual, population or activity requires to produce all the resources it consumes and to absorb the waste it generates, using prevailing technology and resource management practices. The Ecological Footprint is usually measured in global hectares. The total biologically productive area on land and water in 2019 was approximately 12.2 billion hectares gha. Because, trade is global, an individual or country`s Footprint includes land or sea from all over the world. Without further specification, Ecological Footprint generally refers to the Ecological Footprint of consumption. Ecological Footprint is often referred to in short form as Footprint.
The consumption Footprint of a nation is calculated in the National Footprint and Biocapacity Accounts as a nation`s primary production Footprint plus the Footprint of imports minus the Footprint of exports, and is thus, strictly speaking, a Footprint of apparent consumption. The national average of per capita Consumption Footprint is equal to a country's Consumption Footprint divided by its population.

equivalence factor: A productivity-based scaling factor that converts a specific land type (such as cropland or forest) into a universal unit of biologically productive area (gha). For land types (e.g., cropland) with productivity higher than the average productivity of all biologically productive land and water areas on Earth, the equivalence factor is greater than 1. Thus, to convert an average hectare of cropland to global hectares, it is multiplied by the cropland equivalence factor of 2.51. Grazing lands, which have lower productivity than cropland, have an equivalence factor of 0.46. In a given year, equivalence factors are the same for all countries.

carbon Footprint: The carbon Footprint measures CO2 emissions associated with fossil fuel use. In Ecological Footprint accounts, these amounts are converted into biologically productive areas necessary for absorbing this CO2. The carbon Footprint is added to the Ecological Footprint because it is a competing use of bioproductive space, since increasing CO2 concentrations in the atmosphere is considered to represent a build-up of ecological debt. Some carbon Footprint assessments express results in tonnes released per year, without translating this amount into the area needed to sequester it.

Ecological Footprint Standards: Standards are established by the Global Footprint Network Standards Committee, composed of scientists and Footprint practitioners from around the world. The latest ones are from 2009. Standards serve to produce transparent, reliable mutually comparable results in studies done throughout the Footprint Community. Further information on: www.footprintstandards.org.

The following steps serve the identification of a sustainable development path:

- Options of substituting Fossil energy with Non-fossil alternatives is surveyed in 4.2
- General Options of reducing Waste of materials and pollution is outlined in 4.3 on Circular Economy
- Combined agricultural productivity growth with less Pesticides and Fertilizers is outlined too in 4.3
- Based on 4.2-3 an integrated strategy for sustainable carbon neutral growth is advanced in 4.4

4.2 ECONOMIC ALTERNATIVES TO FOSSIL ENERGY

In the 70es scientists discovered that Freon destroyed the Ozone-layer. 10 years later the exact mechanism was discovered. Especially in Antarctica is Freon able to layer on the Top of clouds which starts a chemical chloride-reaction which subsequently destroys Ozone with severe health risks to the general population e.g. skin cancer. By effective political intervention at the Montreal Protocol 1987 this serious global health risk was recognized and combated with effective out-phasing of emission of CFC-gasses. Today, it is estimated that the Ozone-layer is completely healed about 2060 which so far represents the most successful correction of Anthropogenic global ecological risks to human health. Below important alternatives to fossil energy are reviewed:

4.2.1 Nuclear Energy Alternatives

An obvious alternative to fossil energy has since the 60es been nuclear electricity plants. The productivity of nuclear energy plants has improved very much and is now at the level of the most productive energy plants. Nuclear energy plants are an important source of electricity production in more countries e.g. Belgium, Finland, France, Hungary, Japan, South Korea, Slovakia, UK, USA and China. Nuclear energy plants are sensitive to the price of Uranium, a redoubling of the price of Uranium increases nuclear electricity about 10%. China has a comparative advantage in production of nuclear electricity due the low labor-costs related to the undervalued Chinese Yuan.

Despite the green character of nuclear electricity plants, they do face two severe challenges. Firstly, a technical challenge is the handling of radioactive nuclear waste (Uranium), which is difficult as it remains radioactive for thousands of years. A solid solution to this problem is storing in large mountain reservoirs and the costs of this process are included in the price of nuclear electricity. Secondly, an even larger emotional challenge is the risk of nuclear accidents of which the consequences can be extremely catastrophic e.g. the Chernobyl disaster 1996 with thousands of immediate casualties, long-term radioactive pollution of the local region and long-term cancer casualties. From the onset of nuclear electricity plants, there has been strong awareness of the potential hazard release of radioactive materials from generating electricity with nuclear power. As in other industries, the design and operation of nuclear power plants aims to minimize the likelihood of accidents and avoid major human consequences when they occur. The safety is summarized based on statistics from the World Nuclear Association:

- There have been three major reactor accidents in the history of civil nuclear power – Three Mile Island, Chernobyl and Fukushima. One was contained without harm to anyone, the next involved an intense fire without provision for containment, and the third severely tested the containment, allowing some release of radioactivity.
- These are the only major accidents to have occurred in over 17,000 cumulative reactor-years of commercial nuclear power operation in 33 countries.

The evidence over six decades shows that nuclear power is a safe means of generating electricity. The risk of accidents in nuclear power plants is low and declining. The consequences of an accident or terrorist attack are minimal compared with other commonly accepted risks. Radiological effects on people of any radioactive releases can be avoided. The actual nuclear electricity technology is based on fission (division of Uranium atoms). A completely different nuclear electricity technology is that of fusion reactors. This line of research faces the gigantic challenge of heating a plasma of hydrogen to the level of the core of the sun (millions of degrees of Celsius). A private nuclear-fusion company (UK-based Tokamak Energy) announces Autumn 2018, it has heated a plasma of hydrogen to 27 million degrees Fahrenheit (15 million degrees Celsius) in a new reactor, for the first time — hotter than the core of the sun. The company behind the fusion reaction, announced the creation of the superhot plasma inside its experimental ST40 fusion reactor. The successful test means the reactor will now be prepared to test for an even hotter plasma. That will put the ST40 reactor within the operating temperatures needed for controlled nuclear fusion; the company plans to build a further reactor by 2025 that will produce several megawatts of fusion power.

Tokamak Energy is one of several privately funded companies racing to create a working fusion reactor that can supply electricity to the grid, perhaps before the mid-2040s. It could take another decade before the experimental ITER reactor is ready to create sustained nuclear fusion — and even then, the reaction will not be used to generate any electricity. The vision of nuclear fusion electricity is exciting and important as a long-term alternative to fossil energy. However, it is not solid enough to be part of the solution to the present energy challenges.

4.2.2 Renewable Energy Sources

Renewable energy is energy that is collected from renewable resources, which are naturally replenished on a human timescale, such as sunlight, wind, rain, tides, waves, and geothermal heat. Based on IEA 2018-report (5), renewables contributed one fourth of the generation of electricity in 2016. 10% coming from traditional biomass, 5% is heat energy (modern biomass, geothermal and solar heat), 5% hydro-electricity and 3% is electricity from wind, solar, geothermal, and biomass. Worldwide investments in renewable technologies amounted to more than US$ 286 billion in 2015, with countries such as China and the United States heavily investing in wind, hydro, solar and biofuels. Globally, there are an estimated 10 million jobs associated with the renewable energy industries, with solar photovoltaics being the largest renewable employer. Worldwide, more than half of all new electricity capacity is renewable. Modern renewable energy often displaces conventional fuels in three areas:

1. Renewable power generation
2. Renewable heating resources
3. Non-electric alternatives for transport

Renewable Power Generation

By 2040, renewable energy is projected to equal coal and natural gas electricity generation.

Several jurisdictions, including Denmark, Germany, the state of South Australia and some US states have achieved high integration of variable renewables. For example, in 2015 wind power met 42% of electricity demand in Denmark, 23.2% in Portugal and 15.5% in Uruguay. However, due unpredictable fluctuations in wind and sunshine, limits of 40-50% have been claimed on reliance on renewables. In Denmark, the Power from wind plants varies from 0 through 130% of national consumption. Part of the technical solution to this limitation is interconnected electricity plants across regions to reduce stochastically variation in the supply from renewables as well as increasing options of mutual transfers. Such collaboration is established in NordPool, an integrated power market comprising 13 members of the European Union in Northern Europe. Other means to suspend the limits to renewables are new means to store electricity e.g.

1. Conversion of wind to hydrogen for storage or use in transport
2. `Green` gas
3. Other new storage concepts, e.g., thermal electricity storage.

Also, consumers may contribute directly e.g., charging electrified cars in windy times. Traditional limits to renewables are outdated in NordPool and replaced by a cybernetic planning system focusing on the conditions of supply of energy, current adaptation and long-term development. This is expected to suspend classical limitations in the use of renewables in the NordPool-region. The same may happen in Southern Europe with the difference that the primary renewable energy source is not wind, but sunshine.

Different sources of energy are compared by the Levelized Cost of Electricity which indicates the in USD per MWH produced over the life of a new plant (LCOE). Calculate LCOE for new plants starting in 2022 are shown in Table 3 (US EIA, 2018). For illustration, the LCOE including ET is added to Table 3 which makes it clear that already both Onshore Wind Plants and Photovoltaic Solar Panels are competitive with conventional fossil sources of electricity such as coal and natural gas. Offshore Wind Plants are still more expensive, but the productivity is rising rapidly.

Table 3. Levelized costs for new electricity plants 2022 (USD/MWH)

Energy form	Coal	Natural Gas	Onshore Wind	Offshore Wind	Solar by PV[1]	Nuclear 3%[3] 7%[3]
LCOE	48	48	48	80[3]-125	59	50 70
CO_2 Metric ton/MWH		0.2[2]				
LCOE + ET	55	55	48	80	59	50 70

Source: US EIA 2018. Notes: [1]PV is Photovoltaic / [2]Juhrich 2016 / [3]Discount rate for capital investments.

Renewable Heating Sources

Solar water heating makes an important contribution to renewable heat in many countries, most notably in China, which now has 70% of the global total (180 GWh). Most of these systems are installed on multi-family apartment buildings and meet a portion of the hot water needs of an estimated 50–60 million households in China. Worldwide, total installed solar water heating systems meet a portion of the water heating needs of over 70 million households. The use of biomass for heating continues to grow as well. In Sweden, national use of biomass energy has surpassed that of oil. Direct geothermal for heating is also growing rapidly. The newest addition to Heating is from Geothermal Heat Pumps which provide both heating and cooling, and also flatten the electric demand curve and are thus an increasing national priority.

Other Energy Alternatives for Transport than Electricity

1. Bioethanol is an alcohol made by fermentation, mostly from carbohydrates produced in sugar or starch crops such as corn, sugarcane, or sweet sorghum. Cellulosic biomass, derived from non-food sources such as trees and grasses, is also being developed as a feedstock for ethanol production. Ethanol can be used as a fuel for vehicles in its pure form, but it is usually used as a gasoline additive to increase octane and improve vehicle emissions. Bioethanol is widely used in the USA and in Brazil. Biodiesel can be used as a fuel for vehicles in its pure form, but it is usually used as a diesel additive to reduce levels of particulates, carbon monoxide, and hydrocarbons from diesel-powered vehicles. Biodiesel is produced from oils or fats using transesterification and is the most common biofuel in Europe. Biofuels look like a great solution, but cars are a major source of atmospheric carbon dioxide. But since plants absorb carbon dioxide as they grow, crops grown for biofuels should suck up about as much carbon dioxide as comes out of the tailpipes of cars that burn these fuels. Unlike underground oil reserves, biofuels are a renewable resource since we can grow more crops to turn into fuel. Countries around the world are using various kinds of biofuels. Much of the gasoline in the United States is blended with a biofuel—ethanol. For decades, Brazil has turned sugarcane into ethanol, and some cars there run on pure ethanol. Biodiesel—a diesel-like fuel made from palm oil—is generally available in Europe. Biofuels as jet fuel offers a solution to carbon emissions from air travel. Unfortunately, it's not so simple. Growing the crops, making fertilizers and pesticides, and processing the plants into fuel consumes a lot of energy. It's so much energy that there is debate about whether ethanol from corn actually provides more energy than is required to grow and process it. Biofuels don't replace as much oil as they use. The primatologist Jane Goodall warns that harvesting sugarcane and oil palms for biofuels devastates the rainforests. For the future, a better way of making biofuels is from grasses and saplings which contain more cellulose. Cellulose is the tough

material that makes up plants' cell walls, and most of the weight of a plant is cellulose. More research and development are required before cellulose can be turned into biofuel.

A novel alternative, especially to civil air flight is *electrofuel* where CO_2, extracted from the atmosphere, is converted to fuel by electricity. Already, Demo-plants exist. However, so far, the production price is twice the price of fossil sources, but like other new forms of energy the production price is expected to decline markedly due economies of scale.

2. Hydrogen is another non-fossil energy source for transport. More hydrogen cars exist as prototypes. However, the total energy efficiency of hydrogen engines is only a fraction of that of electric cars due extra energy transformation processes. Firstly, renewable energy sources must be used to produce hydrogen for storage. Secondly, the stored hydrogen must be used in combustion cells to produce the necessary electricity for transport. On this background, it seems much simpler to use renewable energy sources directly for electrified transport.
3. Solar electrification is also a transport option. Usually, photovoltaic (PV) cells contained in solar panels convert the sun's energy directly into electric energy. The term "solar vehicle" usually implies that solar energy is used to power all or part of a vehicle's propulsion, but can power communications, controls or other auxiliary functions. Solar vehicles are not yet sold as practical day-to-day transportation devices. However, solar boats are available commercially.

4.2.3 Nanotechnology

Nanotechnology basically means any kind of technology in a nanoscale, which can be applied in the existent world. It is a comparatively new research field, but it is not a completely new area and the research draws insights from many other research areas. Nanotechnology may enable a Fifth Industrial Revolution since it has the potential for a reflective impact on modern society and economy in the early 21st century, similar to that of information technology, electronics technology, especially in semiconductor technology or molecular and cellular biology (Barua et al., 2020).

It is widely felt that nanotechnology will be the next industrial revolution. Today, many of the world's most creative scientists and engineers are finding new ways to use nanotechnology to improve the world in which we live. So, doctors detect disease at its earliest stages and treat illness such as heart disease, cancer and diabetes with further effective and safer medicines. Although there are many research challenges ahead, nanotechnology already is producing a wide range of beneficial materials and pointing to breakthroughs in many fields. However, within the narrow time window for prevention of global warming beyond <2°C, nanotechnology has a low probability of becoming a factor of major importance.

4.2.4 Extraction of CO_2

Carbon removal takes different forms from new technologies to land management practices. The big question is whether these approaches can deliver carbon removal at the scale needed in the coming decades. There are 6 options for removing carbon from the atmosphere:

Forests

Removes carbon dioxide naturally—and trees are especially good at storing carbon removed from the atmosphere by photosynthesis. Restoring or even expanding and managing forests to encourage more carbon uptake can leverage the power of photosynthesis to convert carbon dioxide in the air into carbon stored in wood and soils. The carbon-removal potential for this measure is hundreds of millions of metric tons per year. For example, sequesters every acre of land restored to temperate forest 3 metric tons of CO2 per year. This is relatively inexpensive (generally less than $50 per metric ton) and yields cleaner water and air in the process.

Reforesting farmland can reduce the supply of food. Similarly, not harvesting timber from one forest may result in overharvesting in another. This makes restoring and managing existing forests, and reforesting land outside of farmland, especially important.

Farms

Soils naturally store carbon, but agricultural soils are running a big deficit due to intensive use. There are many ways to increase carbon in soils. Planting cover crops when fields are otherwise bare can extend photosynthesis throughout the year, sequestering about half a metric ton of CO2 per acre per year. Using compost can improve yields while storing the compost's carbon content in the soil. Scientists are also working to breed crops with deeper roots, making them more resistant to drought, while depositing more carbon into the soil.

Bioenergy with Carbon Capture and Storage (BECCS)

BECCS uses photosynthesis to combat climate change, but it is far more complicated than planting trees or managing soils—and it does not always work for the climate. BECCS is the process of using biomass for energy in the industrial, power or transportation sectors; capturing the embodied carbon before it is released back to the atmosphere; and then storing it either underground or in long-lived products like concrete. If BECCS causes more biomass to grow than would otherwise, or more carbon to be stored where it would otherwise be released back into the atmosphere, it can provide net carbon removal. But it Is not always straightforward to determine whether those conditions are met. Moreover, if BECCS relies on bioenergy crops, it could displace food production or natural ecosystems, erasing the apparent climate benefits and exacerbating food insecurity and ecosystem loss.

Direct Air Capture

Direct air capture is the process of chemically scrubbing carbon dioxide directly from the ambient air, and then storing it either underground or in long-lived products. This new technology is not unlike the carbon capture and storage technology for various emissions sources like power plants and industrial facilities. The difference is that direct air capture removes carbon from the atmosphere instead of reducing emissions. It is relatively straightforward to measure and account for the climate benefits of direct air capture, and its potential scale of deployment is enormous. But the technology remains costly and energy intensive. It is often difficult to pin down costs for new technologies, but a recent study estimates cost about $94-$232 per metric ton. However, direct air capture also requires substantial heat and power inputs wherefore it must be powered by low- or zero-carbon energy sources to result in net carbon removal. Multiple companies have already developed working direct air capture systems, despite the near absence of public research and development spending on the technology. The bottom line is that direct air capture is still a new technology, and the existing systems are just the first generation of their kind.

Seawater Capture

Seawater capture is akin to direct air capture, except CO2 is extracted from seawater instead of air. By reducing CO2 concentration in the ocean, the water draws in more carbon from the air to regain balance. Seawater is a more concentrated solution of CO2 than the ambient air, which means less work is required to separate it out. But seawater is also considerably heavier than air, which means more work to move it through the system. Seawater capture will also have to grapple with the added complexities of technology deployment in harsh maritime environments.

The U.S. Navy has developed a prototype seawater capture device. Because CO2 can be converted to fuel by adding energy, such a technology allows vessels to create their own fuel and avoid having to stop to refuel. Captured carbon is converted to fuel and combustion returning to the atmosphere. Future application can provide long-term storage for captured carbon.

Enhanced Weathering

Some minerals naturally react with CO2, turning carbon from a gas into a solid. The process is commonly referred to as "weathering," and it typically happens very slowly—on a geological timescale. But scientists are figuring out how to speed up the process, especially by enhancing the exposure of these minerals to CO2 in the air or ocean. That could mean pumping alkaline spring water from underground to the surface where minerals can react with the air; moving air through large deposits of mine tailings that contain the right mineral composition; crushing or developing enzymes that chew up mineral deposits to increase their surface area; and finding ways to weather certain industrial byproducts, like fly ash, kiln dust, or iron and steel slag. Enhanced weathering is definitely possible, but there is much more work to be done to map out cost-effectiveness.

The Future of Carbon Removal

We don't know today which of these strategies can provide the most large-scale carbon removal in the future, and which may ultimately prove less useful. Each approach offers both promise and challenges. But what we do know is that if we are to avoid dangerous levels of global warming, capturing and storing carbon already in the air must be part of the climate protection toolbox.

4.3 Redesign for Circular Economy

4.3.1 Comparison of Linear and Circular Economy

To find an effective way of transition from linear to circular economy, it is necessary to understand the full scope of the task. For that purpose, the European Energy Agency (EEA) has published a comprehensive report on the subject (9). The transition to a circular economy requires according to EEA a fundamental change in products and the way they meet societal demand. Products are a tangible part of the socio-technical systems people use to fulfil their needs and wants, for example regarding housing, mobility, energy, and food. Understanding the key mechanisms shaping the design, production, use and end-of-life treatment of products in a linear economy is a prerequisite to identify effective measures to alter system dynamics and drive the shift to circular material use.

Reconfiguring societal systems requires innovation across a wide range of sectors — from farming to finance. It includes not only new technologies, but also novel social practices and business models, and change of consumer behavior, beliefs, and basic values. This will inevitably create tension and produce a mix of societal costs and benefits, falling unevenly on different groups. The creative destruction inherent in entrepreneurial innovation will affect jobs and economic interests, creating conflict and power struggles. Other trade-offs that may arise as benefits in one system are offset by harms in another. Table 4 summarizes findings on the difference between linear and circular economy referring to. The findings are structured in accordance with two general aspects of socio-technical systems that are shaped by an array of interrelated factors.

4.3.3 Recirculation of Plastics

One of the largest waste problems in the post-industrial economy is plastics. Info Box 2 presents a practical solution to recirculation of plastics by the Finnish research company VTT.

Table 4. Characteristics of linear versus circular economy

Linear System Mechanisms	Circular System Mechanisms
Business Perspective	
Product as value creation source Technological innovation urges consumers to buy new. Main source of value is intellectual property by protective design measures e.g. barriers to repair	**Functionality/performance as source of value creation** Competition is mainly based on the creation of added service value of a product. Cost minimization drives product longevity, reuse, repair and remanufacturing.
Economies of scale in global production chains Cost-efficiency drives global production chains, minimizing costs of resources, labor and transport	**Better linking of location of production and use** Service is physically linked to the location of the customer with incentive to produce products used close to user
Steer consumer needs towards product offer Products with short lifespans are preferred as they are cheaper to make and support a market for new one`s	**User needs/wants drives the role of a product** Offering the best service means matching the (intangible) needs of the user combining services and products
Tendency to Disregard End-of-Life Phase	**Incentive to Include End-of-Life Phase in Business Model**
Consumer Perspective	
Consumerism follows marketing Consumers want new products that keep pace with fashion and technological advances.	**Customer satisfaction is an important driver** The customer experience feeds better back to the service provider, raising consumers' awareness of his needs
International opportunities for cost reduction Consumers seek the cheapest version of a product on international markets, enabled by e-commerce	**Local-first attitude** Accessibility to the service provider is part of the service experience making proximity a customer choice criterion
Ownership Is the Norm	**Accessibility Is the Norm**
Low/no residual value of products End-of-life products (broken or obsolete) are considered a burden, to deal with as cheap as possible	**End-of-use incentives incorporated** If products are part of a service, there are incentives to return them to the provider after use, avoiding stocks
Policy Perspective	
Dependence on existing production system A strong between mass production of goods, cost reduction, and efficient production.	**More focus on facilitating skilled workforce** More local service demanding a skilled workforce. Facilitated by shifting taxes from labor to resources
Global playing field Economic competition on the international market steers national social and environmental policies	**Less risk for outsourcing jobs** As management of products as local assets is less likely to be outsourced, giving less incentive to race-to-the-bottom
Balance consumer protection with economic stakes Protection of consumer safety and health is mostly reactive and geared to protect economic stakes	**Facilitate safe and healthy services with regulation** Safety and consumer health are business incentives for high-quality performance to focus on
Action prompts by health or environmental concerns There is no inherent incentive for regulation of the waste phase of products. Only waste-related health or environmental concerns arise regulatory action	**Facilitation of end-of-life management** Extended producer responsibility creates incentives for companies to focus end-of-life management. Government provides infrastructure and supportive fiscal measures

Source: Rework of Table 2.1 in EEA 2017.

Box 2. The VTT Vision of Circular Economy of Plastics

Plastics are used in many applications as food packaging, drinking bottles, caps and closures, pipes, automotive parts, agricultural films, window frames, paints and wall coverings, cable insulation, optical fibres, eyeglasses, touch screens, medical implants, membranes, toys, clothes and shoes, building insulations, mattresses, etc. The main application sectors for plastics are:

1. Packaging (40%) 2. Buildings and Construction (20%) 3. Mobility (10%)

Food waste is already a major concern because of its direct contribution to climate change. A 2016-study by Zero Waste Scotland calculated that the carbon footprint of food waste from Scottish households was almost three times that of plastic waste collected. On average redoubles the shelf life of different food products.
In the medical sector, high performance plastics play a major role and are used in a wide variety of essential applications: prostheses, hearing aids, implants, sutures, syringes, blood bags, and so on.
In the mobility and automotive sector, plastic components weigh 50% less than similar components made from other materials, which means a 25 to 35% improvement in fuel economy. Plastics offer lightweight solutions that fulfil essential safety requirements such as fire safety and personal protection.
The Vision of VTT is to establish material circularity while maintaining performance and economic feasibility of plastics. The main technical solutions are ECODESIGN and PAWN SYSTEMS. Other means are Collection & Separation, reuse and recycling.
Reference: Review of Tenhunen A and Pöhler H (2020): A Circular Economy of Plastics. VTT Technical Research Center of Finland Ldt.

4.3.4 Ecological Agriculture

Ecological farming includes methods, including organic, which regenerate ecosystem services: prevention of soil erosion, water infiltration and retention, carbon sequestration in the form of humus, and increased biodiversity. Substantial research in Eco-agriculture raises a prospect of combining continued expected growth of the world population and growing demand for agricultural products with an cost-effective transition to an organic Low-carbon agriculture. However, this transition faces the following problems:

- Fertilizers for accelerated growth have negative side-effects as pollution of the subsoil water, over-growth of seaweed with deoxidation and eventual health risks (nitrate)
- Pesticides to fight noxious animals for crops have in some cases negative health effects as cancer
- Livestock needs carbon neutral buildings and minimization of methane emission e.g. by new foods

Analyses show that ecological farming makes sense economically. First, this modern farming method leads to increased crop yields. Globally, ecological farming can produce an average of approximately 30% more food per hectare than conventional agriculture. In developing countries, ecological farming can produce roughly 80% more food per hectare. The cost efficiencies arise from using natural, locally available fertilizers and organic pest control saving costs on synthetic polluting chemical inputs.

Box 3. Vision of Climate Neutral Danish Agriculture by 2050

The Danish food industry is already well advanced and has one of the most climate-friendly productions in the world. For example, Danish milk production has the lowest greenhouse-gas emission per liter of milk produced in Europe, and the second-lowest emission when it comes to beef production. In the decades to come, this development will be taken a step further. The Danish Agriculture and Food Council has announced a strategy to become completely climate neutral by 2050, meaning that it will not emit more greenhouse gasses than it absorbs. The first step, halving carbon emission is assured by the agricultural sector itself. Methods already in use can be expanded to help reach the full 2050 target. These include excluding low-lying earth, often in areas close to water, from use in food production, since this type of earth emits relatively high amounts of carbon dioxide. However, this is a rather expensive and major exercise, but also it is one of the most effective areas (to focus on) to reduce CO2 (emissions). "For this to happen in such a fast and efficient manner economic backing from the state is needed. This support is assured as part of the Danish plan for 70% carbon reduction 2030. Other potential methods for reducing emissions include converting slurry to biogas, improving animal feed and breeding animals that emit less CO2. But new methods and solutions must also be found in the upcoming years, should the target be achieved. Research in the area is vital!

Finally, ecologically farmed products taste better and promote better health. A recent study in California shows that organically grown strawberries taste sweeter than their conventional, chemically grown counterparts. The organic variety also contains 10% more dietary antioxidants, which are known to protect against disease. Effective Eco-agriculture develops along the 3 tracks:

1 Biodiverse farming—using a mix of different crops and plant varieties in a given field—is a reliable, proven ecological-farming method. In conventional farming, monocultures are used: growing a single crop over a wide area was standard practice. In contrast, biodiverse farming has emerged as the single most important modern approach to achieving food security.

Specifically, biologically diverse farming, also called intercropping, increases plants' resilience to erratic weather changes. Scientists have shown that biodiversity provides a natural insurance policy against major climate changes, both in the wild and in agriculture.

2 Organic pest control is another feature of ecological farming. Instead of using chemical pesticides, ecological farmers use non-polluting, long-term pest protection. One method is to introduce beneficial insects to the field. Another method is to plant crop fields strategically and to use "low-input" technologies that are available locally. As a result, crops are less vulnerable to pest invasion. In China, disease-susceptible rice varieties inter-planted with resistant varieties had an 89% greater yield. The incidence of disease was 94% lower compared to that of conventional monoculture.

3 Natural fertilizers are also key to ecological farming. Achieving fertile soil entails growing green manures such as legumes. Adding compost and animal dung can also enrich soil. These are just some of the effective ways of boosting the soil's organic matter and fertility without synthetic fertilizers. Using natural fertilizers also saves on farmers' costs; it eliminates the need for artificial inputs. With natural fertilizers, soil is richer in organic matter, better able to retain water, and better protected against erosion.

The eco-agricultural environmental problems of *intensive agriculture* are concentrated in the industrialized world. One of the most intensive agricultural systems is the Danish one. The Danish Agricultural sector has committed itself to reduce carbon emission by 50% 2050 and offers collaboration with the government for complete carbon neutrality 2050, see Info Box 3

4.3.5 A Doughnut City Planning Model

Raworth has down-scaled Doughnut Economics to the City level in a model of local-global and social-ecological giving in all 4 categories. Amsterdam is the prototype of a Doughnut City (Amsterdam, March 2020). A start for new ways of thinking, shared inspiration, and transformative action towards becoming a city that thrives for people both community and planet with a strong engagement of local people.

1. A city target is Formulated for in all 8 issues and Confronted with the Actual State:
    a. Equal chances for healthy living for all is confronted with a state of 40% being overweight and 49% having a moderate-to-high risk of depression or anxiety.
    b. Sufficient affordable and decent homes are confronted with that almost 20% of inhabitants are unable to cover their basic needs after paying their monthly rent.
    c. Access to clean and safe public water for all! The tap water is found to br well above the legal standard.
    d. A Food target is still under development. Recently, 1200 households make use of the city`s food banks.
    e. Safe and livable for both residents and visitors is confronted with that 25% in 2017 were victims of a crime. 39% said they experienced domestic violence over the last 5 years
    f. Greater independence and seldom experience of unequal opportunity is confronted with that 16% of residents or more than

earlier experience lack of control over their lives in lower-income neighborhoods.

g. Increased say, involvement and decision role confronts with 52% turning out for the 2017 city election.
h. Amsterdam as an inclusive and connected city confront that 15% reported discrimination 2017.

2. City targets inspired by nature is formulated and reality checked for 4 issues:

The Sand Motor Project for dune development along the coastline is supported to secure drinkable water as renewable water only accounts for 12% of the city supply.

Reduce CO2-emission by 55% of the 1990-level in 2030 and by 95% in 2050. 2018 CO2-emission was 15% lower than 1990.

Could create oyster substrates to support a reef barrier and bolster erosion protection. 12 million m3 of sand is replenished annually, but 20 million m3 would be needed to keep pace with rising sea levels.

Biodiversity is promoted and tracked by sedum, grass and herb roofs, as well as rooftop gardens. In 2018, Amsterdam had at least 200 green roofs, with a total surface area of approximately 120,000 m^2.

3. City Targets Shaping the Respect of the Health of the Whole Planet
   a. Reduce the city's in-boundary CO2 emissions to 55% below 1990 by 2030, and to 95% below by 2050. CO2 dissolved in seawater has increased ocean acidity by 30% during the Industrial Revolution.
   b. Reduce emissions of Nitrogen caused by fertilizers! The Dutch agricultural sector is responsible for 61%.
   c. REDUCE OVERFISHING. Fish consumption has more than doubled in the Netherlands since 1990, putting the country in the top 25% of fish-consuming nations in the world.
   d. FRESHWATER WITHDRAWALS. The Netherlands has the highest water footprint in Europe, with almost 90% of total water consumption embedded in imports such as meat, cotton and food.
4. Regarding the global wellbeing of people, the authors refer to the 17 UNSG

Pluralist Doughnut Economic interventions to strive for the environmental UNSG are presented in 4.4.

The City Doughnut is useful to engage the local community in debating their own future. The lack of connection between the local engagement of Citizens and the democratic city decision-makers make the first version a lightweighter in city planning but renewal is difficult. A `heavy` city plan on environmental protection must deliver action plans on all of these issues: 1) Power supply, 2) Water supply, 3) Collective traffic systems, 4) Construction planning, 5) Garbage systems and 6) Specific local climate change threats such as raising water levels in Amsterdam.

4.4 STRATEGY FOR SUSTAINABLE DEVELOPMENT

4.4.1 Experiences with Pigouvian Carbon Emission Tax (ET)

How to Add a Green Thumb to `The Invisible Hand`?

To minimize negative third-party effects of economic transactions imposing a tariff on the production source is well-known and today termed emission tax (ET) (Pigou, 1920). Due to the high elasticity of the demand for fossil energy e.g. coal (Johnson, 2011) and large economies of scale in the production of electricity, the effect is strong of ET on CO_2-emission at the level of electricity plants as illustrated in Figure 6 ET reduces the Demand markedly from Q_{t0} to Q_{t1}. A model of dynamic integration of climate and economy (DICE) by ET was awarded with the Nobel Prize 2018 (Nordhaus, 2007 and 2018). According to DICE, ET is the most economic accelerated transition from fossil energy to alternatives. The unique advantage of ET is to reinstall profit-seeking as a driver of an appropriate technological development as ET affects the price of each production factor individually in proportion to their content of carbon giving a new set of relative prices for manufacturers to restructure their production. So, ET builds on the same entrepreneurial ingenuity that delivered industrialization. However, a broad study of transition to renewables expresses some doubt that even ET can accelerate the transition to RE enough without additional massive public financial support to rebuild important infrastructure (Solè et al., 2018).

A review of 27 different implemented ET-projects located in both Europe and North America whereof the most important is from the Canadian Province "British Columbia" (Metcalf 2019 and 2020). The conclusion is, that carbon tax is a cost-effective policy tool towards greenhouse gas emissions. Further, it is easy to implement, easy to administer, and straight forward for firms to comply with. It entails costs to the economy, we cannot clean up the environment for free, evidence shows that a carbon tax need not impose large costs on an economy.

Figure 6. Effect of Pigouvian carbon tax on production of electricity
Legend: *The Demand for Fossils is many times more price elastic (Relative flat curve) than the direct Demand of Households wherefore ET at the source of emission is far more effective!*

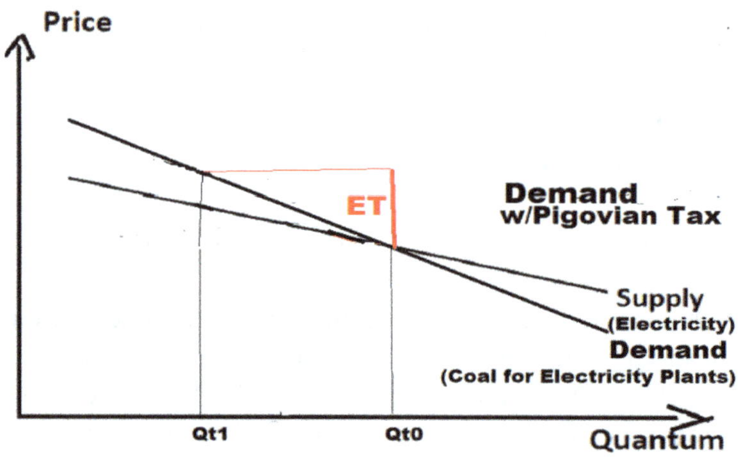

1 Revenue Neutrality With Focus on Fairness

Often the motive for tariffs is the need for public revenue to finance public expenses. Regarding ET, it is going to affect goods and services for the broad population and therefore "Turns the heavy side downwards" like a general added-value tariff. Simple fairness implicates that a major part of the revenue from ET must be used to compensate clients and businesses. Residual revenue serves public investments in related infrastructure to get the full transitional benefit of ET e.g. charging stations for electric cars.

2 Collection at the Source of Emission to Minimize Manipulation

ET should be *collected at the source* where carbon enters the economy, at the wellhead, mine shaft, or import terminal. A full ET 2020 would ultimately cover more than 80 percent of the economy's total emission of greenhouse gas. The importance of collection at the source is illustrated by the flight-sector. ET at the import terminal gives flight companies a strong incentive to search for aircrafts with lower consumption of petrol per mile. A passenger tariff of equal size has little incentive to search non-fossil alternatives but an incentive for passengers to search cheaper but eventually even more polluting alternative means of transport as an individual car.

Figure 7. Global coverage with carbon emission tax systems 2020

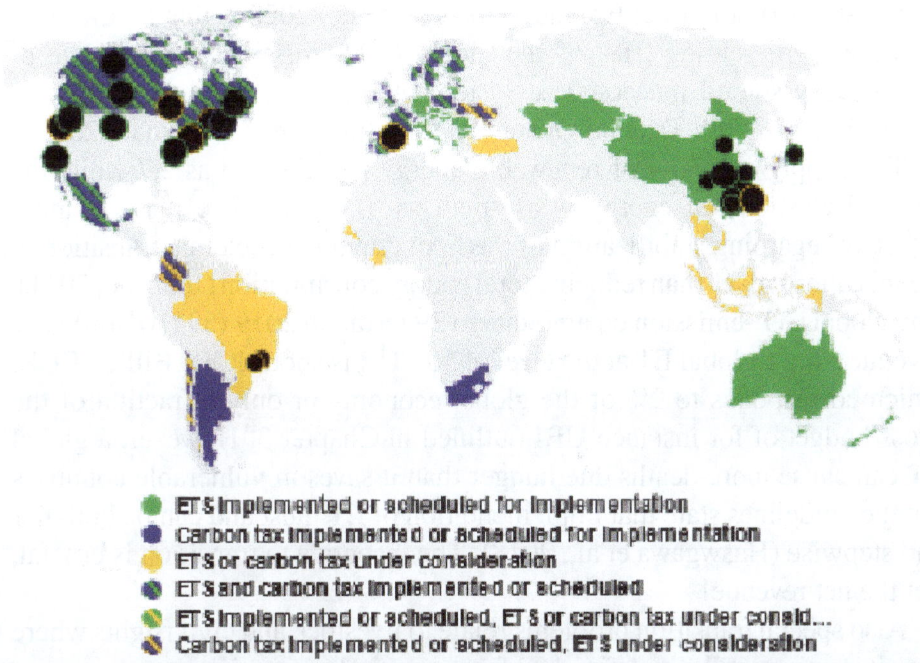

3 Stepwise Implementation to Maximize Learning by Doing

ET is not a stand-alone-project but must include stepwise follow-up investments in both new infrastructure and new technologies. The First Phase must build on contemporary knowledge of alternatives to fossil energy and can be partial e.g. addressing the sectors with the best transition alternatives, for instance the power sector where wind and solar energy are obvious. In the next phase ET could be lifted to encourage more heavy problems.

ET can be implemented either as a "Cap" meaning a company is imposed a fixed charge proportional to the CO2-emission caused by this company. Reducing the CO2-emission the company saves money in the following periods. Alternatively, a "Market" for CO2-emission quotas may be established. In this case, companies with CO2-emission must buy corresponding emission quota. Both forms are included in the global statistics of the ET coverage. During the Kyoto Protocol EU established a market for CO2-emission and in 2017 China has followed this example.

The Global State of Carbon Emission Tax Systems 2020

The World Bank statistics in Figure 7 shows the global state of Emission Tax Systems (both direct ET and Quotas systems) 2020 is that 60 different countries representing 21% of the global CO2-emission already have or plan to levy some Emission Tax System. A line of research confirms the applicability of both Tax and Quatas systems functions (Weitzman, 2009)

The supply elasticity of renewable energy is estimated as 2.7 while the demand elasticity of energy is as small as -0.4 wherefore it is far more effective regarding stabilization of the Ecosystem to accelerate transition to cleaner alternatives than reducing total energy consumption (Johnson, 2011). The global CO_2-emission eq amounts to 39 terra ton 2019 ($39*10^9$ ton). The revenue from a global ET at the level of 50 EUR is about 1.500 Billion EUR, which corresponds to 2% of the global economy or only a fraction of the gross budget of for instance UBI outlined in Chapter 3. However, a global ET can cause more deaths due hunger than it saves in vulnerable countries but the guidelines state that implementation of ET must and can be both fair and stepwise (Haswgawa et al., 2018). The incentive to transition is crucial, not the net revenue!

Also special transition problems relate to livestock and civil flights where the alternatives still are unfinished for mass implementation.

4.4.2 Political Options of Pigouvian Carbon Tax (ET)

The public opinion on global heating is what in neuroeconomics is termed a `Protracted Decision`, where the neural presentation of Reward-seeking respective fear, accumulates over time (Bastena et al., 2010). As the global state of ET is that it already covers 21% of emissions, marketing experiences show that Mankind is at a state where massive *persistent public information on the action mechanism of ET* can provide the necessary public good-will for political implementation.

In accordance with Neuroeconomic Psychology, the emotional resistance to ET can be either fear-based or over-optimistic.

The fear-based resistance to ET has different forms of verbalization that must be considered before elaboration of the intervention (ET):

- Left-wing politicians fear that ET makes the low-income population pay the most. As already explained these problems can be prevented by compensations, because the incentive to transition rather than the revenue, is the key point.
- Right-wing politicians claim that ET like other taxes are bureaucratic means to deteriorate the international competitiveness of business wherefore they prefer subsidized research and development of alternatives to fossil energy. This problem depends on the state of development of alternative non-fossil energy sources. Sun, wind and thermal energy are today so close to be competitive to fossil energy on market terms that the effectiveness of ET must be exploited.
- A widely shared objection to ET is that early-moving countries risk to invest in new technology that rapidly become replaced by cheaper and/or better versions due to fast technological progress in alternatives. However, this worry must be counterbalanced by cognition of:
    - Sharply rising social costs due to environmental damages by unnecessary delay of transition to carbon neutrality
    - Loss of the technological spin-offs of participation in the early state of development
    - Options of minimizing the extra costs for the national sectors that are most exposed to international competition

The over-optimistic view is driven by impatience with the established political system. The over-optimist fraction engages in extra-parliamentary activism. However, the large majority of the population does not identify with that level of enthusiasm wherefore the behavioral recommendation is that the energy is better used more effectively within the framework of democratic activity.

4.4.3 A Multilevel Transition to Carbon Neutrality (MTCN)

The long-term prognosis for ET is promising but the urge for implementation is that strong, that all complementary measures must be used, too. A varied toolbox for accelerated transition to carbon neutrality based on socioeconomic levels of optional influence is summarized in Table 5 with a view on the global economy:

1. The National Level

1.1 Pigouvian Emission Tax (ET)

The optimal economic intervention towards global warming is as soon as possible to levy a Pigovian Tax on CO_2-emission (ET). Based on Figure 1, even a moderate ET can accelerate the transition to carbon neutrality for >80% of the CO2 eq emission while the remaining <20% requires ASAP investment in new energy sources for 1) Air and SeaTransport and 2) Agriculture.

A practical example of operation ET is presented by the Danish Climate Council, see Appendix by Bendtsen and Stewart. However, due to lack of a broad enough political recognition of the comparative advantage of ET, other elements of the toolbox must be used actively, too. A long-term advantage of ET is that it combines entrepreneurial ingenuity with social responsibility which opens for stronger political coalitions across the center. Also, it must be noted that the energy sector only accounts for about 2% of GDP wherefore it should be possible politically to restructure it as part of national long-term planning.

1.2 Public Subsidies to Infant Energy Industries

Besides obvious non-fossil energy alternatives such as sun, wind, thermal and water-falls morem other alternatives are required to complete carbon neutrality without restrictions in the modern way of life. In these cases, the Infant-industry case is relevant. In the 70s scientists discovered that Freon destroyed the Ozone-layer. 10 years later the exact mechanism was discovered. Especially in Antarctica is Freon able to layer on the Top of clouds which starts a chemical chloride-reaction which subsequently destroys Ozone with severe health risks to the general population e.g. skin cancer. By effective political intervention Montreal Protocol 1987 this serious global health risk was recognized and combated with effective out-phasing of emission of CFC-gasses. Today, it is estimated that the Ozone-layer is completely healed about 2060. Another contemporary example of accelerated technological development is the development of Covid-19 vaccines in 1 year or 10-times faster than the typical development of new vaccines.

The next priority of the strategy is public support to accelerated development of the specific transition problems identified in 4.2. Implementation of this strategy element depends very much on good collaboration between government and involved organizations in the respective sectors:

1. None of the existing renewables fit well to heavy transport in air or sea that accounts for 5% of the total CO2-emission (a third of transport in Figure 3). However, already technical solutions as electrofuel functions in small-scale and it is expected that large-scale plants have the same economies of scale as seen for instance in the windmill industry. So, accelerated R&D in electrofuels must have high priority
2. Agriculture accounts for 24% of total emissions in Figure 3 whereof one third is due to Methane related to domestication. Already a number of measures are available to reduce CO2 eq from agriculture. There is no single solution to remove CO2 from agriculture but it takes a number of different means to accomplish, for instance 50% reduction in 2050

The effectiveness of the national actions 1.1-2 have crucial economies-of-scale wherefore the ability to international collaboration is crucial:

- Is the EU able to coordinate independent member-countries?
- Is the US able to coordinate the policies of the different States that formally are responsible for environmental protection policies?

2. The Community Level

Political motivation to develop public-business collaboration towards carbon neutrality at the community has got an important profile in the C40 collaboration among leading Metropoles. Although national policy is definitely the most important, the community level is a very important complement to assure both involvement of the population and their local organizations as well as knowledge about end-user conditions.

The community level has got a common analytical framework in the `Doughnut City` model where Amsterdam has been a frontrunner, see 4.3.5. The Amsterdam City Doughnut expresses high ambitions regarding fulfilment of the Paris Agreement, however, the specific implementation measures need far more experience to mature. Special attention deserves the plans on protection of Amsterdam towards rising sea levels beyond what's expected by the Paris Agreement. In all, the `City Doughnut` seems to engage rather many citizens in planning of their city in general and not at least specific action to protect the environment towards further future water threats.

General environmental issues at the level of Metropoles that are well fit for collaboration with sector organizations, include the collective infrastructure regarding 1) Production and distribution of electricity 2) Heating of houses,

3) City transport systems, 4) Garbage handling systems, 5) Cooking habits in institutions, etc.

3. The Consumer Level

An important strategic element is bottom-up initiatives Voting green with the consumer basket. Figure 5 shows that individual consumer behavior directly affects most CO_2-emission (Electricity and Heating, Transportation, Construction and Agriculture). Already, more ecological living is a substantial driver behind the fast-growing bottom-up movements for "Simple Living" and Ecological Design as elaborated in 1.2. Green NGOs support special activities for sharing of domiciles and cars and reuse of a diversity of household items and clothes grow fast in these years

4. The Scientific Level

The "Dynamic Interaction of Carbon and Ecology"-model (DICE) is an econometric transition tool. The core of DICE is a Cobb-Douglas production function that is expanded with equations on behavioral economics as determined by Multiple Linear Regression (MLR). However, the transition to green technology is not random, but a targeted process where feedback reinforcing successful outcomes coordinate classical cause-and-effect logic e.g. that of DICE. The new cybernetic approach calls for a frontline of specialists in economic ecology to explain the action-mechanism of ET. An *independent national climate council is formed* with representatives of both economic ecologists and other specialists in various domains of ecology. Such a council is recently formed both in Denmark and British Columbia. The major intervention to accelerate transition to carbon neutrality according to the Danish Council of Climate is ET, see Appendix by Bendtsen & Stewart.

Table 5. Multilevel strategy for carbon neutrality (MSCN)

1 The National Level
1.1 A Universal Pigouvian CO2 Emission Tax (ET)
1.2 Subsidies to Infant Energy Industries for instance Electrofuels and Agriculture
2 The Community Level w/Advancement of Doughnut City Proliferation (Must include safety projects for the case of global heating >2°C)
3 The Consumer Level for `Voting by the Consumer Basket`
4 The Scientific Level w/Formation of National Climate Councils and Economic Enlightenment of the General Public
5 International Economic Solidarity with Poor Regions

Box 4. Chinese 2050 High Penetration Scenario for Renewable Energy (Summary by the T. Larsen of Chinese Energy Center Report 2015)

I CONSENSUS ON DEVELOPMENT *Strengthen Environmental Constraints* The goal is to build a beautiful China and realize sustainable development. To achieve this grand objective, China needs to significantly cut back on pollution emissions and restore to levels of the 1970s and 1980s. Based on the environmental constraints, a back-casting mechanism is formed to reduce coal and oil consumption. The study also sets restrictions on greenhouse gas (GHG) emissions - as 3.5 billion tons for the whole energy sector and 1.5 billion tons for the power sector in 2050. 3.5 billion tons corresponds to 2.5 tons per capita or the level in 1980 before the modern focus on industrialization. A halving of the Chinese emission level 2020 despite the Chinese GDP is expected to triple in the period 2020 through 2050.
Optimize Development Paths On the base of broadly seeking expert advice, as well as learning and summarizing the contents and methodologies of advanced international researches, this study establishes a decision-making framework for development of high renewable energy penetration in China. The decision-making process is carried out by integrating techno-economic appraisal, energy system optimization, socio-economic assessment, and externality analysis. In-all, the development paths are optimized across technical, economic, social and ecological conditions as they prevail 2015. Employing a power system optimization model as the research tool and taking 2010 as the baseline year, the optimal operation is analyzed of power system and system expansion plan meeting various constraints under the reference and high penetration scenarios in 2050. It analyzes the energy substitution as well as environmental, economic, and social benefits, and calculates the direct and indirect cost of developing renewable energy. The study optimizes the development paths for the power system between 2015 and 2050 under different scenarios of the perspectives of geographical distribution, distribution of time and operation of the power system.
Adopt Target-Oriented Approach China needs to press ahead with significant reforms in energy production and consumption patterns to fully realize its goal of a clean, low-carbon, secure and reliable energy system by 2050. China must take into account the lock-in effect of traditional energy systems. Fossil energy for end-use and energy conversion processes will be significantly reduced, totaling no more than 1 billion tons by 2050. Renewable energy will be vigorously developed, accounting for over 60% of the energy consumption and over 85% of electricity.
II LONG-TERM VISION *1 Social Economy - Reach the Level of Medium-Developed Countries* By 2050, China's per capita gross national product (GNP) will reach the level of medium-developed countries by the middle of the century. At that time, China will realize modernization, restore a clean environment, and become a prosperous, democratic and civilized socialist country. This is a scientific consensus reached in the whole Chinese society. However, the real Chinese dominance is even stronger as measured by Purchasing Power Parities (PPP) as the Chinese Yuan is strongly under-valued.
2 Ecological Environment – Bring Back Clear Water and Blue Skies for "Beautiful China" "Beautiful China" is a strategic target with abundant meanings, and the key is to realize harmony between man and nature, between people, and between man and society. A beautiful homeland must feature intensive and efficient production, comfortable living, healthy ecosystem, clear water and blue skies. The action plan is mainly manifested in the following three aspects: Firstly, by 2050, energy, water and land consumption per unit GDP will be down by 60-70% of today. Secondly, emission of various kinds of air pollutants should be at least 50% lower than the current level. Thirdly, China will try to construct a scientific urbanization pattern, agricultural development pattern and ecological security pattern implementing protection and construction of ecological function zones e.g. national parks, integrated treatment of water and soil loss, land desertification, and protect biodiversity.

continued on following page

Box 4. Continued

<table>
<tr><td>
3 Energy Development – Embrace A Low-carbon and Green Electricity Future
The socio-economic development level of OECD countries 2010 is the reference for China's 2050 socio-economic development. Under this high renewable energy penetration scenario, China's end-use energy demand is projected to be 3.2 billion tce, in which over 60% is electricity and per capita 10,000-11,000 kWh. Putting electricity at the central position of realizing high renewable energy penetration is objectively determined by electricity characteristics, resource endowment and energy development law.
</td></tr>
<tr><td>
III PATHWAY
1. By 2050, Renewable Energy Will Meet 60% of the Primary Energy Demand
91% of power will be generated from non-fossil energy whereof 5% comes from nuclear fission.
2. Fossil Energy Consumption and Carbon Emission peaks 2025
China has made the commitment to peak CO2 emission before 2030. The high penetration scenario will drive carbon emission to peak in 2025 at 9.23 billion tons, and then decline constantly to 3 billion tons by 2050, taking up 20% of the world's total compared to 1/3 in the reference scenario.
3. Renewable Power is the Essential Replacement for Fossil Energy
China's total power generation will be 15.200 billion kWh in 2050 including 1038 billion kWh of coal power, 466 billion kWh of natural gas power, 649 billion kWh of nuclear power, 2187 billion kWh of hydropower, 5350 billion kWh of wind power, 4130 billion kWh of solar power and 1100 billion kWh of biomass power.
The renewable energy deployment model (EDO) optimizes the deployment of commercialized technologies under different levels of renewable energy development, and the diversity of geographical distribution and time distribution in which renewable energy is generated. The contribution of onshore wind power is the most prominent, while offshore wind power is playing an increasingly important role in realizing high renewable energy penetration. Among solar power technologies, open field photovoltaic (PV) power stations play a more prominent role than distributed solar. Concentrated solar power (CSP) grows rapidly, largely because CSP with heat storage can offer greater adjustability. Biomass power generation also has a place in the renewable energy mix, as there will be a shift from forest and agricultural biomass power stations to municipal waste power plants along with the increase in the proportion of renewable energy. Given resource and techno-economic constraints, geothermal energy and ocean energy contribute less.
</td></tr>
<tr><td>
4. Wind Power and Solar Power Become Important Pillars of Future Power Supply
The economic advantages of wind power will become visible before 2030. The market size of wind power will expand with the simultaneous development of onshore and offshore wind. Newly installed wind capacity will be around 80 million kW each year, accounting for roughly 50% of China's total annual installed power capacity. As for onshore wind facilities, the focus is to build large wind power stations in North, Northeast and Northwest China, which will account for over 70% of total installed wind power capacity. Distributed wind power in Central China and East China will develop more rapidly. Offshore wind power is an additional option for coastal provinces like Hebei, Shandong, Jiangsu, and Zhejiang.
Solar energy is China's most abundant renewable energy resource, particularly in western China. The average annual growth rate will be maintained at 25-30% between 2020 and 2030. Through large-scale development of CSP, China will develop mature solar parabolic trough and solar power tower chains.
Solar PV power can be classified into the following types: (1) electricity development and off-grid micro grid projects for providing electricity to areas without electrification in China's western provinces and offshore islands; (2) distributed PV power stations mainly concentrated in economically developed provinces in mid-eastern China; (3) large PV power stations concentrated in 6 provinces in Western China and coastal provinces in Eastern China. CSP will mainly concentrate in Tibet and five Northwestern provinces.
5. Higher Electrification Rate Enables Renewable Energy to Grow to a Higher Level.
Electricity is a kind of energy with the highest use efficiency yet without any emissions among all end-use energy varieties. The electrification level of a country, that is, the level of electricity use in production, living and mobility, represents the degree of civilization of that country. By 2050, more than 80% of kitchen work of Chinese residents will be completed mainly via electricity. The future era is an information era with a high-degree integration of communication, energy, and logistics over the Internet.
6. Transform Electricity Transmission Network for Optimizing Resource Allocation
There will be three cross-regional transmission lines with a capacity of more than 100 million kW - the Northwest, Central, Central China-East China line and North China-East China line. New transmission under the high renewable energy penetration scenario, will concentrate in China's middle and western regions and will be mainly used to connect the high quality wind power and solar power resources in the central and western regions and transmit that renewable energy power to load centers in eastern China.
</td></tr>
</table>

continued on following page

Box 4. Continued

7. Technological and Institutional Innovation is the Foundation

To adapt to the increase in renewable power generation, China needs to deploy a more flexible system. System flexibility enhances multiple options on the supply and demand side. However, China needs to improve technology, formulate new operational procedures, and develop new business models and new market rules. Renewable power generation increases from 46% in the reference scenario to 85% in the high penetration scenario 2050, the contribution rate of variable power will rise from 30% to 60%, making it more challenging to maintain the real-time balance between electricity supply and demand. Variability and uncertainty will be managed by adding flexible power capacity, improving the flexibility of coal power plants, using energy storage devices (including pure electric vehicles) and demand response mechanisms, and expanding transmission infrastructure. The contribution of nuclear fission energy plays an important role during the peak load in normal work hours on a typical day.

8. High Renewable Energy Penetration Power System at a Small or Non-Incremental Cost

The average cost is pretty close to that of the reference scenario. The average cost per kWh of electricity will rise slightly between 2030 and 2050, basically remaining about RMB0.68/kWh..

Similar to other high penetration studies, fuel costs drop drastically while capacity costs and power transmission costs increase. Major factors contributing to a decrease first and then an increase in relevant costs are: capacity cost - new power equipment replaces existing power plants and additional cost for gas turbines, energy storage equipment and construction of power transmission lines. Most of the incremental capital investment related to these factors will be offset by the reduced fuel costs from fossil energy plants not generating as much as in the reference scenario. Furthermore, the analysis of incremental costs does not take into consideration existing social costs (e.g. GHG emission and air pollutants) or economic impacts.

9. Renewable Energy significantly Improve the development quality of the overall economy

Wind power, solar energy, electric vehicles and other emerging industries become a new economic growth point. China's projected aggregate economic performance will increase 7-fold. In 2050, the contribution of the total added value of related renewable energy industries is estimated to increase from a mere 0.9% in 2010 to 6.2%. In addition, renewable energy industry's technical and industrial demands for equipment manufacturing, electronic instruments, and weather forecast, etc., will stimulate the manufacturing of machinery, electronic products, research & development (R&D) and service industries.

In the meantime, the development of more renewable energy plants will create 12 million jobs (in 2050) in the renewable energy industry and related industries. Research demonstrates that the number of workers in traditional fossil energy industries such as coal mining and the washing industry, oil refining industry, and transportation is declining year by year. In the next 40 years, China will minimize the impact on employment of traditional energy sectors by the development of new employment opportunities in renewable energy industries, and the retirement and transfer of staff in some traditional energy industries to other industries after receiving job training and career guidance.

10. High Renewable Energy Penetration Help Bring Back Clear Water and Blue Skies

If the entire international community could work together to control the temperature rise to less than 2 degrees Celsius, China's CO_2 emission in 2050 will be only about 1/4 of the world's total or online with the share of China's GDP in the world's total. So, China will make a great difference in improving the world's ecological environment.

IV ACTION PLAN

China shall regard the realization of high renewable energy penetration as an important part of the national energy strategy. This objective shall be substantially demonstrated in all energy-related development plans to be rolled out. China needs to formulate a high renewable energy penetration roadmap, break down the general objective into specific objectives at different development stages; prioritize and define tasks in the national energy strategy; identify necessary conditions, major obstacles, key fields to realize high renewable energy penetration at different development stages. The asks at Top, Meso and Bottom levels are:

● Government departments shall enhance guidance and promotion in terms of strategic planning and policy management from now to future stages; renewable energy industries shall vigorously pursue technological innovations and the development and utilization of renewable energy:

1 Formulate and Implement Clean Low-Carbon Energy Revolution Strategy and Action Plan
2 Establish Power Market Mechanism Adaptable to Handle Renewable Power
3 Improve Green Tax Systems and Carbon Trading Market System to Create Fair Play for Renewable Energy
4 Establish Sound Systems of Legal Protection, Comprehensive Management and Professional Regulation

● The electricity sector shall adapt to the features of new renewable energy technologies and construct a public grid service platform and work on developing a more flexible power system

1 Build Major Public R&D Platforms, Strengthen Technology R&D, and Accelerate Industrialization Process
2 Develop Demand Response Mechanisms and Energy Storage in a Large Scale, Keeping sustained large-scale development of renewable power generation
3 Fully Promote Renewable Energy Heating and Fuel Use

● The building industry, transportation and other end-use sectors shall advocate the replacement of fossil energy by clean electric power and renewable energy, build urban clean energy systems, and develop a smart energy Internet, thereby jointly establishing the future energy system and realizing the energy revolution.

1 Optimize the Deployment, Structure and Operation of Flexible Power

Besides the specific tasks at different levels of society Broad Joint Actions of Society comprise:

1 Transform the energy development mindset and make everybody a renewable energy prosumer
2 Promote application of renewable energy heating and Solar PV Power in to residential and commercial buildings
3 Promote electrification and renewable energy heating in industry sector
4 Promote electrified transport to increase valley load and improve system flexibility through energy storage
5 Build urban renewable energy system and energy internet

The political impact of bodies like the Climate Council depends heavily on the support from a well-informed public. This book may hopefully contribute to improved mutual understanding between the economic profession and the general public. Already 2002 the Chinese Communist Party established a central body for planning sustainable development by transitioning to a circular economy. Summary of their 2015 Report in Info Box 4.

5. The Global Level

The overall conclusion from the strategy levels 1-4 is the dominance of ET in a credible transition scenario. In reality ET alone is about 70% of the transition. The strongest limitation of ET is insufficient international collaboration of who the framework is the Paris Agreement 2015. Midst 2019, 195 countries signed the Paris Agreement and 175 countries, representing 88% of global CO2-emission have ratified it, too. Ratification requires that they have a national plan to fulfil it. The most important country that has signed but not ratified is Russia representing 5% of global CO2-emission. The USA, representing about 14% of global CO2-emission, did leave 2020 but reentered during Biden 2021. A potential positive surprise to the MSCN is launched in the book `How to avoid a Climate Disaster` [Gates, 2021]. Gates states a number of options for MNC to contribute to MSCN with an internal ET as Top priority, too. So, Microsoft is engaged to become carbon neutral 2030. More MNC and most B-Corporations have similar initiatives, however, it needs more research to assess the overall effect of this line of voluntary corporate initiatives.

The long-term goal is to keep the increase in global average temperature to well below 2 °C above pre-industrial levels; and to limit the increase to 1.5 °C, since this would substantially reduce the risks and effects of climate change. Under the Paris Agreement, each country must determine, plan, and regularly report on the contribution that it undertakes to mitigate global warming. No mechanism forces a country to set a specific target by a specific date, but each target should go beyond previously set targets. So, the Paris Agreement has a 'bottom up' structure in contrast to most international environmental law treaties, which are 'top down', characterized by standards and targets set internationally, for states to implement. Unlike its predecessor, the Kyoto Protocol, which sets commitment targets that have legal force, the Paris Agreement emphasizes consensus-building, allowing for voluntary and nationally determined targets. The specific climate goals are thus politically encouraged, rather than legally bound. Only the processes governing the reporting and review of these goals are mandated under international law. This situation gives a unique freedom for the scientific society to propose new solutions to the political level. A potential positive surprise to the MSCN is launched in the book `How to avoid a Climate Disaster` [Gates, 2021]. Gates states a number of options for MNC to contribute to MSCN with an internal ET as Top priority, too. So, Microsoft is engaged to become carbon neutral 2030. More MNC and most B-Corporations have similar initiatives, however, it needs more research to assess the overall effect of this line of voluntary corporate initiatives.

These conditions vary a lot from country to country wherefore the Paris Agreement promises *economic solidarity from the industrialized world with poor countries especially exposed to the `Green-house effect`*. Most exposed regions to rising sea levels by global warming are low-income countries in East Africa, Honduras in Central America and Vietnam and Bangladesh with 165 million inhabitants in East Asia. Poor countries need by 2030 to spend $140-300 bn USD each year on coastal defenses to avoid the harm caused by climate change (UN Environment Program).

Review Questions

1 Review the Figures below explain the economic impact?

Figure 8.

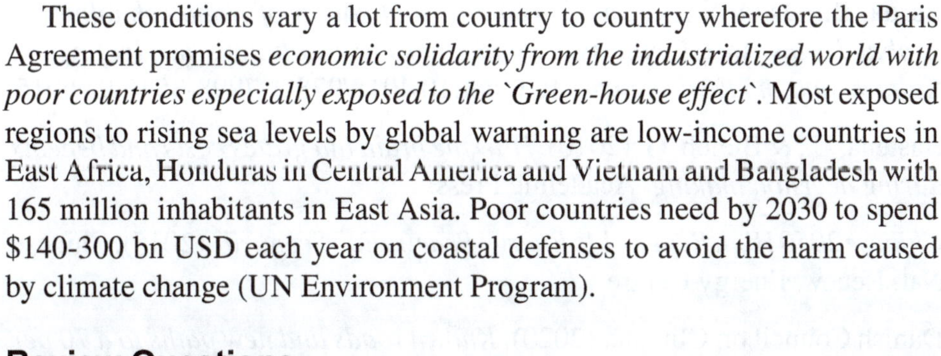

2 What's an ecological tipping point? (Read eventually 4.1)

3 Explain the risk of rising the global temperature >2° Celsius? (Read eventually 4.1)

4 What is the most effective economic means towards global warming? (Read eventually 4.4)

5 When are financial incentives effective to promote recirculation of materials? (Read eventually 4.3)
6 How to overcome unpredictable fluctuations in the use of sun and wind? (Read eventually 4.2)
7 What`s a Doughnut City? (Read eventually 4.3.5)

REFERENCES

Barua, B., Datta, S., & Das, J. (2020). *Application of Nanotechnology in Global Issues*. In *Global Issues and Innovative Solutions in Healthcare, Culture, and the Environment*. IGI. doi:10.4018/978-1-7998-3576-9.ch015

Bastena, U., & Bieleb, G. (2010). *How the brain integrates costs and beneðts during decision making*. Academic Press.

Chinese 2050 High Renewable Energy Penetration Scenario. (2015). Chinese Nat. Renew. Energy Centre.

Danish Council on Climate. (2020). *Known roads and new paths to a 70 per cent reduction – direction and measures for the next ten years of climate action in Denmark. Author. Gates B. (2021). How to avoid a Climate Disaster. The Solutions we have and the Breakthrough we need*. Allen Lane.

Hasegawa, T. (2018). *Risk of increased food insecurity under stringent global climate change policy*. Na Clim Ch.

IPBES Report. (2019). *Nature's dangerous decline 'unprecedented,' species extinction rates 'accelerating' Physical Meteorological Observatory Davos (PMOD)*. IPBES.

Johnson, E. (2011). *Price Elasticity of Supply of Renewable Electricity Generation: Evidence from State Renewable Portfolio Standards*. Georgia Institute of Technology. Working Paper 001.

Juhrich, K. (2016). *CO2 Emission Factors for Fossil Fuels*. Umwelt Bundesamt.

Metcalf, G. E. (2019). On the Economics of a Carbon Tax for the United States. *BPEA Conference Draft*.

Metcalf, G. E. (2020). An emissions assurance mechanism: Adding environmental certainty to a US carbon tax. *Review of Environmental Economics and Policy*, *14*(1), 114–130. doi:10.1093/reep/rez013

Nordhaus, W. (2007). *The Challenge of Global Warming: Economic Models and Environmental Policy*. Yale U.

Nordhaus, W. (2018). Projections and Uncertainties about Climate Change in an Era of Minimal Climate Policies. *American Economic Journal. Economic Policy*, *10*(3), 333–360. doi:10.1257/pol.20170046

Pigou, A. C. (1920). The Economics of Welfare. Academic Press.

Schmutz, W. (2017). *Human-induced global warming to tail off slightly over the next few decades*. Academic Press.

Schoenmaker, M., & Gillabel, J. (2017). *Circular by design Products in the circular economy*. EEA.

Solè, J., García-Olivares, A., Turiel, A., & Ballabrera-Poy, H. (2018). Renewable transitions and the net energy from oil liquids: A scenarios study. *Renewable Energy*, *116*, 258–271. doi:10.1016/j.renene.2017.09.035

Steffen, W. (2015). Trajectory of the Anthroposcene: The Great Acceleration. *Anthrop*, 2(1), 81–98.

Tenhunen, A., & Pöhler, H. (2020). *A Circular Economy of Plastics*. VTT Technical Res. Center Ltd.

U.S. EIA. (2018). *Levelized Cost and Levelized Avoided Cost of New Generation Resources*. Author.

Weitzman, M. L. (2009). On Modeling and Interpreting the Economics of Catastrophic Climate Change. *The Review of Economics and Statistics*, *91*(1), 1–19. doi:10.1162/rest.91.1.1

Zhong, W., & Haigh, J. D. (2013). The greenhouse effect and carbon dioxide. *Weather*, *68*(4), 100–105. doi:10.1002/wea.2072

APPENDIX

Proposal for a Danish Tax on Carbon by the Danish Council on Climate Change

Ulla Blatt Bendtsen, senior climate adviser and Louis Birk Stewart, economist and climate analyst

1. A global price on carbon is the most cost-effective way of reducing emissions

In order to limit global temperature increase and avoid overstepping the planetary boundaries while still obtaining economic and social development and sustainability, policies to limit climate change must be designed in a way that limits the cost. Climate change is a global problem because a tonne of CO_2 emitted in one country is just as harmful as a tonne emitted in another country – greenhouse gas emissions affect the global temperature in the same way. A cost-effective policy to limit climate change is to put a global price on carbon (greenhouse gas emissions), regardless of the origin of the emissions.

A price on carbon helps shift the burden for climate damage back to those who are responsible for the pollution, and who can reduce emissions. Instead of dictating who should reduce emissions where and how, a carbon price gives an economic incentive and polluters decide for themselves whether to discontinue their polluting activity, reduce emissions, or continue polluting and pay for it. The carbon price will incentivize businesses and citizens to change technologies and behaviour in a more climate-friendly direction, and thus stimulate the development of new, climate-friendly technologies and products. In this way, the overall environmental goal is achieved in the most flexible and least-cost way to society.

A global price on carbon can be obtained either in the form of a global carbon tax or through an emissions trading system e.g. the EU emissions trading system which is described in more detail below. The climate regulation, either the level of the tax rate or the amount of emission allowances, should reflect the external costs of greenhouse gas emissions – costs that the public pays for in other ways, such as damage to crops and health care costs from heat waves and droughts or to property from flooding and sea level rise. In practical terms, the price should reflect the political ambition to limit temperature increase to well below 2 degrees Celsius as stated in the Paris

Agreement, and hence the global emissions reductions needed to fulfil the Paris Agreement. However, there is currently no global regulation that meets global ambitions concerning greenhouse gas emissions. At the moment climate regulation must therefore be carried out at the national or regional level.

The focus of this appendix is to describe the proposal of the Danish Council on Climate Change (hereafter the Climate Council) on how to meet the Danish climate goals in a cost-effective way. The main element in the proposal is a general carbon tax across all Danish sectors. According to estimations made by the Climate Council, the current carbon tax levels are far from high enough to reach the Danish reduction ambitions. To sufficiently reduce emissions according to Danish climate goals, the general carbon tax should reach a level of around 200 EUR per tonne of greenhouse gas in 2030. A unilateral carbon tax increase is not unproblematic, as there is a risk of carbon leakage and loss of jobs in an open economy. This should be taken into account when designing the tax. The Climate Council's proposal has been presented to the Danish government and the government is considering a green tax reform including the possibility of a general carbon tax but no decision has yet been made on the reform.

2. The Danish Climate Law 2020

In June 2020, the Danish Parliament approved the new Danish Climate Law. For the first time, the law includes the Danish climate targets:

- 70 percent reduction in GHG emissions by 2030 compared to 1990 level
- Net-zero emissions no later than 2050

Implementation of the law shall take into account a number of guiding principles:

1. Climate change is a global challenge, and therefore Denmark shall strive to be a role model that can inspire other countries to reduce the emissions of greenhouse gasses
2. Denmark shall meet its climate goals in a **cost-effective manner** while at the same time taking into account the long-term transition to a green transition, sustainable business sector development, and maintaining Danish competitiveness and employment, and healthy public finances.

3. Denmark shall demonstrate that transition to a net-zero carbon economy can go hand in hand with a strong welfare society and social balance
4. Danish greenhouse gas mitigation shall lead to real domestic reductions, and limit carbon leakage to other countries outside Denmark.

The role of the Climate Council is to provide independent advice to the Minister of Climate, Energy and Utilities on national climate objectives and make recommendations on climate efforts agreed by the Government. In the recommendations, the Climate Council must assess whether the Government's climate efforts are likely to be sufficient to ensure that the climate goals are met. Furthermore, the Climate Council must provide a status of Denmark's international objectives and comment on the annual climate status and outlook. The Climate Council must also prepare a catalogue of possible instruments to meet the climate targets. Finally, the Climate Council must contribute to the public debate, and it may prepare analyses of and recommendations for climate efforts.

3. The Climate Councils proposal for a general tax on greenhouse gas emissions

General carbon tax across all sectors

A wide range of political instruments are required to realise the Danish reduction target in 2030, but the main and most important instrument is a general carbon tax on greenhouse gas emissions across all sectors based on the polluter-pays principle. This will lead to a cost-effective transition to a low-carbon economy as required by the climate law. The tax should cover not only CO_2 but also all greenhouse gas emissions. CO_2 equivalents (CO_2e) are a way of converting various greenhouse gasses like CO_2, methane and dinitrogen oxide to the same scale. The Climate Council recommends that production facilities covered by the EU ET receive a reduction in the tax corresponding to the EU ET allowance price as is also practiced in the implementation of the UK carbon price floor.

Current carbon and energy taxes in Denmark

Since 2005, Denmark has been part of the EU Emission Trading Scheme (ET) that today covers the energy sector, energy-intensive industry and aviation. In Denmark, the scheme covers approximately 350 production facilities and 10 aviation operators. The EU ET covers less than 40 percent of all Danish greenhouse gas emissions as transport and agriculture are not part of the scheme, and these sectors constitute an increasing share of Danish emissions. The EU carbon price is quite volatile but has been in the range of 20-30 EUR per tonne of CO_2 during the last 2 years. Denmark also has a CO_2 tax that covers the non-ET sectors, which corresponds more or less to the EU ET price.

The current tax system in the energy field is a cacophony of different taxes and subsidies. Figure 11 provides an overview of energy and carbon taxes (CO_2 tax and the price of CO_2-allowances) on fossil fuels in different sectors in Denmark. Currently, it is practically cost-free to emit greenhouse gas emissions from some sectors, e.g. the agricultural sector that only pays the CO_2 tax on its use of fossil fuels but no tax on other greenhouse gas emissions (such as methane and N_2O), while other sectors pay considerable CO_2 and energy taxes. Industry and agriculture are practically free from paying energy taxes, whereas high energy taxes are paid by households for individual heating, by district heating companies (both those covered by the EU ET and those not covered) and by the transport sector. Electricity production is free from energy taxes, as the tax is instead levied on the electricity consumers (not shown in the graph). Process emissions, e.g. from the cement sector, are covered by the EU ET but are not shown in the graph.

The large difference in tax levels between sectors show the need to reform the system with CO_{2-}equivalents at the center and with the aim of ensuring that it is equally costly to emit an extra tonne of greenhouse gas in all sectors. Energy taxes should be reformed depending on the purpose they serve. If the purpose is to reduce greenhouse gas emissions, the energy tax should instead be converted into a carbon tax instead. As an example, the current energy taxes are higher per tonne of CO2 emitted from the burning of natural gas that from the burning of coal. This does not give the right incentives to reduce emissions in a cost-effective way.

The level of the tax

To drive a cost-effective transition to a low-carbon economy, the tax level should be determined according to the price of the last mitigation effort needed to meet a given reduction goal at any given time, i.e. the marginal cost of abatement. The Climate Council has estimated that the marginal abatement cost of reaching the 70 percent reduction goal in 2030 is approximately 200 EUR per tonne of CO_2e. The estimate of 200 EUR per tonne of CO_2e derives from the current estimate of the cost of producing an extra tonne of biogas which is the most expensive technology needed to close the reduction gap.

Figure 9. Overview of energy and carbon taxes in Denmark

Note 1: *Environmental taxes such as the NOx and SO_2 tax are not included. Methane tax on the use of natural gas and bio natural gas in gas engines is not included either. In the transport sector, implicit CO_2 taxes from registration and owner taxes have not been included, even though these have an element differentiated by fuel efficiency.*

Note 2: *District heating plants with capacity of more than 20 MW are covered by the EU-ET and are therefore in the category "District heating ET", while plants with capacity of less than 20 MW are in the category "District Heating non-ET"*

Note 3: *Taxes on electricity consumption are not displayed in the figure.*

Note 4: *ET refers to industrial companies covered by the EU emissions trading system. An allowance price of €26 per tonne is applied in the figure.*

Note 5: *Taxes and prices are converted from Danish kroner to Euro with exchange rate 744.8.*

Source: *PwC, the Danish Ministry of Taxation, the Danish Energy Agency and the Climate Council*

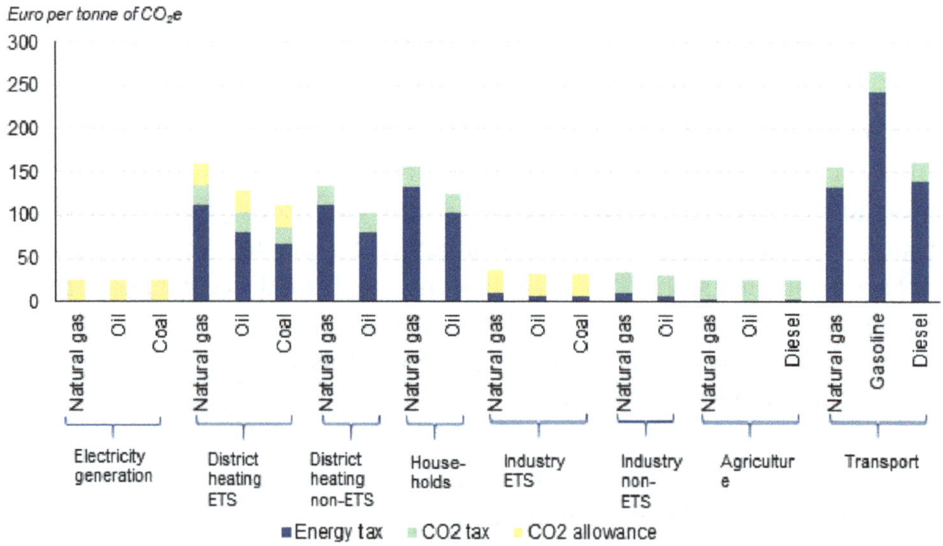

There is, however, substantial uncertainty surrounding this estimate. Hence, if future technology prices drop more than expected in the calculations, a lower tax level might be sufficient to reach the climate goal, and vice versa if abatement costs increase compared to current expectations. Therefore, the Council recommends to follow the development in abatement costs closely and to adjust the tax level accordingly.

Gradually increasing carbon tax to 2030

A gradual phasing in of the carbon tax will give businesses and households the possibility of adjusting production and consumption patterns without having to pay the full tax from the beginning. It is important however, that the tax increases are announced right away and that there is credibility about the future climate policies, as this in itself will provide an important incentive for businesses and households to start now planning the introduction of alternative technologies, for example the change in oil-fired boilers. Figure 10 gives an example of the possible development in the carbon tax level for different uses of fossil fuels.

Figure 10. Example of phasing in the greenhouse gas tax in selected sectors
Note 1: *For some sectors reservations for leakage can be made, which gives the right to a deduction in the total tax payment*
Note 2: *Fuel oil indicates taxes on households' consumption of fuel oil for heating.*
Note 3: *The taxes on the use of coal and natural gas in district heating are for plants with a power input of more than 20 MW.*
Note 4: *Taxes are converted from Danish kroner to Euro with exchange rate 744.8.*
Source: *PwC, the Danish Ministry of Taxation, the Danish Energy Agency and the Danish Council on Climate Change.*

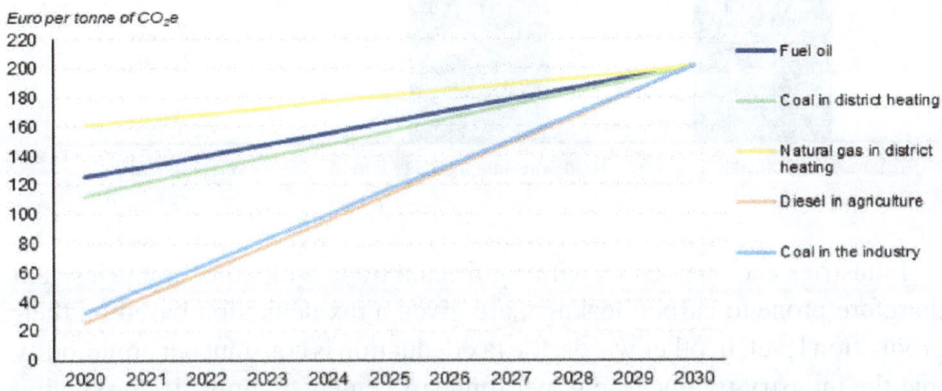

Tax deduction to limit carbon leakage

A general and uniform tax on greenhouse gas emissions will immediately mean that many Danish industrial companies and farms have their tax burden significantly increased with an unchanged production pattern. This is the intention, as the tax should encourage more climate-friendly production, but it also presents a significant risk of carbon leakage, where the tax undermines Denmark's competitiveness and to some extent moves production and emissions to other countries. Therefore, the Climate Council proposes that the general tax is to be supplemented by a deduction in the tax level for industries particularly vulnerable to international competition. Considering carbon leakage stresses that the Danish climate efforts must be viewed from a global perspective.

There are different ways to calculate the tax reduction but the Climate Council recommends the model shown in Figure 11

Figure 11. Illustration of deduction model to counteract leakage
Source: The Danish Council on Climate Change

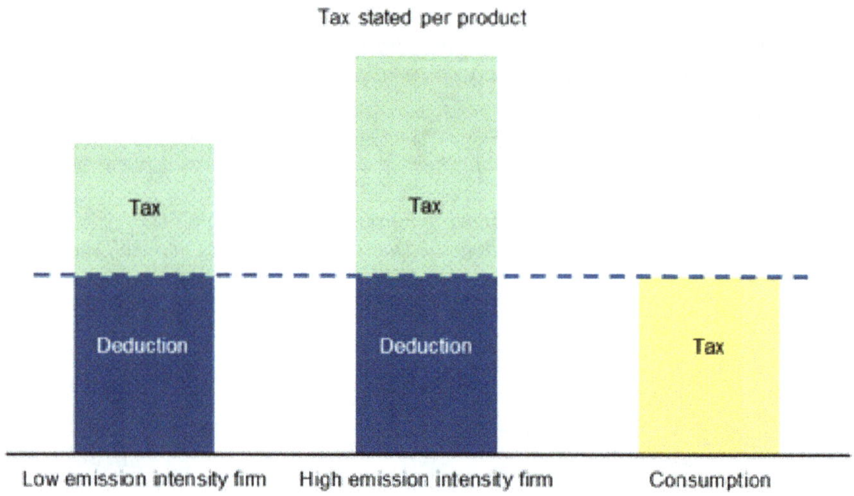

Industries and businesses with significant trade with other countries, and therefore prone to carbon leakage, are given a tax deduction based on their production level. In other words, the tax deduction is constant per commodity that the industry produces, e.g. per tonne of cement. Companies producing the same product get the same absolute tax deduction but the company with a low emission intensity pays an overall lower tax than the company with a high emission intensity. At the same time, the Council proposes that the tax deduction on the production of a given commodity is instead added to the price of the commodity at the consumer level. Again, to use cement as an example, the price of cement is increased by the tax deduction at the cement plant and added to all Danish cement consumption whether the cement is produced in Denmark or it is imported from abroad. Thereby, emissions from Danish produced commodities are fully taxed. There is a limited incentive to move production outside Danish borders and consumers have an incentive to reduce the consumption of commodities with a high carbon footprint both from Denmark and from abroad.

The tax deduction will vary across sectors and depend mainly on leakage rate, defined as the extra emission outside Danish borders that are a consequence of reducing one tonne of emission inside Denmark. The higher the leakage rate, the higher the tax allowance. Furthermore, the higher the general tax, the higher the tax deduction measured in absolute terms.

The advantage of the proposed model is that industries that are prone to carbon leakage have the same incentive to reduce the emission intensity of the production as industries where carbon leakage is not an issue.

The downside of the proposed model is that it requires a substantial amount of information, including estimates of the relative emission intensities in Denmark and abroad. These can be difficult to calculate for all commodity groups meaning that it is easier to use the model for relatively homogeneous goods such as electricity, cement and milk. An alternative model is to give a production independent tax deduction based for example on historic emissions. This model will also give the right incentives to reduce emissions on the margin but it will lead to more carbon leakage than the more sophisticated model.

On this background, the Climate Council suggests to divide companies in three groups:

1. Companies that are not prone to carbon leakage, producing mainly for the Danish market. These companies should not have a tax deduction.
2. Companies that are prone to carbon leakage and produce very heterogeneous commodities. These companies should have a production independent tax deduction based e.g. based historic emission levels.
3. Companies that are prone to carbon leakage and produce homogeneous goods. These companies should have a production dependent tax deduction based on the model proposed by the Climate Council.

How to determine the tax base in the agricultural sector

In principle, the tax also covers farming, land use and forestry. Today, hardly any of the greenhouse gas emissions from this sector are subject to a carbon tax. What makes agriculture special is that it is difficult to calculate the emissions for each farm accurately, and it is therefore necessary to develop true and fair farm accounts before the sector can be included in the general tax system. However, farmers should already be encouraged to limit their emissions. This can be done with a simpler tax based on observable measures such as number of livestock and amounts of fertilizer, and with a deduction for verifiable climate initiatives. The incentive could also be given through actual requirements or subsidies to encourage farmers to use climate-friendly technology.

What about the transport sector?

As seen in. Figure 10 the combined energy and carbon tax on gasoline and diesel are the highest of all sectors, and in the case of gasoline, the tax is above 250 EUR per tonne of CO_2e, and thus higher today than the estimated marginal abatement cost to reach the 2030 reduction target. However, the high energy tax on transport cannot be considered as a "hidden" tax on greenhouse gas, as opposed to the energy tax in other sectors, because there are other non-marketed externalities such as accidents, congestion etc. in the transport sector. These external costs outweigh by far the energy tax on gasoline and diesel. Therefore, the Climate Council proposes that for transport, it is the current CO_2 tax that is gradually increased to 200 EUR per tonne in 2030, and not the overall energy and carbon tax. This will imply a considerable increase in the price of fuel at the gas station, which could lead to more border trade. Hence, it should be considered to convert the energy tax on fuel to a tax the kilometres driven in Denmark instead of the amount of gasoline and diesel used.

Low income groups not likely to hit the hardest but distributional effects can be addressed if necessary

The tax proposed by the Climate Council will not affect all citizens and companies equally, and this could raise concerns that increasing greenhouse gas taxes will have a social impact. However, there is much to suggest that the lowest income groups are unlikely to be hit the hardest by the Climate Council's proposal for a green tax reform. Even so, the tax reform can still be viewed as unfair for people who are mostly affected by the tax increase. As an example, increasing fuel prices will primarily affect people who need a car for their work and have difficulty switching to an electric car.

According to the Climate Council, distribution effects should not stop the use of taxes as an effective climate instrument. However, knowledge of the distribution effects should be considered in the political debate. This will enable a better framework for redistribution elsewhere in society in order to counter what politically may be seen as unfair consequences of climate policy. Distributional effects can be addressed by repaying some of the tax revenue, for example in the form of a lump-sum payment, or by initiating other political or social measures not directly linked to the climate field.

Section 3
Human Resource Development (HRD)

Chapter 5
Cognitive Training

ABSTRACT

Modern economics must reflect that most modern people strive for personal development for self-actualization (HRD). The Ancient Greeks discovered in the 5th century BC the dialectic nature of excellent thinking. Continental Europe (Hegel) rediscovered dialectics as the method of history and Anglo-Saxon empiricism claimed the importance of falsification. Relating to contemporary scientists such as Kahneman and Baddeley, the dialectics and empiricism are combined to positivist dialectics as the primary method PDE. The chapter is complemented by appendices of Anna Vedel on the "big five" taxonomy and Torben Larsen reviewing neuroeconomic research.

INTRODUCTION

Human resources is the set of people making up the workforce of an organization, business sector, industry, or economy. A narrower concept is human capital, the knowledge which the individuals embody. Similar terms include manpower, labor, personnel, associates or simply people. The modern affluence replacing scarcity, gives high priority to HRD in business management.

This new approach to HRD departs from the Neuroeconomic Psychology presented in Chapter 1.1. 4 Heuristics are presented here and further Heuristics for Ratio and Visualization are presented in Chapter 5. Guidance for Stressmanagement is presented in Chapter 6.

DOI: 10.4018/978-1-7998-6424-0.ch005

Figure 1. HS5: `Transparent Brain` by Hiltrud Schinzel

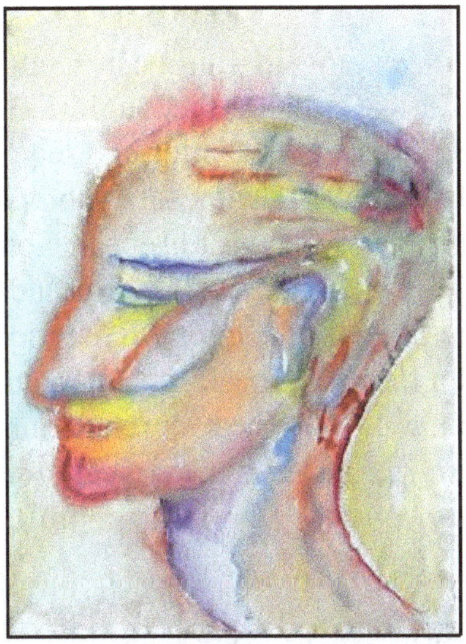

The Chapters are complemented by Appendices from specialists. Psychologist, PhD A. Vedel writes on the `Big Five` Taxonomy and Professor Emeritus, MD A. Holen on de stressing by meditation. The front cover painting of the transparent brain is by Artist Hiltrud Schindler.

5.1 FROM BRITISH EMPIRICISM TO MODERN SCIENCE

The method to construct social justice originated according to the Humanities by Plato 380 BC as Hermeneutics referring to Hermogenes (the son of Hermes, the God of trade and theft). The hermeneutic method interprets human cognition as a recurrent circular process between Analysis and Synthesis (Anna, 1981). Hermeneutics is an early application of the recognition that systemic human cognition must be circular as rediscovered in the modern cybernetic approach to Neurobiology.

Classical hermeneutics was reframed for the social sciences in Continental Europe in the 19th Century by Hegel as the comprehensive method of cognition termed the Dialectical Method (Hegel, 1812):

Thesis vs. Antithesis towards Synthesis

The Hegelian logic was leading in European Continental philosophy as creed in an absolute historical truth. In the Anglo-Saxon world, the Antique heritage was revitalized claiming association and sequencing as the two basal dialectical processes (James, 1907). James *Pragmatism* claims *utility* as the root of utility rather than philosophy of European Continental Hegelianism. This gave later rise to the principle of falsification and a relativist (Agnostic) view as crucial to improve human adaptability. Historically, positivism arising from British Empiricism forms the background for industrialism in the 17th Century, e.g. Hume (Hume, 1742). The game changing recognition of British Empiricism is, that *we see the world as we expect to see it,* wherefore we are subject to prejudices that need to be falsified to improve human understanding and collaboration:

The Illusion of the Philosophical Tradition

The cultural legacy from Aristoteles and Plato which considers itself to represent a Metaphysical recognition of the human conditions beyond sensory logic. Considering other fallacies of the philosophical tradition stated below, metaphysics diverts the focus from pragmatic problems as poverty and lack of social relations

The Fallacy of the Language

Humans accept the language literally, despite its imprecise due morefold meanings. If we are talking about persons of a specific nationality, then different persons have different associations

The Cognition Illusions

Humans are inclined to see intentions and purposes behind all actions, over-simplify situations to gain overview and become complacent having too much success due to Hemispheric dominance

Prejudices due to Temper and Personal Experiences

Modern social psychology has more fold confirmed how important the early childhood and later social relations are for the shape of our values

British empiricism coined the term "Tabula Rasa" to characterize the Open-minded state of the mind. This reorientation towards human self-recognition was already coined by the Antique with the saying `Know yourself`. The concept of `Tabula Rasa` installs self-recognition and control of prejudices as the higher standard of knowledge. The Empiricist concept of `Tabula Rasa` corresponds to the psychological term Open-minded who integrates emotional empathy and cognitive integration.

The problem of prejudices is far heavier than that of simple belief. The primitive way of thinking is, that when we have 2-3 parallel observations, we typically conclude it as a general law. For example, when we experience that 2-3 foreigners of a different color commit crime then many conclude that all foreigners of that color are criminals. The core of modern positivist science is falsification by statistical laws as the basic standard of modern positivist science (Popper, 1959). The secret of *falsification* is that when you have some observations in favor of a conclusion, you must always ask why the opposite could not be true? This feeds the recognition scheme illustrated in Table 1, where every question has not just two, but at least four possible empirical answers. Important characteristics of good scientific hypotheses are that they are simple, specific and advanced before onset of testing.

Table 1. Options of positivist dialectics

Value of Thesis	Supported by data	Rejected by data
True	**Action Plan**	*Type 2 Error* (False negative)
False	*Type 1 Error* (False positive)	**Worst-case-alternative**

Note: Notice that `False` is not simply nothing, it's a real option!

An excellent exhibition of widespread modern cognitive prejudices is presented as 10 global learning examples in the book FACTFULNESS [Rosling, 2018]. The negative bias behind all these examples demonstrates the dominance of pessimism compared to optimism in human nature as presupposed in Neuroeconomic Psychology.

Falsification implies that a true thesis is rejected by empirics if there are shortcomings or failures in the experimental design. History is rich with examples of innovative ideas that firstly become rejected and then accepted with honor to the author after a couple of years (Type 2 Errors). A specific example is the Monocular of Galilei which opposed the Christian world order giving evidence to the reduction of the Earth from the center of the Universe to a simple planet in the solar system. However, due to religious prejudices Galilei had to reject his "Proof" of the Solar system to avoid execution, because they lacked understanding of the validity of positivist design. The good news to original thinkers in the 21th Century is, that experimental design now proceeds so fast that it seems improbable that true innovators have to die before they become recognized. However, the case of Galilei underlines the crucial importance of a thorough planning/falsification process before deciding new important problems.

Falsification implies too, that false theories may be confirmed by sampling (Type 1 Error). A common Type 1 Error is conclusions based on time series. Most phenomena grow or diminish over time. So, many pure fantasies on the growth/diminishing of an object over time are easily confirmed by time series without any scientific justification. For example, in the 70s, it showed up that American metropoles with >1% organized meditators had higher than average economic growth. This finding was claimed to prove a special spiritual effect of meditation. However, the opposite explanation is at least as plausible: Strong economic growth in a city affects many changes whereof a growing interest in meditation is an example. Another is relative more cars and more physical travels. Intuitively, Type I errors can be thought of as errors of *commission*, i.e. the researcher unluckily concludes that something is the fact. For instance, consider a study where researchers compare a drug with a placebo. If the patients who are given the drug get better than the patients given the placebo by chance, it may appear that the drug is effective, but in fact the conclusion is incorrect. In business life, the falsification principle implicates the recognition of a *worst-case-alternative* to the expected outcome of a *business plan*. In case the worst-case-alternative is unacceptable to the entrepreneur, the whole business project should be abandoned, preventing decisions during the implementation from becoming biased. In the case of ambiguity, the cognitive analysis is incomplete!

Nietzsche and Freud told us unanimously that we are ignorant of ourselves. This idea surged in the 20th century and became a commonplace phrase. The deep explanation of our astonishing ability to be unaware of our true motives, and of what is real, lay in our hidden hang-ups. The bulk of the explanation is the lack of dialectics in ordinary *Action Planning*. The book *Strangers to Ourselves* (Wilson, 2004) has inspired the following "Plain-language" recapitulation: To set dialectics going ask yourself `What is 13 x 27?` then Ratio takes over, rather unwillingly, when things get difficult, It is the cognitive 'I', but this is only a half-truth! You are wrong to identify with *Ratio*, for you are also and equally profound your imagination! This is analogous to an actor who believes herself to be the lead actor and often has little idea of what is going on in the play. Also, *Ratio* is slothful and tires easily – so it usually accepts what *Expectation* tells it. It is often right to do so, because imagination for the most part is pretty good as highly sensitive to subtle environmental cues, signs of danger, and so on. *Expectation has her reasons as Ratio does not understand* to cite Pascal. It does, however, pay a high price for speed. It loves to simplify (assuming `what you see is all there is`), even as it gossips and embroiders and confabulates. It is hopelessly bad at the kind of statistical thinking often required for good decisions. It jumps wildly to conclusions and it's subject to a fantastic suite of irrational biases (the halo effect, the "Florida effect", framing effects, anchoring effects, the confirmation bias, outcome bias, hindsight bias, availability bias, the focusing illusion, and so on).

The general point about our self-ignorance is incorporated in a famous (pre-mobile phone) experiment centered on a New York City phone booth. Each time a person came out of the booth after having made a call, an accident was staged – someone dropped all her papers on the pavement. Sometimes a dime had been placed in the phone booth, sometimes not (a dime was then enough to make a call). If there was no dime in the phone booth, only 4% of the existing callers helped to pick up the papers. If there was a dime, no fewer than 88% helped. Since then, thousands of other experiments have been conducted, right across the broad boulevard of human life, all to the same general effect. We don't know who we are or what we're like, we don't know what we are really doing and we don't know why we're doing it. That is a typical exaggeration by *Ratio*, but there's more truth in it than you can easily imagine. Judges think they make considered decisions about parole based strictly on the facts of the case.

We also hugely underestimate the role of chance in life. Analysis of the performance of fund managers over the longer term proves conclusively that you would do just as well if you entrusted your financial decisions to a monkey. Kahneman explains how the illusion works: `Performance bonuses` are awarded for luck, not skill. They might as well be handed out rolling a dice.

5.2 POSITIVIST DIALECTIC TRAINING

5.2.1 The Neural Root of Economic Decision-Making

The historical tradition of cognitive dialectics is revitalized into a modern neuro-oriented context by Kahneman with his formulation of thinking as a dual process between *System 1* (Emotional empathy and Intuition) that is fast and instinctive and *System 2* (Rationality) that is slow and deliberate (Kahneman, 2003). Figure 1 shows the neural correlates of System 1-2. The neural base of *System 1* is Mesolimbic Dopamine Activity (MLDA) reaching the Frontal Cortex (FC) from Ventral Tegmentum (VTA) in the BrainStem and Hippocampus in the Midbrain. The neural center of *System 2* is Dorsolateral Prefrontal Cortex (dlPFC ~ Ratio) within FC. The neural basis of dialectics is now identified as that between MLDA and FC.

Figure 2. A tripartite neurodynamics
Legend: *Brain Dynamics is tripartite between 1) Passion (Dopamine Activity,* **MLDA***), 2) Fear-center (Amygdala,* **AM***) and 3) Cognitive Function in Frontal Cortex (***FC***)*

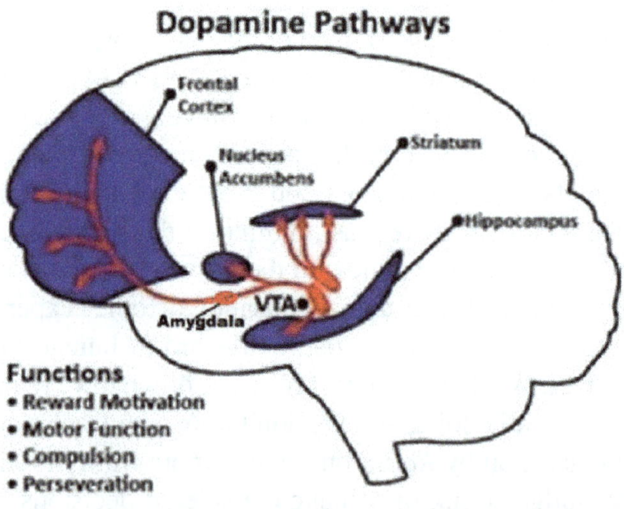

The extra recognition by Neuroeconomics is that besides MLDA and FC, the Fear-center (Am) within MLDA, inhibits Passion arising towards the FC. So, neurodynamics is a tripartite complex which explains that the cognitive integration of Passion and Ratio can be disturbed by 2 different types of emotional biases: fearfulness and over-optimism. Two phenomena known in experimental economics as Risk-aversion and Risk-love and discussed in 1.1 in relation to the model of Neuroeconomic Psychology (Figure 6). In order to strengthen the harmonic integration of Passion and Ratio known as economic rationality (Figure 1 in Introduction) the following 2 Heuristics are developed to minimize emotional biases in decision-making:

- 5.2.2 focuses training of Ratio
- 5.2.3 focuses reinforcement of the whole thought process

5.2.2 Improvement of the Working Memory (Ratio)

One of the most important contributions to understanding the neural base of the cognitive function is Baddeley's model of the `Working Memory` (WM) (Baddeley, 2010). WM is the system of memory processes according to his persistent research during half a Century. Long-Term Memories (LTM) are the outcome of WM by continued internal dialogue on the interpretation of memories. The determinants of LTM are specified in Figure 3.

Figure 3. Determinants of long-term memories (LTM)

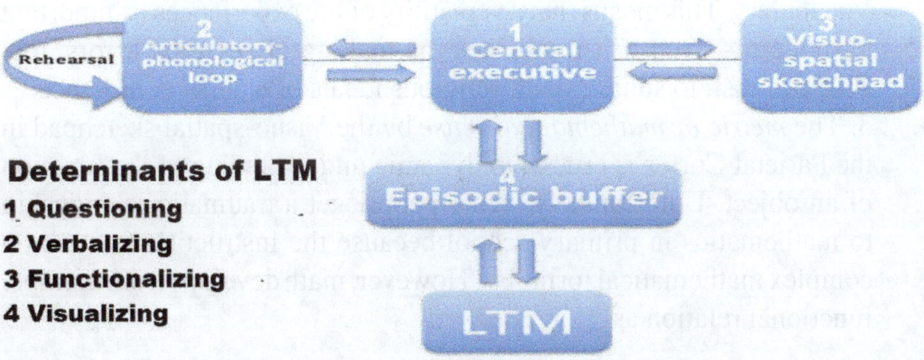

1. The Central Executive of WM is identified as dlPFC termed *Ratio*. *Ratio* activates WM by questioning. There are 7 elementary question words regarding the substance of an object: What, Who, Why, When, Which, Where and How. Try out if you have understood all these aspects of your leading thoughts and do it by open-ended questions without ex ante answer.

Adding `else` after the question word opens another array of comparisons with the substance i.e. the opposite. The critical aspect of this line of work is crucial to the development of new concepts.

A third group of questions addresses similarities to the object (verbal or visual) which activates the imagination (Associations). Imagination is not a gift you have or have not, it is actively stimulated searching similarities to your actual situation. Psychology tells us that *free associations* reveal the emotional root of our thoughts. So, openness to free associations is crucial to reveal your true individuality. Free associations are stimulated writing them down on a piece of clean white paper. The technique is known as Mind mapping.

A fourth type of questions address the emotional level and seek the root of a feeling of inconsistency for instance wondering. In all, inner dialogue by questioning is a crucial tool to mark improvement of the LTM establishing inner peace for more energetic Action Planning.

More sub-tools serve further improvement of LTM in the Baddeley model, too:

2. The *Vocabulary* is important to improve linguistic sensitivity and expressivity in the Articulatory-phonological loop between the Temporal Cortex and CE. Education and other personal experiences expands the Vocabulary. This means that a versatility of life experiences is important to modern – even if it implicates the making of personal errors, too. This contrast, to some extent, religious ideals of a clean conscience.
3. 3. The *metric or mathematical sense* by the Visuo-spatial sketchpad in the Parietal Cortex is crucial to dynamic understanding of the function of an object. Unfortunately, many people get a traumatic relationship to mathematics in primary school because the instruction focuses on complex mathematical formulas. However, math develops from a simple functional relation as

$y=f(x)$

Develop your mathematical imagination considering how **y** varies with **x** instead of assuming simple proportionality. For example, when you loan money in a bank your debt doesn't grow linear but exponential with the borrowing rate of interest.

4. *Visualization* is the most potent means to develop imagination for goal-directed behaviors as it reinforces existing and includes non-processed personal perceptions in the autobiographical *Episodic Memory Buffer* in Hippocampus. The procedure of visualization is elaborated in 2.1.3.
5. Another benefit of a strong LTM is instinctive formation of *intuitive understanding of complex experiences* as demonstrated in a study of experienced versus inexperienced chess players. So, Intuition is not a special gift to a few people, but an ordinary gift of non-verbal understanding arising from vast experience.
6. An additional type of cognitive benefit beyond the individual LTM may arise from group brainstorming that follows the following principles as good as possible:
   a. 1 Organize a meeting for participants that differ as much as possible regarding knowledge on the subject
   b. 2 Do not prejudge any proposal, but encourage free associations, even if they seem foolish at first glance
   c. 3 Write down all ideas – the more the better!

In all, Baddeley's WM-model presents a simple checklist for marked improvement of individual memory performance by inner dialogue as preparation for personal improvement of cognitive performance by Visualization training.

5.2.3 Reinforcement of Cognitive Performance by Visualization

In order, to improve multidisciplinary collaboration and reach a common synthesis beyond the listing of different disciplinary approaches, each disciplinary representative must adopt an unbiased attitude towards his own discipline which presupposes strong cognitive training as all young people are ruled by strong emotions. Cognitive training is widespread used by Top athletes to improve their sports performance by persistent *visualization* of the performance task. For broad use in business life, the final product development goal is typical even further ahead of the individual than that of an individual athletic performance which makes the individual control of emotions at least as important as in competitive sports.

Visualization is not something fluffy used by dreamers not living in the real world. It is quite the opposite! It is used by a whole array of people who know how to bring about positive outcomes in their life. Many athletes including Olympians use it to excel in their sports, in the same way ordinary people can use it to improve a specific cognitive performance regarding a product or service. The benefits of visualizing are also for children. Research shows that child table tennis players between the ages of 7 to 10 performed better using visualizations (mental imagery). Research also shows that people who did a virtual workout over three months in their minds were able to increase their muscle strength by 13.5% compared to 30% by the people who actually did work out.

Top athletes typically start cognitive training at an advanced state of their career where they have already gained specialist competence in a particular field. In a broader application, the first step of cognitive training is to reveal the direction of individual abilities. The general framework for this task in business life is a *personal SWOT-analysis* giving valid and reliable knowledge of Strengths, Weaknesses, Options and Threats, reread eventually 2.5. A good start is experience with identification of different personality types by Template 1. For each SWOT-aspect 2 or 3 items must be identified:

1. To identify your Strengths, list projects with a satisfactory outcome and judge which aspects of your cognitive approach helped you and how you could have done even better
2. To identify your Weaknesses, list projects with an unsatisfactory outcome and judge which of the standard advices you have missed
3. To identify your Options, list some job advertisements that matches your competences
4. To identify Threats, list some business trends that undermine your competence

Template 5 guides your personal reinforcement using the dialectic model for mental imagery adopting mental training as well documented especially by modern sports psychology.

The selection of a career or profession is one of the most important things of life, but it is equally difficult. The lack of guiding services, proper counseling and risk of unemployment has further complicated the matter. Therefore, many young men and women in search of suitable jobs are confused, indecisive, and frustrated generating a deep sense of frustration and indecision. Make use of Template 1-2 as early as possible in your adult life!

Box 1. Visualization Heuristic 5

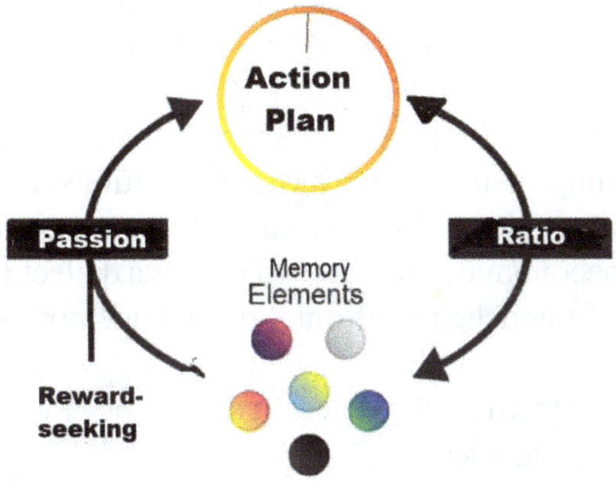

Above image illustrates 5 steps to reinforce *visualized production goal*s like sportsmen do:

Step 1: Visualize your Passion
To visualize and manifest the kind of life you want, it is crucial to clarify what you want and why. You must understand what you value and what brings you the most joy in life. Have you ever had that moment when doing something made you joyful? If yes, it's a good sign of what you want!

Step 2: Associate details to your Passion making it a Vision
This is one of the most important steps. When you want to manifest the life you want, you must create a clear vision of what it should look like. Write this down in detail or create a vision board. This helps you to create a clear and full picture of what your life would look like.

Step 3: Relate emotions to your Vision
Once you are ready, take a moment to start envisioning the actual outcome. Start to imagine the sights, sounds, smells and even the taste of achieving what you want. As you go along, do not forget to feel the emotions you would feel, as if this "life" was your reality now.

Step 4: Take regular (daily) actions to improve your Vision by rehearsal
A saying is that "Rome was not built in a day." Similarly, the life you want to create won't happen in one day but will eventuate in a series of weeks/months by actions of working towards your goal. Don't get too caught up with how far you are, instead focus on the present and set yourself daily/weekly visionary goals and benefit from the reinforcement illustrated above

Step 5: Have grit and rehearse perseverant to complete your `Action Plan`!
When creating the life you want, you will be faced with challenges. An important tip doing your visualizations is to imagine yourself facing and overcoming these challenges.
Mental imagery uses these 5 steps to ANCHOR your vision in your mind. Many celebrities use and praise visualization, but started without much in their lives. Be open, try it out, see where it takes you and learn from your experiences. The more associations and emotions involved the better!

5.3 CONCLUSION

Already the Antique discovered 2.500 years ago cognition as a dialectic rather than linear process. In the beginning of the 19th Century Hegel revived dialectics and used it as a method to explain human social history.

Hegel's `Dialectic Method` became soon challenged by the British Empiricism founded in the 18th Century by philosophers as Bacon and Hume. Empiricism roots scientific quality specific to falsified knowledge. Since a gap has existed between `Continental Dialectics` and Anglo-saxon Empiricism. The development of modern brain scanners to a level of `Mind Reading` gives rise to understanding of the neural basis of emotions and thoughts (Neuroeconomics) and integration of Continental and Anglo-saxon traditions of social science.. Neuroeconomics reveals cognition as a dialectic process between autonomic emotions and their confrontation with memories by Ratio in the left hemisphere.

Firstly, the neural base of Ratio identifies the determinants of our long-term memory who is crucial to our judgement.

Secondly, understanding of the root of Ratio enables the design of Visualization as means for cognitive reinforcement.

REVIEW QUESTIONS

1. Explain the Learnings from Each of the Figures:

Figure 4.

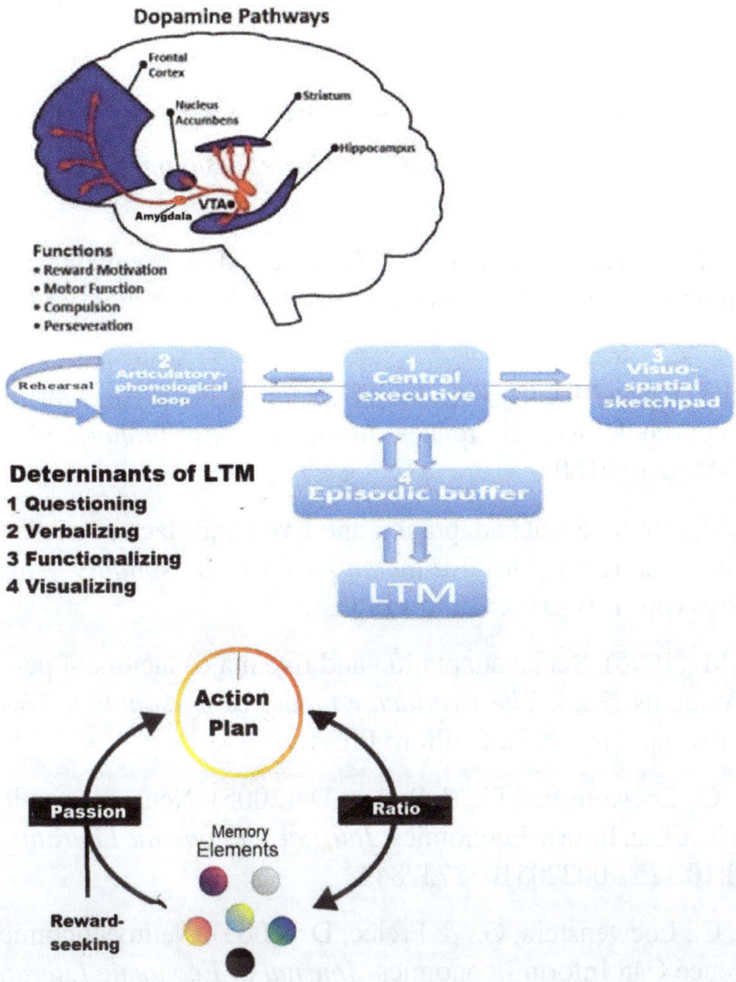

2. How can you Improve your Long-term Memory? (Read eventually 5.2.2)
3. What`s the elements of Visualization (Reread eventually 5.2.3)

REFERENCES

Allik, J., & McCrae, R. R. (2004). Toward a Geography of Personality Traits: Patterns of Profiles Across 36 Cultures. *Journal of Cross-Cultural Psychology*, *35*(1), 13–28. doi:10.1177/0022022103260382

Allik, J., & McCrae, R. R. (2004). Toward a Geography of Personality Traits: Patterns of Profiles Across 36 Cultures. *Journal of Cross-Cultural Psychology*, *35*(1), 13–28. doi:10.1177/0022022103260382

Annas, J. (1981). *An Introduction to Plato's Republic*. Oxford University Press.

Baddley, A. (2010). Working Memory. *Current Biology*, *20*(4), 136–140. doi:10.1016/j.cub.2009.12.014

Bouchard, T. J. Jr, & McGue, M. (2003). Genetic and environmental influences on human psychological differences. *Journal of Neurobiology*, *54*(1), 4–45. doi:10.1002/neu.10160

Bouchard, T. J. Jr, & McGue, M. (2003). Genetic and environmental influences on human psychological differences. *Journal of Neurobiology*, *54*(1), 4–45. doi:10.1002/neu.10160

Buss, D. M. (1996). Social adaptation and five major factors of personality. In J. S. Wiggins (Ed.), *The five-factor model of personality: Theoretical perspectives* (pp. 180–207). Guilford Press.

Buss, D. M. (1996). Social adaptation and five major factors of personality. In J. S. Wiggins (Ed.), *The five-factor model of personality: Theoretical perspectives* (pp. 180–207). Guilford Press.

Camerer, C., Loewenstein, G., & Prelec, D. (2005). Neuroeconomics: How Neuroscience Can Inform Economics. *Journal of Economic Literature*, *43*(1), 9–64. doi:10.1257/0022051053737843

Camerer, C., Loewenstein, G., & Prelec, D. (2005). Neuroeconomics: How Neuroscience Can Inform Economics. *Journal of Economic Literature*, *43*, 9–64.

Camille, N., & Corricello, G. (2004). The involvement of the orbitofrontal cortex in regret. *Sci*, *304*(5674), 1167–1170. doi:10.1126cience.1094550

Camille, N., & Corricello, G. (2004). The involvement of the orbitofrontal cortex in regret. *Sci*, *304*, 1167–1170.

Cattell, R. B. (1943). The description of personality: Basic traits resolved into clusters. *Journal of Abnormal and Social Psychology*, *38*(4), 476–506. doi:10.1037/h0054116

Cattell, R. B. (1943). The description of personality: Basic traits resolved into clusters. *Journal of Abnormal and Social Psychology*, *38*(4), 476–506. doi:10.1037/h0054116

Costa, P. T. Jr, & McCrae, R. R. (1985). *The NEO Personality Inventory manual*. Psychol Assessm Res.

Costa, P. T. Jr, & McCrae, R. R. (1985). *The NEO Personality Inventory manual*. Psychol Assessm Res.

Daw, N. D., O'Doherty, J. P., & .... (2006). Cortical substrates for exploratory decisions in humans. *Nat*, *441*, 876–879.

Daw, N. D., O'Doherty, J. P., Dayan, P., Seymour, B., & Dolan, R. J. (2006). Cortical substrates for exploratory decisions in humans. *Nat*, *441*(7095), 876–879. doi:10.1038/nature04766

Farb, N A S. (2013). Can Neuroimaging inform economic theories of decision-making? *Neuroscience and Neuroeconomics*, *2*, 1–10. doi:10.2147/NAN.S39339

Farb, N A S. (2013). Can Neuroimaging inform economic theories of decision-making? *Neuroscience and Neuroeconomics*, *2*, 1–10.

Galbraith, G. (1967). *The New Industrial State*. Houghton Mifflin.

Galbraith, G. (1967). *The New Industrial State*. Houghton Mifflin.

Goel, V., Tierney, M., Sheesley, L., & .... (2006). Hemispheric specialization in human prefrontal cortex for resolving certain and uncertain inferences. *Cerebral Cortex*, *17*(10), 2245–2250.

Goel, V., Tierney, M., Sheesley, L., Bartolo, A., Vartanian, O., & Grafman, J. (2006). Hemispheric specialization in human prefrontal cortex for resolving certain and uncertain inferences. *Cerebral Cortex (New York, N.Y.)*, *17*(10), 2245–2250. doi:10.1093/cercor/bhl132

Goldberg, L. R. (1992). The development of markers for the big-five factor structure. *Psychological Assessment*, *4*(1), 26–42. doi:10.1037/1040-3590.4.1.26

Goldberg, L. R. (1992). The development of markers for the big-five factor structure. *Psychological Assessment*, *4*(1), 26–42. doi:10.1037/1040-3590.4.1.26

Hegel, C. W. F. (1812). The Science of Logic. Academic Press.

Hogan, R. (1996). A socioanalytic perspective on the five-factor model. In J. S. Wiggins (Ed.), *The five-factor model of personality: Theoretical perspectives* (pp. 163–179). Guilford Press.

Hogan, R. (1996). A socioanalytic perspective on the five-factor model. In J. S. Wiggins (Ed.), *The five-factor model of personality: Theoretical perspectives* (pp. 163–179). Guilford Press.

Hume, D. (1742). *A Treatise in Human Nature*. University of Edinburgh.

James, W. (1907). *Pragmatism's Conception of Truth. Lecture 6 in Pragmatism: A New Name for Some Old Ways of Thinking*. Longman Green and Co. doi:10.1037/10851-000

Kahneman, D. (2003). Maps of bounded rationality: Psychology for behavioral economics. *The American Economic Review*, *93*(5), 1449–1475. doi:10.1257/000282803322655392

Karven, A., Strømlandc, E., & Wollbrante, C. (2019). *The Intuitive Cooperation Hypothesis Revisited: A Meta-analytic Examination of Effect-size and Between-study Heterogeneity*. MetaArXiv Preprints.

Karven A, Strømlandc E, Wollbrante C et al. (2019): The Intuitive Cooperation Hypothesis Revisited: A Meta-analytic Examination of Effect-size and Between-study Heterogeneity. MetaArXiv Preprints.

Kenning, P., & Plassmann, H. (2005). Neuroeconomics: An overview from an economic perspective. *Br Res Bul*, *67*(5), 343–354. doi:10.1016/j.brainresbull.2005.07.006

Kenning, P., & Plassmann, H. (2005). Neuroeconomics: An overview from an economic perspective. *Br ResBul*, *67*(5), 343–354. doi:10.1016/j.brainresbull.2005.07.006

Larsen, T. (2017). Homo Neuroeconomicus – a Neuroeconomic Review of Functional Magnetic Resonance Imaging of Economic Choice. *IJUHD*, *7*(1), 44–57.

Larsen, T. (2017). Homo Neuroeconomicus – a Neuroeconomic Review of Functional MagneticResonance Imaging of Economic Choice. *IJUHD*, *7*(1), 44–57.

Laurie-Martinez, D., & Canessa, N. (2004). Frontopolar Cortex decision-making efficiency: Comparing brain activity of experts with different professional background during an exploration-exploitation task. *Frontiers in Human Neuroscience*, *7*, 1–10.

Laurie-Martinez, D., Canessa, N., & .... (2004). Frontopolar Cortex decision-making efficiency: Comparing brain activity of experts with different professional backgrounds during an exploration-exploitation task. *Frontiers in Human Neuroscience*, *7*, 1–10.

McClure, S. M., Laibson, D. I., Loewenstein, G., & Cohen, J. D. (2004). Delayed monetary rewards separate neural systems value immediate and delayed monetary rewards. *Science*, *306*(5695), 503–507.

McClure, S. M., Laibson, D. I., Loewenstein, G., & Cohen, J. D. (2004). Delayed monetary rewards separate neural systems value immediate and delayed monetary rewards. *Science*, *306*(5695), 503–507.

McCrae, R. R., & Costa, P. T. Jr. (1987). Validation of the five-factor model of personality across instruments and observers. *Journal of Personality and Social Psychology*, *52*(1), 81–90. doi:10.1037/0022-3514.52.1.81

McCrae, R. R., & Costa, P. T. Jr. (1987). Validation of the five-factor model of personality across instruments and observers. *Journal of Personality and Social Psychology*, *52*(1), 81–90. doi:10.1037//0022-3514.52.1.81

McLean, P. (1973). *The Triune Conception of Brain and Behavior*. Academic Press.

McLean, P. (1973). *The Triune Conception of Brain and Behavior*.

Myers, I. B., & McCaulley, M. H. (1985). *Manual: A guide to the development and use of the Myers-Briggs Type Indicator*. Consulting Psychologists Press.

Myers, I. B., & McCaulley, M. H. (1985). *Manual: A guide to the development and use of the Myers-Briggs Type Indicator*. Consulting Psychologists Press.

Oosterbeek, H., Sloof, R., & van deKuilen, G. (2004). Cultural Differences in Ultimatum Game Experiments: Evidence from a Meta-Analysis. *Experiment Econ*, *7*, 171–188.

Oosterbeek, H., Sloof, R., & van deKuilen, G. (2004). Cultural Differences in Ultimatum Game Experiments: Evidence from a Meta-Analysis. *Experiment Econ*, *7*, 171–188.

Pareto, D. (1906). *Manual of Political Economy*. Academic Press.

Pareto, D. (1906). *Manual of Political Economy*.

Popper, K. R. (1959). *The Logic of Scientific Discovery*. Routledge.

Roberts, B. W., & DelVecchio, W. F. (2000). The rank-order consistency of personality traits from childhood to old age: A quantitative review of longitudinal studies. *Psychological Bulletin*, *126*(1), 3–25. doi:10.1037/0033-2909.126.1.3

Roberts, B. W., & DelVecchio, W. F. (2000). The rank-order consistency of personality traits from childhood to old age: A quantitative review of longitudinal studies. *Psychological Bulletin*, *126*(1), 3–25. doi:10.1037/0033-2909.126.1.3

Rosling, H. (2018). FACTFULNESS. Factfulness AB.

Sanfey, A. G. (2007). Social Decision-Making: Insights from Game Theory and Neuroscience. *Science*, *318*, 598–602.

Sanfey, A. G. (2007). Social Decision-Making: Insights from Game Theory and Neuroscience. *Sci*, *318*, 598–02.

Segal, N. L. (2012). *Born together—reared apart: The landmark Minnesota Twin Study*. Harvard University Press. doi:10.4159/harvard.9780674065154

Segal, N. L. (2012). *Born together—reared apart: The landmark Minnesota Twin Study*. Harvard University Press.

Singer, T. (2007). The neuronal basis and ontogeny of empathy and mind reading: Review of literature and implications for future res. *Neuroscience and Biobehavioral Reviews*, *30*, 855–863.

Singer, T. (2007). The neuronal basis and ontogeny of empathy and mind reading: Review of literature and implications for future res. *Neuroscience and Biobehavioral Reviews*, *30*, 855–863.

Vedel, A. (2017). *Personality, academic performance, and study choices* (PhD dissertation). Aarhus University, Department of Psychology and Behavioural Sciences.

Vedel, A. (2017). Personality, academic performance, and study choices : PhD dissertation. Aarhus University, Department of Psychology and Behavioural Sciences, Aarhus.

Wiener, N. (1962). *Cybernetics; or, Control and communication in the animal and the machine* (2nd ed.). Academic Press.

Wiener, N. (1962): Cybernetics; or, Control and communication in the animal and the machine 2nd Edition Hardcover. Amazon.com.

Wilson, T.D. (2004). *Strangers to Ourselves Discovering the Adaptive Unconscious*. Harvard Uni. Press.

APPENDIX 1

Big Five and Their Association With Study Choices

The following chapter is a brief review of the history and research on the Big Five personality traits and represents a condensed version for informed laymen of my PhD (1). The chapter covers areas such as the lexical background for the traits, theory on the nature of the traits, heritability and biological underpinnings, stability and change over time, cross-cultural research, and sex differences. The chapter also covers important outcomes associated with the Big Five, in particular how the traits relate to study choices.

1 The lexical background for the Big Five

The Big Five refer to five broad personality dimensions: *Neuroticism* (moody, ruminating, irritable) or denoted by its opposite pole, *Emotional stability* (relaxed, balanced, patient); *Extraversion* (outgoing, sociable, active); *Openness* (curiosity about and tolerance for diverse cultural and intellectual experiences), sometimes denoted *Intellect, Culture,* or *Open-mindedness*; *Agreeableness* (friendly, modest, and accommodating); and *Conscientiousness* (dutiful, diligent, and orderly). The Big Five personality traits originate in the lexical approach to personality research. The lexical approach is based on a specific assumption known as the Goldberg lexical hypothesis: "Those individual differences that are the most significant in the daily transactions of persons with each other will eventually become encoded into their language". Therefore, the analysis of language should yield the most important personality attributes, since these have been encoded in the language and stood up to the test of time, hence proving their usefulness.

The history of the lexical personality-taxonomic research is long and stretches back to 1884, but it was a systematic work from 1936 that really laid the groundwork for lexical personality research examining *Webster's New International Dictionary* and constructing a list containing all personality-relevant terms in the English language. The final list contained almost 18,000 words, and these were divided into four categories: 1) neutral stable trait terms, 2) temporary state terms, 3) socially evaluative terms, and 4) terms that were either unclear or deemed of limited relevance to personality. This final list and its four categories influenced subsequent lexical personality research greatly developing a comprehensive personality model, ultimately developing the Sixteen Personality Factors Questionnaire measuring various personality traits, but also an intelligence factor. Firstly, the non-evaluative stable trait terms were added to the appropriate temporary state-terms. Similar terms were grouped in clusters, and opposite or redundant semantic clusters were eliminated. Starting out with a rigorous lexical approach, he revised his clusters and variables multiple times based on his own ideas about dimensions of personality, though, before boiling them down to first 67 clusters and later 35 trait variables. Based on a factor analysis of 35 trait variables 12 factors was extracted (2)—which with the addition of four additional personality factors were used to construct the 16PF.

Cattell's 12 factors are now widely regarded as an over extraction, and studies reanalyzing Cattell's trait variables suggested the extraction of only five factors similar in content to what we now know as the Big Five. A thorough lexical study and independent scanning of the updated *Webster's New International Dictionary* and subsequent analysis also replicated these five factors, and throughout the 1970's and 1980's Goldberg conducted multiple empirical studies confirming the robustness of five broad personality factors, which Goldberg was the first to coin the "Big Five" 1981. With the empirical support for the Big Five laid out, Goldberg and colleagues proceeded to develop instruments measuring the Big Five using adjective markers (3).

In parallel with Goldberg and colleagues' lexical studies, other researchers analyzed existing personality questionnaires to identify major personality factors, assuming personality measures developed by psychology experts would reflect the most important dimensions of personality. Costa and McCrae used 1976 this approach to examine data from Cattell's 16PF questionnaire and argued that these represented the *Extraversion* and *Neuroticism* dimensions, respectively. *Openness to experience* is a concept largely similar to the Culture/Intellect factor found in the lexical approach. Costa and McCrae then proceeded to construct a personality questionnaire measuring Neuroticism, Extraversion, and Openness (to experience); the NEO Personality Inventory (4). However, after a visit by Goldberg at their institute and hearing about the lexical discovery of the Big Five, Costa and McCrae added scales measuring Agreeableness and Conscientiousness to their questionnaire and eventually published a revised NEO Personality Inventory. In addition to measuring the five broad factors, this questionnaire included the measurement of narrower lower-level facets subsumed under each of the factors to provide a richer description. Other Big Five measures also include facets, though not identical in their number or content. Throughout the 1980's, Costa and

McCrae published multiple studies demonstrating correspondence between the lexically derived adjective measures and their NEO inventories. This is where the lexical tradition and the questionnaire tradition converged on the Big Five factors.

There were (and still are) some divergences in the conceptualization and labeling of the five factors. However, these differences are relatively small, hence the high correspondence between the lexically derived adjective measures and the NEO inventories. In both the adjective measures and the NEO inventories, personality is conceptualized dimensionally; the individual is scored on each of the Big Five dimensions, but is not categorized as a "type" as is the case in typological measures such as the Myers–Briggs Type Indicator (MBTI) (5), and this comes with some advantages. Taking Extraversion as an example, the individual is not either an Extravert or an Introvert, but simply falls somewhere on the normally distributed Extraversion–Introversion continuum. No arbitrary cut-offs place people in fixed—and potentially undesirable—categories; instead, each individual's score on each Big Five dimension can be interpreted in light of the norm for the population, and the dimensional approach therefore enables a more precise and meaningful personality description. Moreover, the Big Five dimensions can be used as continuous variables in research, which enables more powerful statistical analyses than what is possible using categorical variables such as personality types.

2 Theories on the Big Five

It has been argued that Big Five advocates implicitly adopt the basic tenets of *trait theory*: that personality traits exist and can be measured. However, the lexical approach is theoretically agnostic, since it is only concerned with the mapping of personality description encoded in the language; not with the conceptual status of personality, the causal origin of personality, the mechanisms underlying behavior, etc. Different theories behind the Big Five have been proposed. One of the most influential ones is the Five-Factor Theory (FFT) (6) which provides a theoretical context for the Big Five. The FFT conceptualizes personality as a dynamic system with a fundament of endogenous and stable "basic tendencies"; that is, personality traits with the Big Five as the organizing structure. These basic tendencies influence the next component in the personality system; the "characteristic adaptations" encompassing personal strivings, goals, attitudes, and self-concept. "External influences" such as cultural norms and life events affect the characteristic adaptations, and these can therefore change over the life course, but the basic tendencies are largely unaffected by the environment. Personality traits are conceived of as largely derived from biological structures and processes such as specific brain regions, genes, hormones, and neurotransmitters, and—like other biological structures—personality traits are proposed to be developing through childhood, reaching maturity and stability in young adulthood.

The FFT has received much attention, but several other theories incorporating the Big Five have been proposed. Interpersonal theory, for example, is less interested in the biological underpinnings of the Big Five and interprets the Big Five in terms of how they relate to interpersonal dynamics and the two broader concepts of *Agency* and *Communion,* conceptualized as two orthogonal axes that constitute the *interpersonal circumplex.* In short, Agency refers to the individual's striving to master the environment, to assert the self, and to experience competence, achievement, and power. Communion, on the other hand, refers to the desire to relate to and cooperate with others; to belong with a group. Depending on whether the individual is Agency-oriented or Communion-oriented, he/she will experience fulfillment through individual accomplishments and independence or relationships and belongingness, respectively. Among the Big Five dimensions, Extraversion is most clearly conceptually related to Agency due to its dominance aspect, and Agreeableness most clearly to Communion due to its affiliation aspect. Consequently, Extraversion and Agreeableness are given priority over other Big Five dimensions in interpersonal theory given their comparatively greater influence on interpersonal situations and their prominence in the interpersonal circumplex.

Another theoretical alternative is socioanalytic theory (7), which focuses on status hierarchies always present in the groups people live and work in. Two broad motives resembling the Communion and Agency concepts lie at the core of this theory, *getting along* (with other members of the group) and *getting ahead* (compared to other members of the group). People's behavior reflects their efforts to gain acceptance and/or status within their group, and these efforts and the ensuing behaviors are evaluated by others. Personality is defined from an actor–observer perspective, where the Big Five represent a taxonomy of reputation and self-presentation; a structure of observers' (and actors') trait descriptors encoded in language to communicate potential contributions of an actor to the group. Among the Big Five, Agreeableness is the dimension most closely associated with the motive of getting along, and Extraversion with the motive of getting ahead, but the remaining Big Five dimensions are also explained in terms of their relationship with the two motives, and they receive considerably more attention in socioanalytic theory than in interpersonal theory.

Finally, an evolutionary perspective on the Big Five has been offered (8). Humans, it is argued, have faced many different problems of survival and reproduction, and this has led to the evolution of many different psychological mechanisms addressing such problems. Consequently, personality traits are conceptualized as inherited adaptations; solutions to problems faced by our ancestors and passed down through many generations. No single personality configuration has been unambiguously adaptive in relation to all problems and in all environments; instead, individual differences in personality reflect a variety of different, but all viable, evolutionary strategies. According to evolutionary theory, the Big Five traits represent important personality dimensions, because they distinguish such evolutionary strategies from each other. A high level of Extraversion, for example, may foster exploration of the environment and success in finding a mate and social allies, but it also exposes the individual to dangers in the environment. A low level of Extraversion, on the other hand, may make it more difficult to find mates and allies, but in return it protects the individual from dangers in the environment. Depending on the environmental demands, each of these strategies could be useful, and the same cost–benefit logic applies to the other Big Five traits. As other human beings have evolutionarily composed our primary environment, it has been adaptive to be able to detect personality differences as these relate to behavior, and humans have evolved the capacity to perceive individual differences and act upon them. With the emergence of language and the encoding of personality trait descriptors in it, such personality perception has become communicable.

These four theoretical perspectives on the Big Five are not mutually exclusive. Evolution may have brought about biologically based personality traits, and these (in particular some of these) traits may be salient due to their impact on interpersonal situations and their connection to the broad motives of getting along and getting ahead. More than being each other's opposites, the different theories offer different lenses through which to look at personality and the Big Five.

3 Heritability and biological underpinnings

Behavior genetic research especially has examined the degree to which personality traits are inherited. Different methods of varying complexity have been used, but they all share the idea that if a trait is influenced by genes, people who are close genetic relatives will generally be more similar on that trait than people who are distant genetic relatives. Twin studies and adoption studies have often been used to tease apart genetic and environmental influences on personality traits, but the twin design and the adoption design have also been combined in studies of monozygotic twins reared apart (MZA) and dizygotic twins reared apart (DZA), thereby overcoming some of the potential problems connected with potential dissimilar treatment of monozygotic twin (MZ) pairs and dizygotic twin (DZ) pairs reared together (i.e., MZ-pairs may be treated more alike than DZ-pairs). A milestone in this research was the Minnesota Study of Twins Reared Apart (MISTRA) conducted from 1979 to 1999 (9). The results from the MISTRA showed that twins reared apart were as alike as twins reared together and that genes accounted for around 50 percent of the phenotypic variance in personality traits. The Big Five were not measured directly in the personality questionnaires used in the MISTRA, but the figure of around 50 percent has since been echoed in behavior genetic research on the heritability of the Big Five (10). This research also finds some influence of nonshared environmental factors (environmental factors not shared by relatives reared together) on phenotypic personality traits, but very close to zero influence of shared family environment (environmental factors shared by relatives reared together). More and more attention is devoted to the study of gene–environment interactions and epigenetics, and this will hopefully generate more knowledge on how (and which) genes and environments work together in creating our personality. For now, we can conclude that the Big Five are moderately heritable with heritability estimates around .50.

The heritability of the Big Five implies a biological basis for the traits, and using different methods, researchers have connected the Big Five to various biological factors such as neurotransmitters, hormones, and brain structures. Some findings from this research seem fairly robust, such as the association between elevated Neuroticism levels and high baseline levels of the stress hormones cortisol and norepinephrine and reduced increase in the cortisol level in response to actual stressors. However, the neuroscientific research on the Big Five is still limited, and its methods have some downsides. Neuroimaging studies, for example, which have generated most of the present neurobiological evidence, are inherently expensive and complicated to conduct. Consequently, many of these studies are underpowered due to small sample sizes, and this may lead both to chance findings and undetected associations. Further, the causal relations among neurobiology, personality, and environment are far from well understood as of now, and the classical philosophical mind–body problem seems more relevant than ever. However, the first steps have been taken towards a greater understanding of the neurobiology of the Big Five, and given the growth in neuroscientific research, we may know much more in just a few years.

4 Stability and change

At first glance, it may seem contradictory that personality should be both consistent and developing throughout life. However, this is entirely possible— it depends on the definitions of consistency and development. Rank-order consistency denotes the consistency of individuals' relative standing (compared with peers) on a dimension over one or more time intervals, whereas mean-level change denotes a sample's or a population's change in absolute scores on a dimension over time and age. Rank-order consistency and mean-level change are not mutually exclusive; individuals can maintain a relative standing on a dimension compared with their peers yet change in absolute scores as they grow older. The seeming contradiction between personality consistency and development therefore disappears, and considerable evidence supports the existence of both rank-order consistency of personality traits and mean-level change over time.

Consistent individual differences emerge very early in life. Research on infants and toddlers has found consistency in cross-time correlations of temperamental factors, such as activity level and positive emotionality, and temperamental factors measured by observation in childhood have been linked to personality traits in adulthood, both theoretically and empirically. The Big Five seem to apply to individual differences among both adults and children, and these traits are increasingly used in studies on personality consistency and change. However, other measures from previously dominating personality taxonomies have been used in longitudinal studies initiated before the Big Five gained currency. Most of the other personality measures and traits can be organized around the Big Five, though, rendering comparisons across studies possible. A meta-analysis of personality rank-order consistency did exactly this and found that the rank-order consistency of Big Five aligned traits estimated through test-retest correlations increased from .31 in childhood to .54 in the college years and .64 at age 30 (11). It then gradually increased until reaching a plateau around .74 between the ages of 50 and 70. As a whole, the longitudinal data currently available suggest that a major increase in rank-order consistency takes place from childhood through adolescence and young adulthood, and that there also is a continuous, though smaller, increase throughout adulthood. The Big Five are therefore relatively stable from early adulthood in terms of rank-order consistency.

In terms of mean-level changes, radical change in personality can take place in connection with various pathological conditions, both physical and psychological, and therapy can also lead to substantial personality change, specifically decreases in Neuroticism and increases in Extraversion. Pathology and therapy aside, some age trends also unfold naturally. In a very large cross-sectional study with over 200.000 subjects found a gradual increase in Conscientiousness with age, particularly during the 20's. Agreeableness also increased with age, especially during the 30's, whereas Openness, on the other hand, decreased somewhat. Neuroticism and Extraversion declined with age for women, but not for men. These findings were generally replicated in a sample of over a million subjects in a subsequent cross-sectional study, which also revealed a temporary dip in Agreeableness and Conscientiousness from late childhood into adolescence, before the positive age trend kicked in. Furthermore, for females, Neuroticism increased from late childhood into adolescence, flattened off in emerging adulthood, and then decreased through adulthood and middle age. Extraversion showed only modest negative trends from late childhood into adolescence and flat trends throughout middle age, and Openness showed negative trends from late childhood into adolescence, but subsequent positive, though modest, trends across adulthood and middle age. Longitudinal studies have also explored age trends in the Big Five. Given the challenge of tracking people over long time periods, the sample sizes in these longitudinal studies do not parallel the sample sizes in the large cross-sectional studies, but the longitudinal studies have the comparative advantage that possible cohort effects are minimized. A meta-analysis of 92 longitudinal studies on personality mean-level change across the life course organized the results around the Big Five and found a general increase in Agreeableness and Conscientiousness aligned traits with age and a decrease in Neuroticism and Openness aligned traits. Extraversion was subdivided into a Dominance and a Vitality aspect, the former showing positive age trends and the latter showing negative age trends. Overall, both cross-sectional and longitudinal studies suggest that some personality change takes place over the life course, and that adolescence and young adulthood is a key period of personality mean-level change, possibly because major role transitions take place in that life period.

5 Cross-cultural research and sex differences

The Big Five were originally identified, described, and theorized about in the United Kingdom and North America, but with the growing consensus on the Big Five, the robustness of these traits has been explored in many different cultures. Cross-cultural studies of the Big Five have employed translations of Big Five measures and successfully replicated the five-factor structure across many different cultures and languages. Such studies have also explored country-level Big Five scores and found both general similarity in country-level scores and some small differences between European and American cultures on one side and Asian and African cultures on the other (12). Europe and America score higher on Extraversion and Openness and lower on Agreeableness than Asian and African countries, and these country-level differences in personality scores are related to country-level differences in cultural values such as individualism and power distance.

Lexical personality studies have also been conducted in many languages and have revealed both cross-cultural universals and culture-specifics. Using personality descriptors extracted from dictionaries, these lexical studies generally reproduced variants of Neuroticism, Extraversion, Conscientiousness, and Agreeableness in many languages. However, the fifth factor was more inconsistent across languages and did not always conform to the Openness/Intellect dimension in the American-English-based Big Five. In Chinese, Interpersonal Relatedness emerged as a culture-specific. Taken together, cross-cultural research supports the universality of the Big Five in the sense that these traits can be measured across diverse cultures, can be connected to cultural values, and seem to be of some importance in different cultures, given their general representation in different languages. However, cross-cultural research also shows that the Big Five are replicated most clearly in cultures of (Northern) European origin.

Cross-cultural research has also provided knowledge on sex differences in the Big Five. Exploration of sex differences in self-ratings across 26 cultures found sex differences in both broad personality factors and narrower personality facets: women scored higher on the Neuroticism and Agreeableness factors, on the Extraversion-facets *Warmth, Gregariousness,* and *Positive Emotions,* and on the Openness-facets *(Openness to) Feelings and Aesthetics*; men scored higher on the Extraversion-facets *Assertiveness* and *Excitement-Seeking* and on the Openness-facet *(Openness to) Ideas*. The sex differences in Neuroticism and Agreeableness have been replicated in many other cross-cultural studies, sometimes obtaining higher female scores on Conscientiousness and Extraversion as well. Interestingly, though these sex differences are found consistently across cultures, the magnitude of the differences varies. Sex differences in the Big Five are more pronounced in European and American cultures than in African and Asian cultures, and are positively associated with country-level wealth and negatively associated with a range of inequality indicators such as women's illiteracy rate relative to men's. In other words, sex differences in personality traits are largest in modern, progressive, and wealthy countries, and smallest in developing countries. This runs counter to arguments from social role theory, stating that psychological sex differences originate in sex role socialization and that comparatively smaller sex differences would be found in egalitarian cultures where men and women occupy similar roles. Instead, the cross-cultural pattern in sex differences may reflect some more biologically rooted sex differences, and it is possible that modern societies afford more freedom to express innate dispositions compared to more traditional societies. If so, sex differences may be more pronounced in wealthy and progressive cultures simply because people are freer to express their given personality. However, it is still an open question what generates the differential magnitude of the sex differences cross-culturally.

6 The Big Five: the relation to study choices

With the growing consensus on the Big Five traits as a viable conceptualization of individual personality differences, the traits have also been employed in much outcome research. This research has shown that the Big Five are good predictors of important outcomes, such as occupational attainment, academic performance, and physical and mental health. High Neuroticism and low Extraversion and Conscientiousness, for example, predict a range of mental illnesses, and high Conscientiousness predicts overall job performance while there are other job-specific effects for the other Big Five traits. High Conscientiousness also predicts academic performance across academic levels, while some subject-specific effects for the other Big Five traits have been found. Importantly, the power of the Big Five traits as predictors of such important life outcomes as mortality or occupational attainment rivals the predictive power of socioeconomic status, underlining the relevance of these traits in social science.

Research has also examined how the Big Five relate to study and career choices, and a review of the research on the Big Five across academic majors found substantial group differences in the traits. Arts and humanities students, followed by psychology students, scored consistently higher on Neuroticism than all other groups, while economics and business students scored consistently lower. Arts, humanities, and science students scored lower on Extraversion than other groups. Humanities, arts, psychology, and political science students scored higher on Openness than economics, engineering, law, and science students. Law, business, and economics students scored consistently lower than others on Agreeableness. Arts and humanities students scored consistently lower on Conscientiousness than other groups and the personality differences often represented medium effect sizes, and for Openness even large effect sizes were found regularly.

Such personality differences across academic majors could be interpreted in (at least) two different ways. They could either be a result of socialization within academic environments where different values, qualities, etc. are endorsed in different environments and change students over time, thereby creating group differences across majors. Or the personality group differences could originate in self-selection where individuals seek out environments consistent with their own characteristics, values, and aspirations and "match" their personality to academic majors. A few studies have measured the Big Five personality traits in newly enrolled students and replicated the group differences even in the very beginning of the education. The results from these studies do not rule out the presence of socialization, but they suggest that self-selection is a major factor in the Big Five group differences consistently found across majors. As students in different majors go on to join the workforce in different professions, these group differences among students have obvious implications in terms of personality differences across occupations.

APPENDIX 2

Review of Neuroeconomic Research: Modern Brain Scanners as "Mind Readers"

Digital electronics has had a pathbreaking influence in general behavioral brain research. A change that correlates with the change of Millennium. In the old Millennium electronic brain research was dominated by Computer Tomography (CT-Scanners). CT is useful for a relative gross scanning of the brain e.g. identification of strong anomalies related to diagnoses as Epileptics. So far, brain scanning was largely an exclusive tool for neurological diagnosis. With the new Millennium new hypersensitive scanners has appeared based on magnetic resonance imaging (MRI). MRI is so sensitive that it identifies activity not only at the level of brain organs but at the level of small groups of nerve cells. The measurement method of Magnetic Resonance Imaging (MRI) is Blood Oxygenation Level Deviation (BOLD). BOLD it is extremely sensitive to small changes in the blood circulation in the brain which again is closely related to nerve cell activity (that requires oxygen). BOLD is that fast that it can be combined with simultaneous mental task solving. This line of combined brain research in BOLD and problem solving is termed functional MRI (fMRI). Ultrashort, fMRI establishes a functional link between problem solving and activation of small groups of nerve cells. From general neurology the detailed relationship subtle mental processes as thoughts, emotions and reflexes and their neural correlates are already well-known. So, fMRI is in plain language explained as a veritable "Mind Reader" in the study of economic choice, see Figure 5.

Figure 5. Functional magnetic resonance imaging (fMRI)
Legend: *Magnetic Resonance Imaging the Brain simultaneously with solving economic problems (fMRI) activates primarily Frontal Cortex*

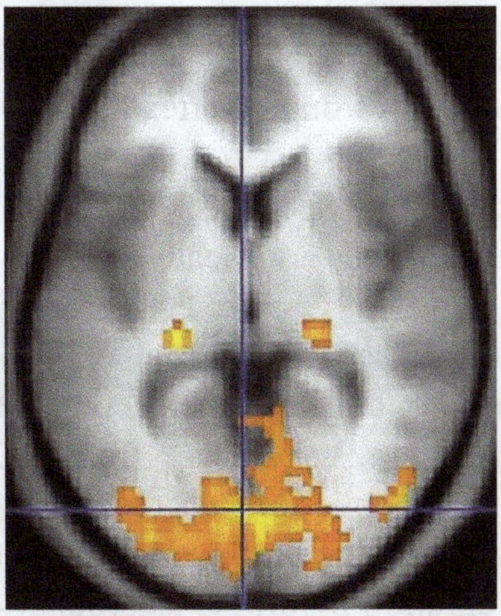

Summary of Key Findings by Neuroeconomics

The principle of thought as a neural circuit between different nodes (groups of connected nerve cells) was revealed by studies of the brain that gave birth to cybernetics as developed in modern computer science (Wiener, 1962). As computer science has developed a general theory of communication in living organisms, that of *Client-Server-Integrator* systems, cybernetics now returns to brain science to explain the secrets of the brain function hidden for former reductionist approaches. Neuroeconomics reveals the brain activation pattern associated with specific mental activity.

Figure 6 illustrates the Triune Brain Conception as the leading approach to a holistic view on the brain (McLean, 1973). According to the Triune Conception of brain function, the BrainStem is the primitive origin of the brain. The Brain Stem is evolutionarily characterized as Pro-Reptile centering brain reflexes. The basal behavioral brain reflex is the fight-or-flight-response as characteristic to Reptile behavior and rooting the fighter-spirit. The midbrain centers the Paleocortex or Anterior Cingulate Cortex (ACC) that forms our Pro-Mammal heritage with the ability to parental care. In-all, passion arising from both the Pro-Reptile and Pro-Mammalian brain levels is indicated by the Meso-limbic Dopamine Activity" (MLDA). ACC is the primary center of consciousness which reflects our overall state of passion. Amygdala (Am) centers a fear network that supports short-term adaptation to insecure situations of any kind, inhibiting passion. The Neo-mammalian Neocortex is on top and around MLDA. It contains the cognitive function who is unique to Man. Major subdivisions within Neocortex is between Frontal Cortex (FC), and Posterior Parietal, Occipital and Temporal Cortices. Within FC the dorsolateral prefrontal Cortex (dlPFC) centers the executive cognitive integration.

So, from a Neuroeconomic perspective, humanity appears as an integrated economic, social and ecological modification of Pro-Reptile and Mammal drivers.

More general reviews of neuroeconomic trials exist. A review focuses on how Neuroscience can inform Economics (Camerer et al., 2005). A complementary review focuses on what economists can learn from Neuroeconomics. A third review focuses on Neuroeconomic findings regarding man as a social being. One of the most recent reviews identifies reward-seeking by MLDA and cognitive executive integration by dlPFC as crucial to economic decision-making (Farb, 2013).

A focused neuroeconomic review with a view on neuroeconomic modelling identifies 7 specific nodes, within MLDA respective FC, that are involved in economic choices across all brain levels (Larsen, 2017). The specific neuroeconomic studies constituting the decision-making model are summarized in the following subsections with a minimum of citations to focus the main line of thought.

Figure 6. Triune conception of the brain

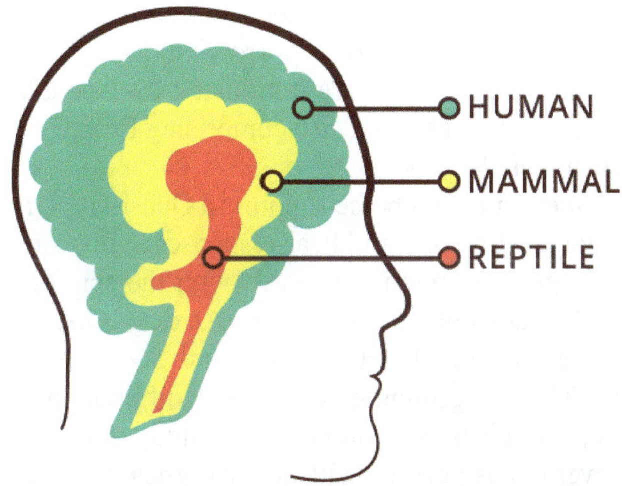

1 Simple Economic Choices

A simple economic choice is investigated in the Ultimatum Game (UG). In UG, an investor promises an agent a reward, for instance 100 EURO, if he agrees with a third person on the sharing of the reward. The UG is a simple economic choice because it involves preferences for a reward and requires cognitive reasoning by the agent on the best decision within a budget restriction (100 EURO). A situation resembling many financial negotiation situations in real life. The UG is reproduced more times and shows repeatedly that Dorsolateral Prefrontal Cortex and ACC are activated simultaneously (Sanfey, 2007). ACC transmits emotions to the Orbitofrontal Cortex forming our Preferences, and saliency signals transmit to Ratio. In broad terms, the UG explains the neural rooting of classical Homo Economicus as illustrated in Figure 1 in Chapter 1 (Pareto, 1906).

The UG represents simple economic decision-making in daily private consumer goods e.g. food, and clothes. Private daily consumer goods amount to 25% of Gross Domestic Product (GDP) in the post-industrial society.

2 Complex Economic Choices

Intertemporal Choice (IC) is a complex economic choice. IC offers a group of persons a choice between rewards at different points of time. A rational IC-choice is according to the borrowing rate. Respondents to IC divide in a group of rationalists dominated by *Ratio* and a subgroup of risk-averters preferring a halving of their reward as paid instantly instead of waiting a year which in comparison with normal borrowing rates of interest is a poor economic decision. Risk-averters are dominated by Amygdala indicating hyper activation of the fear network also comprising Primary consciousness and *Ratio* (McClure et al., 2004).

The study of intertemporal choice supports a Quasi-Hyperbolic model of intertemporal choice with *Ratio* and Fear-responses as opposite poles. Over-activation of Amygdala is often associated with the serotonin transporter (5-HTTLPR). This constitutes too Social Anxiety Disorder wherefore the border between a normal risk-aversion and Social Anxiety Disorder is a gray zone. This subgrouping indicates a different decision-making pattern than simple choices. A neuroeconomic study of consumer behavior identifies risk-averters as persons with relatively few brain connections in the Electroencephalogram (EEG). Risk-averters are pragmatic consumers dominated by fear compared to rationalist consumers dominated by the left hemisphere. Non-neurotic *risk-averters* are a special group of economic agents with a pragmatic consumer pattern.

Complex choices (IC) are representative to economic DM regarding durables (>1 year of function) as houses, cars and consumer electronics as well as production planning and political issues which in-all accounts for a major part of the GDP.

3 Explorative Choices

A game trial within the field of reinforcement learning investigates a switch between normal exploitative choices (EC) and extraordinary explorative choices. Subjects performed a 'four-armed bandit' task involving repeated choices between four slot machines paying out points (to be exchanged for money) around four different means randomly and independently changing from trial to trial. Exploration appears when subjects choose another slot than the one with the highest expected mean (the subjective experience behind these choices were described during a post-task interview). The learning from explorative choices is that it is not a permanent state but the mental faculty to switch from normal rationality to consciously explorative choices from time to time in a period with recurrent choices. The gift to make explorative choices complements sequencing by Ratio and adds passionate imagination/ association by Frontopolar Cortex to normal DM (Daw et al., 2006). This means that creativity is a special ability of volitional switching between exploitation (Ratio) and exploration of Preferences. Where this ability is a secondary faculty in ordinary people, it is the dominant ability in a minority of explorers. Exploration differentiates entrepreneurs managing their own venture from managers without venture experience in a controlled trial. Managing entrepreneurs made more efficient decisions than non-entrepreneur management (Laurie-Martinez & Canessa, 2004).

4 Social Choices

Is man an egoist or an altruist? Empathy and solidarity are evidenced as human qualities originating at the pro-mammal brain level of primary consciousness. These qualities rely on a "mirror"-function by ACC meaning that our response to the pain of other people is nearly as strong as to pain originated in our own body (9). Further, regret as a technical term for conscientiousness is part of *Preferences* (Camille & Corricello, 2004). So, man is definitely neither egoist or altruist but a hybrid of both. Further a review of simple economic choices (UG) indicates the practical balance between egoism and altruism (Oosterbek et al., 2004):

- Shares below 20% of the pie are mostly rejected
- Shares of least 40% of the pie are nearly always accepted

The prototype of classical economic man, deciding sovereign as illustrated in Figure 1 in the Introduction, is that of Robinson Crusoe living alone on an island. A modern approach to economics is a citizen valuing some mutual human solidarity. In plain words, Robinson Crusoe must recognize that he/her is outdated. The hypothesis that human nature is developed for cooperation has attracted considerable research attention. A meta-analysis of 82 cooperation experiments, spanning four different types of intuition manipulations—time pressure, cognitive load, depletion, and induction—includes 29,087 participants in total concludes that to become productive collaborating partners, confidence is required to the collaborative value-setting to turn the social dimension into a productive resource (Karven et al., 2019).

5 Cognitive Errors

A study (MRI) examines hemispheric specialization and decision-making during conditions of resolving certain, respective uncertain inferences. The results provide compelling evidence for hemispheric specialization for reasoning in FC. The right Hemisphere (Imagination) has a critical role to play about incompletely specified situations (ambiguity) which is typical to economic DM). This role involves maintenance of ambiguous mental representations that temper premature over-interpretation by the left hemisphere (*Ratio)*. This special fallacy of *Ratio* is explained as an over-imposed goal-direction blocking interhemispheric communication due to serial processing (with limited capacity) in the left Hemisphere)Goel et al., 2006}. The subjective aspect of this cognitive failure was already described in behavioral economics by Galbraith discovering that when American private corporations went bankrupt the most frequent cause was subjective failures in top-management that from outside appeared as *Complacency* (Galbraith, 1967).

The risk of cognitive error by complacency in powerful organizations is not a modern discovery. Already in Ancient Greece, philosophers discovered the causality between "Hubris and Nemesis". As modern business life develops far more economic and political power-centers than ever seen before the law of "Hubris and Nemesis" is as relevant as ever and rises phenomena as Nepotism, abuse of power and strategic failures in large organizations.

Evaluation of the State of Neuroeconomics

Neuroeconomics has so far explored a diversity of economic choices:

- Simple choices (UG) applied by households for `Daily Consumables`
- Complex Choices for `Durables`, Production Planning and Politics
- Explorative Choices following Passion to identify new means of satisfaction
- The neural root of `Cognitive Errors`
- Social choices to decide moderating the classical choice between Egoism and Altruism

Based on this research a decision-making model was already presented in Figure 6 in 1.1. Based on the aggregated experiences with UG a positive economic behavior is recommended:

- Show moderately solidaric behavior in business relations
- Minimize relations to people that tries to cheat you

Chapter 6
Stress Management

ABSTRACT

The chapter departs from a review of scientific research in job-related stress. A model of neurodynamics explains the action mechanism of classical meditation as in-depth relaxation as effective means to cope with stress. This line of research has so far been considered alternative by the medical healthcare system, but understanding of the neurophysiological action mechanism should lead to inclusion in accordance with the normal standard of modern healthcare. A minireview of "Meditation and Prevention of Stress" by Are Holen complements the chapter.

6.1 JOB-RELATED EPIDEMIC STRESS

The rise of the creative class is a double-edged sword! 50 years ago, young people aiming a social career primarily had to respect the social hierarchy on their career-path and persons with many individual ideas were considered egocentric (Benne & Sheats, 1948). Today, 40% of youngsters aim to engage in self-actualization of their individual faculties and that is the type of persons demanded by advanced companies. However, the expectation of youngsters of self-actualizing is a huge stress-factor, too. More studies link epidemic depression to stresses related to the economic crisis. A study from the American Institute for Occupational Safety and Health finds that 25% of American workers often or very often burned out or stressed in their job (Sauter et al., 1999). The impact of specific modern triggers of stress are

DOI: 10.4018/978-1-7998-6424-0.ch006

ranked, too, see Table 24 (Holmes & Rahe, 1967). Scores >150 points in a 12 month period implies a moderate health risk.

Based on the study of 5000 patients, the experience of 150 stress-points within a year has a risk of 50% to cause illness whereof e.g. marriage accounts for 50. The frequency of most of the stressful events – both positive and negative events - has increased more frequently since 1970. WHO warns that the world faces a mental health crisis by an epidemic raise in diagnosed depressions (Marcus et al., 2912). In 2020, depression will be the second leading cause of world disability and 2030, it is expected to be the largest contributor to the burden of disease.

Open-minded are frontrunners in the adoption into modern Western lifestyle including relaxation exercises inspired by classical yoga and meditation (Hurk et al., 2011). Until recently, yoga and meditation originated in the Veda 1000 years B.C. Modern interest in meditation understands human vulnerability to stress as deeper than modern business life. The human fear response, rooted in the Mammal brain (Amygdala), is shaped by thousands of years in the Stone Age with many acute threats. The Stone Age Syndrome emerges today as *Pride* characterizing a *Conscientious* personality. In the post-industrial society with assurance of physical as well as social survival, acute threats are few while personal long-term planning e.g. regarding education is a crucial quality in modern career development. *Pride* represents in modern business life a narrowmindedness that blocks for personal development. The great evolutionary idea of classical meditation, as reinterpreted in neuroeconomic psychology, is to wipe out fear and defensiveness in favor of positive psychology.

6.2 SCIENTIFIC RESEARCH IN CLASSICAL MEDITATION

6.2.1 Introduction

The primary medical advice for better mental integration is self-control or *stamina* based on physical fitness (Oaten & Cheng, 2006). The long-term effect of regular meditative In-depth-relaxation is illustrated in Figure 1. It is a neuroeconomic EEG-study during meditation (Travis & Arenander, 2006).

Table 1. The impact of stressful life events

Event	High Impact	Event	Moderate Impact	Event	Minor Impact
Death of Spouse	100	New Mortgage/Loan	>100.000 USD 31	Changes in Working Hours	20
Divorce	73	Call in of Mortgage/ Loan	30	Change of Address	20
Separation	65	Change of Job-responsibility	29	Change of School	20
Imprisoning	63	Great Personal Performance	28	Change of Leisure or Social Habits	19
Death of close family-member	63	Son or Daughter leaves the home	29	Mortgage/ Loan	<100.000 USD 17
Personal damage or illness	53	Difficulties with Family-in-Law	29	Change of Sleeping or Eating Habits	16
Marriage	50	Spouse stops or starts to Work	26	Holidays or Christmas	12
Dismissal	47	Starts or finishes school	26	Minor Offences	11
Marriage Reconciliation	45	Difficulties with your Boss	23		
Retirement	45				
Change in Health of Family	44				
Pregnancy	40				
Sexual difficulties	39				
New member of the Family	39				
Job-related Adaptation	39				
Change in Financial Status	38				
Death of close Friend	37				
Change in Job-conditions	36				
More Discussions with Spouse	35				

Source: Holmes and Rahe 1967.

Figure 1. Improved frontal cohesion by regular meditative in-depth relaxation
Source: *Reworked after Travis & Arenander, 2006*

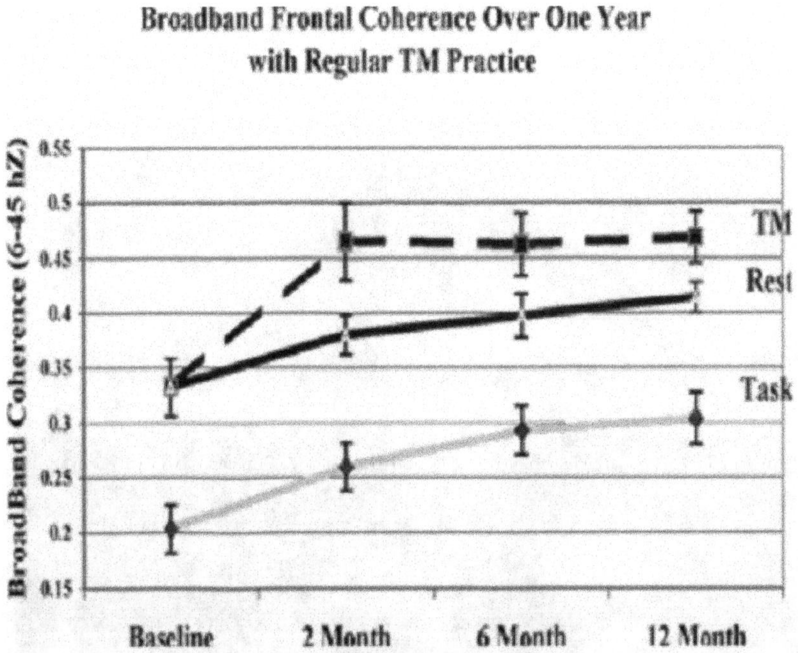

A key indicator of mental capacity is Frontal cohesion as indicated by Electro-Encephalography (EEG). Its broadly accepted that the Frontal Cortex (FC) centers cognitive integration. The degree of Frontal EEG-cohesion indicates how many brain cells are synchronized in the actual process. The more synchronized brain cells the broader the spectrum of included information in the processing. So, the degree of Frontal cohesion indicates mental capacity. A correlation study shows a significant relationship between Frontal cohesion tests and `*General Fluid Intelligence*` (Cox & MacPherson, 2014).

Figure 1 shows that the state of `Task Work` is a more chaotic state than that of `Rest` as the level of Frontal cohesion declines from 33% to 20%. This is because sensory input passing the Pro-Mammal Midbrain activates protective personal memories from the Hippocampus by the Fear-network which desynchronizes the overall impression of the cortical function. A level of 20% Frontal cohesion during Task work is quite low and indicates in itself an option of improvement.

Further, Figure 1 shows that after 2 months of regular meditation, the level of Frontal cohesion improves markedly from 33% to 46%. The improved cohesion is maintained during task work rising from 29% before introduction of meditation to 26% after 2 months of training.

Figure 2. ACEM meditation

Continuation of regular meditation after 2 months does not change a lot on the meditation experience. However, the cohesion during task work continues to rise and reaches 30% after 12 month. In order to assess the importance of this change in cohesion, it's relevant to compare the squares of the starting respective the end point. These squares (R^2) are 4% respective 9% which indicates that one year of regular meditative In-depth-relaxation can redouble mental capacity.

In summary, it seems to be an incredible scenario that ordinary people can redouble their mental capacity by regular meditative In-depth-relaxation two times 20 minutes a day during 12 months. This means that the next section presents a brief review of modern meditation research.

6.2.2 Brief Review of Research in Meditative In-depth-relaxation

The modern breakthrough of medical research in meditation focuses on transcendental meditation (TM) (Wallace, 1970). Medical TM-research comprises >500 scientific studies. These results are later reproduced in more studies, for instance. a series of experiments with mantra-meditation at Harvard Medical School (Benson & Klipper, 1975). Another modern meditation procedure that of ACEM Meditation is illustrated in Figure 2.

Health technology assessment (HTA) is the format of comprehensive evaluation of medical interventions that is recognized by WHO. An HTA of TM identifies the following key studies of long-term effects of regular TM (Larsen, 2006):

- A prospective, randomized trial compared the effect of TM on the stress hormone (cortisol) with a verbal course in Stress Reduction Control during a period of 4 months (MacLean, 1997). The conclusion is a significant decline in plasma cortisol in the TM-group compared to the Stress Reduction Control group. Lowering the level of plasma cortisol is known to 1) Improve the immune response, 2) speeding up healing of wounds and 3) improving learning (mental capacity)
- A meta-analysis finds that regular relaxation exercises complement physical fitness as health activity presenting an option of reinforcement by dissolution of stress and anxiety (Manzoni et al., 2008). In a diversity of physical and mental relaxation procedures, meditation is most efficient
- The long-term effect of meditation on Frontal Cohesion (integration) is indicated by EEG-cohesion (Travis & Arenander, 2006). After two months of regular meditation Frontal cohesion is improved – not only during meditation or in ordinary rest – but in task solving too

The effectiveness of the TM-program arises from the disciplined teaching of the original Vedic mantra-meditation in a modernized, standardized program in 7 steps, see Table 2.

Table 2. Standard introduction program to transcendental meditation

1	**Introduction**	A vision on the potentials by TM	1.5 hours
2	**Preparation**	The technique and origin of TM	1.5 hours
3	**Personal Interview**	Interview with a TM-teacher	10 min.
4	**Introduction to TM**	Individual introduction to TM	2 hours
5	**Verification And Evaluation**	Verification of meditation practice and further practical instruction	2 hours
6		Explanation of TM-effects by varied personal experiences	2 hours
7		Explanation of the development of advanced states of consciousness[1]	2 hours

The individual benefits of TM presuppose a good compliance to the guidelines! A very few persons (shares a promille of all practitioners) with vulnerable minds have experienced states of mania due to uncontrolled prolongation of meditation time.

The Neuroeconomic Psychology presented in 1,1 explains the action-mechanism of meditative In-depth-relaxation in Figure 6 as a movement towards Origo that releases suppressed information for integration and extended flexibility. Neuroscience teaches us that this simple decision-making model in practice is disturbed by Fear-responses (*Am*) which are biological heritage from the Stone Age with many acute threats. In the Stone Age effective Fear-responses were crucial to survival. In the Post-Industrial economy the acute threats to matured adults are few while long-term decisions as choice of occupation and formation of families have enormous influence on the short-term conditions of life. In the adaptation of man to the modern conditions of life, the preservation of Stone Age Fear-responses has become a negative inheritance leading to an enormous split between short-termed useless or even harmful Consumerism and rational `Simple Living` as explained in 1.2. In order, to strengthen focus on the essential task of unfolding individual gifts a method to weaken biological Fear-responses seems crucial. Classical mantra-meditation as described in the Indo-European Veda 1.000 years B.C. presents itself as such a method to calm mind and increase mental stability.

6.2.3 International Meditation NGOs besides the TM Organization

The fast dissemination of TM in the 60s and 70s – especially in the USA – called for more alternatives to TM. Today, the following meditation programs

– differing slightly from TM - have both documented de-stressing effects and public appeal:

ACEM Meditation

A variant of TM (Mantra-meditation) focuses development of modern open-mindedness

(see Fig. 1) is founded by the Norwegian MD (Holen, 1976), see his Appendix

Autogenic Training (AT)

AT is a German relaxation procedure developed by (Schultz, 2004). The technique involves repetitions of a set of visualizations that induce a state of relaxation and is based on passive concentration of bodily perceptions (for instance, heaviness and warmth of arms, legs), which are facilitated by self-suggestions. AT alleviates many stress-induced psychosomatic disorders.

Mindfulness meditation (MFM)

MFM is a meditation procedure referring to the Buddhist tradition. MFM is practiced with open instead of closed eyes involves attention on breathing practice, mental imagery, awareness of body and mind or muscle and body relaxation. MFM does not have a standardized and individualized introduction program like TM. A Mindfulness-Based Stress Reduction (MBSR) focuses on awareness and attention to the present (Stierwalt, 2018)

Meditation Courses as Module in Patient-Centered Healthcare

The growing scientific understanding of the technique of classical meditation is accompanied by growing dissemination of meditation procedures. Millions of persons have learnt in-depth relaxation from the above reviewed programs. Also, several popular science books on meditation help to spread the knowledge of de stressing by meditation. However, recognizing the strong personal effect associated with regular meditation, it is highly recommended to seek guidance from some organization representing a professional guidance to the long-term meditation tradition. Guidance from experienced consultants in meditation is firstly crucial in the introduction phase that may involve strong affections. Also follow-up guidance for inspiration, mentoring and variation of training is very important for the best possible outcome.

At the same time, user-driven healthcare has become an element in medical healthcare for instance parallel to the format of programs for physical fitness. Physical fitness for endurance and mantra-meditation for de stressing are complementary interventions for promotion of mental health for a large share of the population. Medical healthcare, experts in meditation and health economists must collaborate within a scheme of `Integrated Care`-interventions as developed in relation to other modern interventions towards chronic diseases (Larsen, 2011).

6.3 CONCLUSIONS ON STRESS MANAGEMENT BY MEDITATION

Based on a Health Technology Assessment the following conclusions appears (Larsen, 2006):

1. Medical research – based on more specific meditation programs – shows that daily meditation for instance in 3 months distressed the nervous system reducing the level of the stress hormone (cortisol). This medical interpretation of meditation is supported by the Appendix of A. Holen.
2. The psychological effect of regular meditation is demonstrated as release of anxiety which in far the most cases improves mental. However, a low probability of mania-like events may be considered, too.
3. From the point of view of health economics a 5-year follow-up study indicates a significant decline in healthcare costs.
4. The In-depth-relaxation response by meditation is best assured by meditation courses organized by persons with long-term experience in meditation and secular aspirations in their life. Despite the documented benefits from regular meditation, the historic driver of meditation has been religious values.

From a secular point of view, the positive motivation to meditation is the extra mental adaptability following from reduced fear-responses or strong Open-mindedness in the terms of pluralist behavioral economics, see Figure 6.

Facing the reality that job-related stress is a good candidate as the next Pandemic after Covid-19, foresighted health policies should support a liberal dissemination of meditation procedures. The overall target of meditative development is not medical specialist competence but rather a broad competence as a very Open-minded person. So, it is recommended that health policies support NGO`s for meditation, for instance as a fixed subsidy to introductory meditation courses.

Review Questions

1. How do you explain the neurodynamics of meditative In-depth relaxation?

Figure 3.

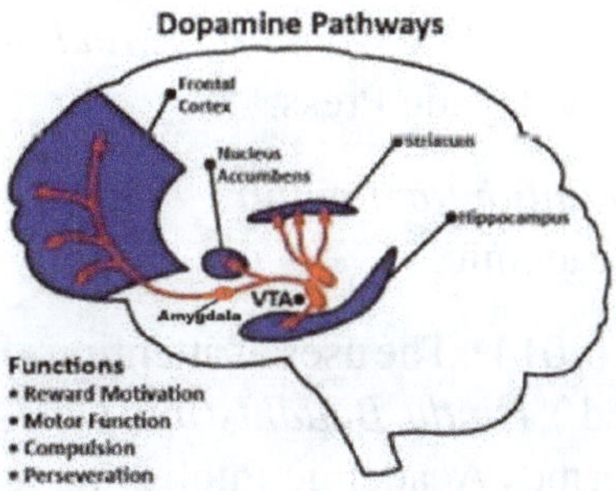

2. Reconsidering Table 2, how many stress events have you experienced during the last 12 months?
3. Could you learn meditation from a book?
4. Do you have to believe in God to learn meditation In-depth-relaxation?
5. What are the Neurophysiologic characteristics of In-depth-relaxation?

REFERENCES

Beaty, R. E., Benedek, M., Wilkins, R. W., Jauk, E., Fink, A., Silvia, P. J., Hodges, D. A., Koschutnig, K., & Neubauer, A. C. (2014). Creativity and the default network - A functional connectivity analysis of the creative brain at rest. *Neuropsychologia*, *64*, 92–98. doi:10.1016/j.neuropsychologia.2014.09.019

Benne, K., & Sheats, P. (1948). Functional roles of group members. *The Journal of Social Issues*, *4*(2), 41–49. doi:10.1111/j.1540-4560.1948.tb01783.x

Benson, H. (1975). *The relaxation response*. HarperCollins Publishers Inc.

Benson, H., & Klipper, M. (1975). *The Relaxation Response*. W Morrow & Co.

Cox, R. C., MacPherson, S. E., Ferguson, K. J., Nissan, J., Royle, N. A., MacLullich, A. M. J., Wardlaw, J. M., & Deary, I. J. (2014). Correlational structure of frontal tests and intelligence tests indicates two components with asymmetrical neurostructural correlates in old age. *Intelligence*, *46*, 96–104. doi:10.1016/j.intell.2014.05.006

Eifring, H. (2016). Types of meditation. In H. Eifring (Ed.), *Asian traditions of meditation* (pp. 27–47). University of Hawai'i Press. doi:10.21313/hawaii/9780824855680.003.0002

Eifring, H. (2019). *The Power of the Wandering Mind - nondirective meditation in science and philosophy*. Dyade Press.

Eifring, H. (2015). *Meditation and culture - The interplay of practice and context*. Bloomsbury Academic.

Eifring, H., & Holen, A. (2014). The uses of attention - Elements of meditative practice. In H. Eifring (Ed.), *Hindu, Buddhist and Daoist meditation - Cultural histories* (pp. 1–26). Hermes Academic Publishing and Bookshop as.

Epel, E., Daubenmier, J., Moskowitz, J. T., Folkman, S., & Blackburn, E. (2009). Can meditation slow rate of cellular aging? Cognitive stress, mindfulness, and telomeres. *Annals of the New York Academy of Sciences*, *1172*(1), 34–53. doi:10.1111/j.1749-6632.2009.04414.x

Fox, K., & Koroma, M. (2018). Wandering along the spectrum of spontaneous thinking - Dreaming, meditation, mind-wandering, and well-being. An interview with Kieran Fox. *ALIUS Bulletin.*, *2*, 1–15.

Hersoug, A. G., Wærsted, M., & Lau, B. (2018). Nondirective meditation used in stress management. *Nordic Psychology*, *70*(4), 290–303.

Holen, A. (1976). *The Psychology of Silence*. Dyade Publishing.

Holen, A. (2016). *Psychology of silence - Perspectives on Acem Meditation*. Dyade Press.

Holmes, T. H., & Rahe, R. H. (1967). The social readjustment rating scale. *Journal of Psychosomatic Research*, *11*(2), 213–218. doi:10.1016/0022-3999(67)90010-4

Hurk, P.A.M., Wingens, T., & Giomni, F. (2011). Relationship Between the Practice of Meditation and Personality – an Exploratory Analysis of the Mediating Role of Mindfulness Skills. *MF, 2*, 194-200.

Lagopoulos, J., Xu, J., Rasmussen, I., Vik, A., Malhi, G. S., Eliassen, C. F., Arntsen, I. E., Sæther, J. G., Hollup, S., Holen, A., Davanger, S., & Ellingsen, Ø. (2009). Increased theta and alpha EEG activity during nondirective meditation. *Journal of Alternative and Complementary Medicine (New York, N.Y.), 15*(11), 1187–1192. doi:10.1089/acm.2009.0113

Larsen, T. (2006). *Neuropsychology for Economists: Health Technology Assessment of Meditation.* Lulu.com.

Larsen, T. (2011). Clinical Continuity by Integrated Care. In Healthcare Delivery Reform and New Technologies: Organization Initiatives. IGI. doi:10.4018/978-1-60960-183-6.ch014

Lehrer, P. M., Schoicket, S., Carrington, P., & Woolfolk, R. L. (1980). Psychophysiological and cognitive responses to stressful stimuli in subjects practicing progressive relaxation and clinically standardized meditation. *Behaviour Research and Therapy, 18*(4), 293–303. doi:10.1016/0005-7967(80)90088-1

Levine, G. N., Lange, R. A., Bairey-Merz, C. N., Davidson, R. J., Jamerson, K., Mehta, P. K., Michos, E. D., Norris, K., Ray, I. B., Saban, K. L., Shah, T., Stein, R., & Smith, S. C. Jr. (2017). Meditation and cardiovascular risk reduction - A scientific statement from the American Heart Association. *Journal of the American Heart Association, 6*(10). Advance online publication. doi:10.1161/JAHA.117.002218

Maclean, C. A., Walton, K. G., Wenneberg, S. R., Levitsky, D. K., Mandarino, J. P., Waziri, R., Hillis, S. L., & Schneider, R. H. (1997). Effects of the Transcendental Meditation program on adaptive mechanisms: Changes in hormone levels and responses to stress after 4 months of training. *Psychoneuroendocrine, 22*(4), 277–295. doi:10.1016/S0306-4530(97)00003-6

Manzoni, G. M., Pagnini, F., Castelnuovo, G., & Molinari, E. (2008). Relaxation training for anxiety: A ten-years systematic review with meta-analysis. *BMC Psychiatry, 8*(1), 41. doi:10.1186/1471-244X-8-41

Marcus, M., Yasami, M. T., & Ommeren, M. (2012). *Depression – A Global Public Health Concern.* WHO. doi:10.1037/e517532013-004

Mason, M. F., Norton, M. I., Van Horn, J. D., Wegner, D. M., Grafton, S. T., & Macrae, C. N. (2007). Wandering minds - The default network and stimulus-independent thought. *Science*, *315*(5810), 393–395. doi:10.1126cience.1131295

Nesvold, A., Fagerland, M. W., Davanger, S., Ellingsen, Ø., Solberg, E. E., Holen, A., Sevre, K., & Atar, D. (2012). Increased heart rate variability during nondirective meditation. *European Journal of Preventive Cardiology*, *19*(4), 773–780. doi:10.1177/1741826711414625

Oaten, M., & Cheng, K. (2006). Longitudinal gains in self-regulation from regular physical exercise. *British Journal of Health Psychology*, *11*(4), 717–733. doi:10.1348/135910706X96481

Ospina, M. B., Bond, K., Karkhaneh, M., Tjosvold, L., Vandermeer, B., & Liang, Y. (2007). Meditation practices for health - State of the research. *Evidence Report/technology Assessment*, (155), 1–263.

Sauter, S., Murphy, L., & Colligan, M. (1999). *Stress...At Work*. NIOSH Publication 99-101.

Schultz, J. H. (2004). *Das original Übungsheft für das autogene Training. Anleitung vom Begründer der Selbstentspannung* (24th ed.). TRIAS.

Stierwalt, S. (2018). Mindfulness: The Science Behind the Practice. *Sci Am*. https://www.scientificamerican.com/article/mindfulness-the-science-behind-the-practice/

Travis, F. T., & Arenander, A. (2006). Cross-Sectional and Longitudinal Study of Effects of Transcendental Meditation Practice. *The International Journal of Neuroscience*, *116*(12), 1519–1538. doi:10.1080/00207450600575482

Wallace, R. K. (1970). *A Hypometabolic State of Wakefulness*. State University of California.

Xu, J., Vik, A., Groote, I. R., Lagopoulos, J., Holen, A., Ellingsen, O., Håberg, A. K., & Davanger, S. (2014). Nondirective meditation activates default mode network and areas associated with memory retrieval and emotional processing. *Frontiers in Human Neuroscience*, *8*, 86. doi:10.3389/fnhum.2014.00086

APPENDIX 1

Meditation for Stress Relief, Renewal and Creativity

In this chapter, practicing non-directive meditation for people in innovative, creative and responsible positions are discussed. These kinds of meditation activate the default network of the brain, which is associated with mind wandering and brain rest. With more ease, the person may be able to disengage from habitual thinking, be more creative and problem-solving in his pursuits. Regular practice will also contribute towards deep relaxation, de-stressing and health.

Why Meditate?

Our forefathers used their bodies to work hard; they rested physically to refresh. Today, work tends to challenge the output of the brain rather than muscular strength. Work nowadays often requires multifaceted problem-solving skills, interpersonal skills, innovation and creativity. Our forefathers did not exercise much, their work sufficed. Modern man, however, hardly moves at work, instead, he concentrates and uses his mental capacities. To refresh himself, he may use his body after work at the gym, in sports, in the garden or in nature, and/or he may engage in good interpersonal relations, cultural activities such as watching moves, reading books, listening to music and its like. The salutary qualities of physical exercise are well acknowledged. Mental stress is still poorly taken care of in the society of today. For some, de-stressing or debriefing mentally may involve the unhealthy use of tranquilizers, alcohol, recreational drugs etc.

Since the late 1950s, the Western world has increasingly seen an influx of Eastern meditative practices. Some are clearly associated with Eastern belief systems and major lifestyle changes; others have little or nothing of that. Most of them promise stress relief. Since the 1970s, a growing number of scientific papers on the effects of meditation have been published every year. With some exceptions, many had for long a poor scientific quality (1), and some were rather promotional. However, lately the level of scientific quality has gone up. There is increased recognition in the scientific community that some meditations have profound physiological and psychological effects pointing in the direction of deep stress relief, and also, some meditations may foster health (2, 3) and longevity (4). Considerable changes in the electric patterns of brain waves related to rest and anxiety reduction have been documented (5). In particular, the fMRI studies of the wandering mind or the default network activity of the brain have led to new insights. Increased default network activity in the brain seems to indicate that the mind is at rest (6). Such default network activity has been linked to lateral thinking, creativity, and problem-solving (7, 8).

What is Meditation?

There are many kinds of meditation. They can be classified according to their cultural origins as Christian-Judaic, Hindu, Buddhist, Daoist meditations etc. Within Islamic traditions, the Sufis are closest to having a meditative orientation. Meditative practices have traveled long before modern times from one culture to another, or between religions as when Buddhist insight meditation was adopted by Daoists, or when Jesuit visualization was brought to China (9). In modern times, Asian meditations have traveled to the West. On the way, they may have been modified to fit the new cultural context, reflected both in the teachings and in the labeling used. For example, Buddhist meditations are now mostly referred to as mindfulness meditation and Hindu practices as mantra meditations etc. The cultural and geographical origins of the various types of meditations, however, do not convey much about their outcome and how they work.

A more suitable classification includes the basic elements of the most widespread meditative practices. Below, we will focus on four such composites:

1 The use of attention
2 Meditation objects
3 Stance towards the wandering mind
4 The context of teaching

One definition emphasizes that meditation is an attention-based mental technique aiming for inner transformation. The nature of the meditation can be suggestive, self-hypnotic, directive, thematic, devotional, or the opposite of these, i.e., they can be non-suggestive, non-directive, non-thematic, and non-religious (10, 11).

1 The Use of Attention

One central and distinguishing feature is related to how the attention is being used during meditation. A few traditions emphasize intense concentration to the exclusion of everything else. More typically, the great variety of mindfulness practices advocate anything from hard concentration to rather mild concentration. The meditator assumes an observant attentional position in relation to what goes on in the body or mind. Some effort is put into keeping the observing position and to avoid being drawn into other mental activities as that would lead to the loss of the mindful, observant position. Finally, there are several schools that emphasize that no effort or directed attention should be used. This mode of attention has by one school been defined as the "free, open mental attitude" (12). To sum up, the ways of using the attention during meditation include those that instruct the meditator to use (a) intense concentration, or (b) modest concentration, or (c) no concentration.

2 Meditation Objects

The point of reference for the attention during meditation is called the meditation object, and practically speaking, all meditations include a meditation object. In one classification, there are three domains from which such meditative objects may be taken – external objects, those related to the body, and those that are mental objects. The choice of meditation object has implications for the outcome of meditation.

A person can meditate on an external object like the flame of a candle, or the sounds of a brook or a waterfall. The meditation object can also be found in the body like the breath or heartbeat, typical for yoga and mindfulness meditations. Finally, the meditation object can be a mental object – an image, a sentence or a quote, a non-semantic sound combination, a mantra, emotions or its like. Within the mental category, there are meditation objects with symbolic or representational qualities, they can have a philosophical, religious or ideological, psychological or contextual meaning. On the other hand, there are those meditation objects that do *not* carry any such representational or symbolic functions or meaning. They have a neutral quality; they are not symbols, and they do not represent anything or carry a meaning, but their effects may be quite strong.

3 The Wandering Mind

In the meditative traditions, almost every school has taken a clear stance on how to relate to the general human tendency sometimes to let the mind wander. Most commonly, the meditator is instructed to control the wandering mind, limit its moves, influence and/or involvements. In a frequently used parable in Asia, the wandering mind is compared to a monkey jumping around, and meditation is to limit by concentration this tendency to wander or jump around. In these schools, the wandering mind should be controlled in order to bring about stillness. The wandering mind is regarded by them as a disruptive agent in meditation.

Some schools have, however, taken the opposite stance. They advise that incoming thoughts and images in the mind should be allowed to come and pass freely during meditation; the wandering mind should not be restricted, but rather be allowed to flow freely. This is supposed to optimize the access to deeper levels of consciousness, provide more profound rest and relaxation plus major autonomic changes in the brain and the organ systems of the body during meditation, and enhanced problem-solving, creative capacities outside of the meditation.

Recently, science has located the wandering mind activity to be related to increased cerebral metabolic activity in the default network of the brain, mostly located along the midline of the two brain halves. High activity in these areas indicates that the brain is resting (6). Moreover, this resting default activity disappears rapidly when a person starts to focus or concentrate on some problem or task.

The two opposite approaches to the wandering mind have resulted in a division between *directive meditations* versus *non-directive* types of meditation, also labeled *concentrative* meditations and *non-concentrative* meditations (13). Scientific studies have to some extent explored these opposites, and the findings seem to demonstrate that both work, and both provide some degree of relaxation and stress relief, but non-directive, or non-concentrative types of meditations seem to bring more comprehensive and profound changes in the autonomic functions of body and the brain (14).

4 Teaching Context

When a person in the West learns to meditate, he may be introduced to an environment that is religious, semi-religious, new-age like, or an environment that is secular, focusing on relaxation, health and stress effects. In the first three types of teaching environments there are tendencies to interpret parts of the meditative experiences within a religious, semi-religious or philosophical framework using quotes from scriptures or other texts with a clear spiritual orientation. The non-cultic alternatives, however, tend to base their perspectives and explanations on science, health recommendations, research, common sense and practical experience.

Physiological Stress Paradigm

During non-directive meditation, a person relaxes deeply. Both in the body and brain, major changes have been measured scientifically. The momentary regulation of a person's level of stress is explained by the functions of the HPA-axis (HPA = Hypothalamus-pituitary-adrenal gland). Hypothalamus is a structure in the middle of the brain that also receives input about the environment. The pituitary gland is linked to the hypothalamus; it is situated at the bottom of the brain inside the skull. To a large extent, these two structures regulate a person's levels of stress by sending varying signals down to the adrenal gland situated at the top of the kidneys. From this gland, stress hormones are secreted into the bloodstream, mainly adrenalin (epinephrine), nor-adrenalin (nor-epinephrine) and cortisol. They affect more than 300 different sites in the body and the nervous system that regulate the autonomic functions. When we are stressed, the activities of organ systems such as the circulatory and respiratory system goes up; the heart beats faster, the blood pressure is elevated, the metabolic rate goes up, and therefore, we consume more oxygen, we breathe faster, our hands get sweaty, we tend to tense our muscles etc. when stressed. In other organ systems, the activity goes down, like the secretion of saliva in the mouth; when we are nervous, we tend to get a dry mouth.

In extreme stress situations, the organism turns into the fight-flight mode, and sometimes into freeze or submission to optimize chances of survival in danger. When stressed, most human beings tend to think and act faster, mobilize their resources to compete and pursue goals, or protect turf, mate and/or offspring. Moderate levels of stress, however, aim for better adaptation and output in daily life to the momentary challenges of the social and/or physical environment. If we hardly ever are stressed, we tend not to mobilize and maintain our resources well. Our muscles get weaker, our knowledge, skills and brain responses tend to get lower outputs. A certain daily dose of stress is healthy, invigorating and improves performance and maintains health.

However, stress can become unhealthy if we are exposed to extreme degrees of it, or if we persistently remain on moderate levels of stress for a very long time without any brake or chance for restitution. People have different levels of stress tolerance; some can take a lot without getting into trouble, others may have very little stress before a breakdown of performance, relations or health. During a normal day, we oscillate between various levels of stress depending on the challenges in front of us from moment to moment; this is generally good and stimulates the organism. Some people quickly mobilize and go up in stress levels but require a lot of time to return to ordinary levels. They are more prone to get into trouble with regard to their performance, relations or health because they do not so easily turn off the stressful arousal even when the challenges are over. Modern man in responsible positions is more exposed to mental stress, which tends to linger longer in the mind. Today, to keep up good performance, creativity, relations and health, humans need to develop ways of destressing. The right type of meditation may be one important remedial tool to handling stress, and also, a key to progress, high capacity output, persistent and solid problem-solving or creative solutions.

More on Non-Directive Meditation

The well-known kinds of non-directive meditation include Acem Meditation (12), Transcendental Meditation, Clinically Standardized Meditation (15), and The Relaxation Response (16). In the following, the focus will be on non-directive meditation in general and Acem Meditation in particular.

For Acem Meditation, the meditation object is a non-semantic sound-combination, the mode of attention is a free mental attitude, i.e., without any concentration. The wandering mind is met with an open and accepting, non-directive attention. Anything that enters the mind should be given a free opportunity to pass. The teaching of Acem Meditation is secular, based on systematized experiences over more than 50 years, explained and interpreted within the framework of modern psychology and health sciences.

The outcome of Acem Meditation is based on regular daily practice, and on the quality of the inner behavior of meditating. Other factors that may play a part include such as the person's personality, lifestyle, readiness to change, and willingness to work with emerging issues and its like.

When it comes to the results of Acem Meditation, there are the direct and indirect effects. The direct effects manifest during the sitting in meditation and amount to deep relaxation and the associated changes in body and brain. The indirect effects may affect life outside of the meditation; it may be experienced as better sleep, less mental distress, less worries and nervousness, and less musculoskeletal pain (17). Some report more energy, increased stress tolerance, and creative thinking and problem-solving capacity. To meditate is a way to turn attention inwards, the meditator becomes more aware of aspects inside himself; this can lead to better self-understanding. When applied to others, this cultivated introspective sensitivity during meditation may be expressed as empathy in the interaction with others at the workplace, at home, or among friends.

Wanting to Try?

For some people, meditation may trigger curiosity, and they may want to try. Before choosing where to learn, explore the available options and the characteristics of the various types of meditation on offer. Also, check the costs and the qualifications of the instructors etc. Note that the language most meditation schools use when presenting their meditation results tend to be rather similar in ways that disguise essential differences. It may be advisable to check the four dimensions mentioned above in this chapter: the use of attention, the kind of meditation object, the stance towards the wandering mind, and the conceptual context of the teaching; this will give a more comprehensive picture of what a particular meditation entails. Going more into the matter is worth the time and effort to arrive at a good choice.

APPENDIX 2

Table 3. UN Sustainability Goals 2015 and Applied Doughnut Economics

No	UNSG	Means by Applied Doughnut Economics (ADE)
1 2 3 5 10 8	**No Poverty** **Zero Hunger** **Good Health and Well-Being** **Reduced Inequality** **Gender Equality** **Decent Work and Economic Growth**	**Chapter 3: New Welfare Economics** Doughnut Economics recommends social welfare policy beyond that of the minimal state. A comprehensive welfare model includes: ● Major components of the stabilization of recurrent business recessions ● Public finance of collective needs regarding healthcare, social security and education is more effective than private finance shows ● Universal Basic Income (UBI) at 50% of the median income is effective both for equalization of income, social security and simplification of the tax system ● Principles of New PublicManagement 2.0 ensure both a market-like effectiveness of services as well as an appropriate level of minimal staffing ● New Welfare policy includes too national accounting of Multinationals
9 12	**Industry, Innovation and Infrastructure** **Responsible Consumption And Production**	**Part 1: Business Economics** Neuroeconomic Psychology guides guides behavioral economics towards: ● `Simple Living` with health and ecology as well as household economies ● Entrepreneur-like business life with Pilot-in-plant as prototype ● Collaborative democratic policies with coalitions across the center
6 7 11 13 14 15	**Clean Water And Sanitation** **Affordable and Clean Energy** **Sustainable Cities And Communities** **Climate Action** **Life below Water** **Life on Land**	**Chapter 4: Economic Ecology** The key climate intervention is a Pigouvian CO2 Tax (ET) as an `Invisible Hand with a Green Thumb`. Complementary targets for different decision-makers: 1. National Level: Implementation of ET and collaboration on R&D in special sectors as electrofuels for transport in air and on the sea 2. Community Level: Especially Metropoles can establish broad collaboration 3. Consumer Level: Propagation of `Simple Living` including more sharing 4. R&D Level: Formation of National Councils on Climate Change 5. International collaboration: Implementation of Paris Agreement requires a marked international economic solidarity with poor regions.
4 16 17	**Quality Education** **Peace, Justice and Strong Institutions** **Partnerships for the goals**	**Part 2: Human Resource Development (HRD)** Modern brain scanners to a level of `Mind Reading` gives understanding of the neural basis of emotions and thoughts. This reveals cognition as dialectics between autonomic emotions and their confrontation with memories by Ratio in the left hemisphere. Firstly, the neural base of Ratio identifies the determinants of our long-term memory who is crucial to our judgement. Secondly, understanding of the root of Ratio enables the design of Visualization as means for cognitive reinforcement. Thirdly, WHO warns that epidemic job-related becomes the next pandemic, but a Health Technology Assessment of meditative In-depth relaxation identifies significant de-stressing effects in an economic setting based on NGO`s.

Compilation of References

Allik, J., & McCrae, R. R. (2004). Toward a Geography of Personality Traits: Patterns of Profiles Across 36 Cultures. *Journal of Cross-Cultural Psychology*, *35*(1), 13–28. doi:10.1177/0022022103260382

Andersen, L.B., Bjoernholt, B., Bro, L.B., & Holm-Petersen, C. (2016). Leadership and motivation: a qualitative study of transformational leadership and public service motivation. *Review of Administrative Sciences*.

Andersen, K., & Lorentzen, M. (2005). *The Geography of the Danish Creative Class – A Mapping and Analysis Danish part of "Technology, Talent and Tolerance in European Cities: A comparative analysis"*. CBS.

Andrews, R. K. (1975). *The Concept of Corporate Strategy*. McGraw Hill.

Annas, J. (1981). *An Introduction to Plato's Republic*. Oxford University Press.

Baddley, A. (2010). Working Memory. *Current Biology*, *20*(4), 136–140. doi:10.1016/j.cub.2009.12.014

Bahl, R. (2013). *Supereconomies. China and the Future of the World*. Allen Lane.

Barua, B., Datta, S., & Das, J. (2020). *Application of Nanotechnology in Global Issues*. In *Global Issues and Innovative Solutions in Healthcare, Culture, and the Environment*. IGI. doi:10.4018/978-1-7998-3576-9.ch015

Bastena, U., & Bieleb, G. (2010). *How the brain integrates costs and beneðts during decision making*. Academic Press.

Beaty, R. E., Benedek, M., Wilkins, R. W., Jauk, E., Fink, A., Silvia, P. J., Hodges, D. A., Koschutnig, K., & Neubauer, A. C. (2014). Creativity and the default network - A functional connectivity analysis of the creative brain at rest. *Neuropsychologia*, *64*, 92–98. doi:10.1016/j.neuropsychologia.2014.09.019

Becker, A., Deckers, T., & Dohmen, T. (2012). The Relationship Between Economic Preferences and Psychological Personality Measures. *Annual Review of Economics*, *4*, 453–478.

Becker, G. S. (1993). *Human Capital: A Theoretical and Empirical Analysis, with Special Reference to Education* (3rd ed.). University of Chicago Press.

Benne, K., & Sheats, P. (1948). Functional roles of group members. *The Journal of Social Issues*, *4*(2), 41–49. doi:10.1111/j.1540-4560.1948.tb01783.x

Benson, H. (1975). *The relaxation response*. HarperCollins Publishers Inc.

Benson, H., & Klipper, M. (1975). *The Relaxation Response*. W Morrow & Co.

Bouchard, T. J. Jr, & McGue, M. (2003). Genetic and environmental influences on human psychological differences. *Journal of Neurobiology*, *54*(1), 4–45. doi:10.1002/neu.10160

Buss, D. M. (1996). Social adaptation and five major factors of personality. In J. S. Wiggins (Ed.), *The five-factor model of personality: Theoretical perspectives* (pp. 180–207). Guilford Press.

Camerer, C., Loewenstein, G., & Prelec, D. (2005). Neuroeconomics: How Neuroscience Can Inform Economics. *Journal of Economic Literature*, *43*(1), 9–64. doi:10.1257/0022051053737843

Camille, N., & Corricello, G. (2004). The involvement of the orbitofrontal cortex in regret. *Sci*, *304*(5674), 1167–1170. doi:10.1126cience.1094550

Cattell, R. B. (1943). The description of personality: Basic traits resolved into clusters. *Journal of Abnormal and Social Psychology*, *38*(4), 476–506. doi:10.1037/h0054116

Cheng, X. (2017). *The Circular State – The Symbolic Labor Politics in Transitional China*. Horizon Res. Publ.

Chinese 2050 High Renewable Energy Penetration Scenario. (2015). Chinese Nat. Renew. Energy Centre.

Clayton Antitrust Act (1914). United States Congress.

Costa, P. T. Jr, & McCrae, R. R. (1985). *The NEO Personality Inventory manual*. Psychol Assessm Res.

Cox, R. C., MacPherson, S. E., Ferguson, K. J., Nissan, J., Royle, N. A., MacLullich, A. M. J., Wardlaw, J. M., & Deary, I. J. (2014). Correlational structure of frontal tests and intelligence tests indicates two components with asymmetrical neurostructural correlates in old age. *Intelligence*, *46*, 96–104. doi:10.1016/j.intell.2014.05.006

Danish Council on Climate. (2020). *Known roads and new paths to a 70 per cent reduction – direction and measures for the next ten years of climate action in Denmark. Author. Gates B. (2021). How to avoid a Climate Disaster. The Solutions we have and the Breakthrough we need.* Allen Lane.

Daw, N. D., O'Doherty, J. P., & … . (2006). Cortical substrates for exploratory decisions in humans. *Nat*, *441*, 876–879.

Dohmen, T., & Falk, A. (2012). *Individual Risk Attitudes: Measurement, Determinants and Behavioral Consequence*. JEEA.

Drummond, M., & Brixner, D. (2009). Toward a Consensus on the QALY. *Value in Health*, *12*(1), 1–5. doi:10.1016/j.jval.2017.01.008 PMID:19250129

Dunning, J. H. (1979). Toward an Eclectic Theory of International Production: Some Empirical Tests. *Journal of International Business Studies*, *11*(1), 9–31. doi:10.1057/palgrave.jibs.8490593

Eifring, H. (2015). *Meditation and culture - The interplay of practice and context*. Bloomsbury Academic.

Eifring, H. (2016). Types of meditation. In H. Eifring (Ed.), *Asian traditions of meditation* (pp. 27–47). University of Hawai'i Press. doi:10.21313/hawaii/9780824855680.003.0002

Eifring, H. (2019). *The Power of the Wandering Mind - nondirective meditation in science and philosophy*. Dyade Press.

Eifring, H., & Holen, A. (2014). The uses of attention - Elements of meditative practice. In H. Eifring (Ed.), *Hindu, Buddhist and Daoist meditation - Cultural histories* (pp. 1–26). Hermes Academic Publishing and Bookshop as.

Epel, E., Daubenmier, J., Moskowitz, J. T., Folkman, S., & Blackburn, E. (2009). Can meditation slow rate of cellular aging? Cognitive stress, mindfulness, and telomeres. *Annals of the New York Academy of Sciences*, *1172*(1), 34–53. doi:10.1111/j.1749-6632.2009.04414.x

Farb, N A S. (2013). Can Neuroimaging inform economic theories of decision-making? *Neuroscience and Neuroeconomics*, *2*, 1–10. doi:10.2147/NAN.S39339

Florida, R. (2002). *The Rise of the Creative Class: And How it's transforming work, leisure, community and everyday life*. Perseus Book Group.

Fox, K., & Koroma, M. (2018). Wandering along the spectrum of spontaneous thinking - Dreaming, meditation, mind-wandering, and well-being. An interview with Kieran Fox. *ALIUS Bulletin.*, *2*, 1–15.

Francese, M., & Mulas-Granados, C. (2015). *Functional Income Distribution and Its Role in Explaining Inequality*. IMF. doi:10.5089/9781513549828.001

Friedman, T. L. (2005). *The World is Flat. A Brief History of the Twenty-First Century*. Picador.

Galbraith, G. (1967). *The New Industrial State*. Houghton Mifflin.

Gentilini, U., Grosh, M., & Rigolini, J. (Eds.). (2020). Exploring Universal Basic Income A Guide to Navigating, Concepts, Evidence, and Practices. WB Group.

Global Top 100 Companies by market capitalization. (2017). PWC: www.pwc.com/top100

Goel, V., Tierney, M., Sheesley, L., & .... (2006). Hemispheric specialization in human prefrontal cortex for resolving certain and uncertain inferences. *Cerebral Cortex*, *17*(10), 2245–2250.

Goel, V., Tierney, M., Sheesley, L., Bartolo, A., Vartanian, O., & Grafman, J. (2006). Hemispheric specialization in human prefrontal cortex for resolving certain and uncertain inferences. *Cerebral Cortex (New York, N.Y.)*, *17*(10), 2245–2250. doi:10.1093/cercor/bhl132

Goldberg, L. R. (1992). The development of markers for the big-five factor structure. *Psychological Assessment*, *4*(1), 26–42. doi:10.1037/1040-3590.4.1.26

Goldberg, L. R. (1993). The structure of phenotypic personality traits. *The American Psychologist*, *48*(1), 26–34. PMID:8427480

Gountas, J., & Ciorciari, J. (2010). Inside the Minds of Trendsetters. *Aus Magazine Sci/Tech*, 14-17.

Gurel, E., & Tat, M. (2017). SWOT analysis: A theoretical review. *J Internat Soc Res*, *10*(51), 1–23. doi:10.17719/jisr.2017.1832

Haagh, L., & Rohregger, B. (2019). *Universal basic income policies and their potential for addressing health inequities. Transformative approaches to a healthy, prosperous life for all. WHO Reg.* Office for Europe.

Hasegawa, T. (2018). *Risk of increased food insecurity under stringent global climate change policy*. Na Clim Ch.

Hegel, C. W. F. (1812). The Science of Logic. Academic Press.

Hersoug, A. G., Wærsted, M., & Lau, B. (2018). Nondirective meditation used in stress management. *Nordic Psychology*, *70*(4), 290–303.

Hoffman, R. (2010). A Cybernetic Approach to Economics. *Hum Know*, *7*(45), 89–97.

Hogan, R. (1996). A socioanalytic perspective on the five-factor model. In J. S. Wiggins (Ed.), *The five-factor model of personality: Theoretical perspectives* (pp. 163–179). Guilford Press.

Holen, A. (1976). *The Psychology of Silence*. Dyade Publishing.

Holen, A. (2016). *Psychology of silence - Perspectives on Acem Meditation*. Dyade Press.

Holmes, T. H., & Rahe, R. H. (1967). The social readjustment rating scale. *Journal of Psychosomatic Research*, *11*(2), 213–218. doi:10.1016/0022-3999(67)90010-4

Hood, C. (1991). Public Management for All Seasons. *Public Administration*, *69*(6), 3–19. doi:10.1111/j.1467-9299.1991.tb00779.x

Hood, C., & Dixon, R. (2015). What We Have to Show for 30 Years of New Public Management: Higher Costs, More Complaints. *Governance: An International Journal of Policy, Administration and Institutions*, *28*(3), 265–267. doi:10.1111/gove.12150

Hume, D. (1742). *A Treatise in Human Nature*. University of Edinburgh.

Hurk, P.A.M., Wingens, T., & Giomni, F. (2011). Relationship Between the Practice of Meditation and Personality – an Exploratory Analysis of the Mediating Role of Mindfulness Skills. *MF, 2*, 194-200.

Intergovernmental Panel on Climate Change (IPCC). (2019). *Summary Report.* https://www.ipcc.ch/2019/

IPBES Report. (2019). *Nature's dangerous decline 'unprecedented,' species extinction rates 'accelerating' Physical Meteorological Observatory Davos (PMOD).* IPBES.

James, W. (1907). *Pragmatism's Conception of Truth. Lecture 6 in Pragmatism: A New Name for Some Old Ways of Thinking.* Longman Green and Co. doi:10.1037/10851-000

Jantzen, R. T., & Volpert, K. (2013). *On the Mathematics of Income Inequality: Splitting the Gini Index in Two.* Mathematical Association of America.

Johnson, E. (2011). *Price Elasticity of Supply of Renewable Electricity Generation: Evidence from State Renewable Portfolio Standards.* Georgia Institute of Technology. Working Paper 001.

Juhrich, K. (2016). *CO2 Emission Factors for Fossil Fuels.* Umwelt Bundesamt.

Kahneman, D. (2003). Maps of bounded rationality: Psychology for behavioral economics. *The American Economic Review, 93*(5), 1449–1475.

Kalic, K. (2017). *Social Vulnerability Assessment Tools for Climate Change and DRR Programming.* UNDP.

Karven A, Strømlandc E, Wollbrante C et al. (2019): The Intuitive Cooperation Hypothesis Revisited: A Meta-analytic Examination of Effect-size and Between-study Heterogeneity. MetaArXiv Preprints.

Karven, A., Strømlandc, E., & Wollbrante, C. (2019). *The Intuitive Cooperation Hypothesis Revisited: A Meta-analytic Examination of Effect-size and Between-study Heterogeneity.* MetaArXiv Preprints.

Kela and the Ministry of Social Affairs and Health. (2019, Aug. 2). Press Release.

Kenning, P., & Plassmann, H. (2005). Neuroeconomics: An overview from an economic perspective. *Br Res Bul, 67*(5), 343–354. doi:10.1016/j.brainresbull.2005.07.006

Kern, M. L., & McCarthy, P. X. (2019). Social media-predicted personality traits and values can help match people to their ideal jobs. *Proceedings of the National Academy of Sciences of the United States of America.* PMID:31843929

Keynes, J. M. (1936). *The General Theory of Employment, Interest and Money.* Palgrave MacMillan.

Lagopoulos, J., Xu, J., Rasmussen, I., Vik, A., Malhi, G. S., Eliassen, C. F., Arntsen, I. E., Sæther, J. G., Hollup, S., Holen, A., Davanger, S., & Ellingsen, Ø. (2009). Increased theta and alpha EEG activity during nondirective meditation. *Journal of Alternative and Complementary Medicine (New York, N.Y.), 15*(11), 1187–1192. doi:10.1089/acm.2009.0113

Larsen, T. (2006). *Neuropsychology for Economists: Health Technology Assessment of Meditation.* Lulu.com.

Larsen, T. (2011). Clinical Continuity by Integrated Care. In Healthcare Delivery Reform and New Technologies: Organizational Initiatives. IGI. doi:10.4018/978-1-60960-183-6.ch014

Larsen, T. (2017). Homo Neuroeconomicus – a Neuroeconomic Review of Functional Magnetic Resonance Imaging of Economic Choice. *IJUHD*, *7*(1), 44–57.

Larsen, T. (2017). Homo Neuroeconomicus – a Neuroeconomic Review of Functional MagneticResonance Imaging of Economic Choice. *IJUHD*, *7*(1), 44–57.

Larsen, T. (2019). Neuroeconomic Psychology: 3 cognitive modules for end-users. *IJPCE*, *9*(1), 1–22.

Laurie-Martinez, D., & Canessa, N. (2004). Frontopolar Cortex decision-making efficiency: Comparing brain activity of experts with different professional background during an exploration-exploitation task. *Frontiers in Human Neuroscience*, *7*, 1–10.

Laurie-Martinez, D., & Canessa, N. (2004). Frontopolar Cortex decision-making efficiency: Comparing brain activity of experts with different professional backgrounds during an exploration-exploitation task. *Frontiers in Human Neuroscience*, *7*, 1–10.

Lehrer, P. M., Schoicket, S., Carrington, P., & Woolfolk, R. L. (1980). Psychophysiological and cognitive responses to stressful stimuli in subjects practicing progressive relaxation and clinically standardized meditation. *Behaviour Research and Therapy*, *18*(4), 293–303. doi:10.1016/0005-7967(80)90088-1

Levine, G. N., Lange, R. A., Bairey-Merz, C. N., Davidson, R. J., Jamerson, K., Mehta, P. K., Michos, E. D., Norris, K., Ray, I. B., Saban, K. L., Shah, T., Stein, R., & Smith, S. C. Jr. (2017). Meditation and cardiovascular risk reduction - A scientific statement from the American Heart Association. *Journal of the American Heart Association*, *6*(10). Advance online publication. doi:10.1161/JAHA.117.002218

Levy, J. (2014). *Accounting for Profit and the History of Capital*. University of Chicago Press.

Luhr, J. (1997). *The Simple Living Guide: A Sourcebook for Less Stressful, More Joyful Living*. Harmony.

Maclean, C. A., Walton, K. G., Wenneberg, S. R., Levitsky, D. K., Mandarino, J. P., Waziri, R., Hillis, S. L., & Schneider, R. H. (1997). Effects of the Transcendental Meditation program on adaptive mechanisms: Changes in hormone levels and responses to stress after 4 months of training. *Psychoneuroendocrine*, *22*(4), 277–295. doi:10.1016/S0306-4530(97)00003-6

Maddison, A. (2003). The World Economy: Historical Statistics. In *OECD: Data 1928-98*. OECD.

Malthus, T. R. (1826). *An Essay on the Principles of Population*. John Murray.

Manzoni, G. M., Pagnini, F., Castelnuovo, G., & Molinari, E. (2008). Relaxation training for anxiety: A ten-years systematic review with meta-analysis. *BMC Psychiatry*, *8*(1), 41. doi:10.1186/1471-244X-8-41

Marcus, M., Yasami, M. T., & Ommeren, M. (2012). *Depression – A Global Public Health Concern*. WHO. doi:10.1037/e517532013-004

Mason, M. F., Norton, M. I., Van Horn, J. D., Wegner, D. M., Grafton, S. T., & Macrae, C. N. (2007). Wandering minds - The default network and stimulus-independent thought. *Science*, *315*(5810), 393–395. doi:10.1126cience.1131295

Mazlow, A. (1962). *Toward a Psychology of Being*. Van Nostrand.

McClure, S. M., Laibson, D. I., Loewenstein, G., & Cohen, J. D. (2004). Delayed monetary rewards separate neural systems value immediate and delayed monetary rewards. *Science*, *306*(5695), 503–507.

McCrae, R. R., & Costa, P. T. Jr. (1987). Validation of the five-factor model of personality across instruments and observers. *Journal of Personality and Social Psychology*, *52*(1), 81–90. doi:10.1037/0022-3514.52.1.81

McLean, P. (1973). *The Triune Conception of Brain and Behavior*. Academic Press.

Meadows, D. H., Meadows, D. L., Randers, J., & Behrens, W. W. I. I. I. (1972). *Limits to Growth*. Rom-klubben.

Metcalf, G. E. (2019). On the Economics of a Carbon Tax for the United States. *BPEA Conference Draft*.

Metcalf, G. E. (2020). An emissions assurance mechanism: Adding environmental certainty to a US carbon tax. *Review of Environmental Economics and Policy*, *14*(1), 114–130. doi:10.1093/reep/rez013

Myers, I. B., & McCaulley, M. H. (1985). *Manual: A guide to the development and use of the Myers-Briggs Type Indicator*. Consulting Psychologists Press.

Nesvold, A., Fagerland, M. W., Davanger, S., Ellingsen, Ø., Solberg, E. E., Holen, A., Sevre, K., & Atar, D. (2012). Increased heart rate variability during nondirective meditation. *European Journal of Preventive Cardiology*, *19*(4), 773–780. doi:10.1177/1741826711414625

Nordhaus, W. (2007). *The Challenge of Global Warming: Economic Models and Environmental Policy*. Yale U.

Nordhaus, W. (2018). Projections and Uncertainties about Climate Change in an Era of Minimal Climate Policies. *American Economic Journal. Economic Policy*, *10*(3), 333–360. doi:10.1257/pol.20170046

Nozick, R. (1974). *Anarchy*. State and Utopia.

Oaten, M., & Cheng, K. (2006). Longitudinal gains in self-regulation from regular physical exercise. *British Journal of Health Psychology*, *11*(4), 717–733. doi:10.1348/135910706X96481

Oosterbeek, H., Sloof, R., & van deKuilen, G. (2004). Cultural Differences in Ultimatum Game Experiments: Evidence from a Meta-Analysis. *Experiment Econ*, *7*, 171–188.

Ospina, M. B., Bond, K., Karkhaneh, M., Tjosvold, L., Vandermeer, B., & Liang, Y. (2007). Meditation practices for health - State of the research. *Evidence Report/technology Assessment*, (155), 1–263.

Pareto, D. (1906). *Manual of Political Economy*.

Peck, J. (2005). Struggling with the creative class. *Internat. J. pf Urban and Reg. Res.*, *29*(4), 740–770.

Petersen, O. H., Hjelmar, U., & Vrangbæk, K. (2015). Is contracting out of public services still the great panacea? A systematic review of international studies from 2000-2014. *Proceedings NormaCare Meeting*.

Petty, T. (2014). *Capital in the Twenty-First Century*. Belknap/Harvard University Press.

Pigou, A. C. (1920). The Economics of Welfare. Academic Press.

Popper, K. R. (1959). *The Logic of Scientific Discovery*. Routledge.

Rae, A. (2012). Assessing the Accountability of the Benefit Corporation: Will This New Gray Sector Organization Enhance Corporate Social Responsibility? *Journal of Business Ethics*, *110*(1), 133–150.

Rasmussen, A.F. (1993). *Fra Socialstat til Minimalstat*. Saxo.com.

Rasnussen, A.F. (1993). *The Minimal State*. Academic Press.

Report on the Execution of the Central and Local Budgets for 2017 and the Draft of Central and Local Budgets for 2018. (n.d.). Chinese Ministry of Finance/Xinhua News Agency.

Roberts, B. W., & DelVecchio, W. F. (2000). The rank-order consistency of personality traits from childhood to old age: A quantitative review of longitudinal studies. *Psychological Bulletin*, *126*(1), 3–25. doi:10.1037/0033-2909.126.1.3

Rogers, E. (1962). *Diffusion of Innovations*. Free Press of Glencoe.

Rosling, H. (2018). FACTFULNESS. Factfulness AB.

Sanfey, A. G. (2007). Social Decision-Making: Insights from Game Theory and Neuroscience. *Sci*, *318*, 598–02.

Sanfey, A. G. (2007). Social Decision-Making: Insights from Game Theory and Neuroscience. *Science*, *318*, 598–602.

Saraswathy, S., & Read, S. (2001). *Effectual Entrepreneurship*. Routledge.

Sauter, S., Murphy, L., & Colligan, M. (1999). *Stress...At Work*. NIOSH Publication 99-101.

Schmutz, W. (2017). *Human-induced global warming to tail off slightly over the next few decades*. Academic Press.

Schoenmaker, M., & Gillabel, J. (2017). *Circular by design Products in the circular economy*. EEA.

Schultz, J. H. (2004). *Das original Übungsheft für das autogene Training. Anleitung vom Begründer der Selbstentspannung* (24th ed.). TRIAS.

Schutt, F. (2003). *The Importance of Human Capital for Economic Growth. IWIM*. Uni. of Bremen.

Schwab, K. (2017). *The Fourth Industrial Revolution*. Penguin Random Books.

Segal, N. L. (2012). *Born together—reared apart: The landmark Minnesota Twin Study*. Harvard University Press. doi:10.4159/harvard.9780674065154

Singer, T. (2007). The neuronal basis and ontogeny of empathy and mind reading: Review of literature and implications for future res. *Neuroscience and Biobehavioral Reviews*, *30*, 855–863.

Smith, A. (1776). *Inquiry into the Nature and Causes of the Wealth of Nations*. doi:10.1093/oseo/instance.00043218

Solè, J., García-Olivares, A., Turiel, A., & Ballabrera-Poy, H. (2018). Renewable transitions and the net energy from oil liquids: A scenarios study. *Renewable Energy*, *116*, 258–271. doi:10.1016/j.renene.2017.09.035

Steffen, W. (2015). Trajectory of the Anthroposcene: The Great Acceleration. *Anthrop*, *2*(1), 81–98.

Stierwalt, S. (2018). Mindfulness: The Science Behind the Practice. *Sci Am*. https://www.scientificamerican.com/article/mindfulness-the-science-behind-the-practice/

Teiling, B. (2018). Accountability of MNCs in Societal Transformation. In *Proc 19. Symposium on Sustainable Development*. International Institute of Advanced Studies (IIAS).

Tenhunen, A., & Pöhler, H. (2020). *A Circular Economy of Plastics*. VTT Technical Res. Center Ltd.

Travis, F. T., & Arenander, A. (2006). Cross-Sectional and Longitudinal Study of Effects of Transcendental Meditation Practice. *The International Journal of Neuroscience*, *116*(12), 1519–1538. doi:10.1080/00207450600575482

U.S. EIA. (2018). *Levelized Cost and Levelized Avoided Cost of New Generation Resources*. Author.

Vedel, A. (2017). *Personality, academic performance, and study choices* (PhD dissertation). Aarhus University, Department of Psychology and Behavioural Sciences.

Vedel, A. (2017). Personality, academic performance, and study choices : PhD dissertation. Aarhus University, Department of Psychology and Behavioural Sciences, Aarhus.

Vedel, A. (2016). The Personality of Academic Majors. *American Scientist*.

Vedel, A., & Thomsen, D. K. (2017). The Dark Triad among academic majors. *Personality and Individual Differences*, *116*, 81–105.

von Neuman, J., & Morgenstern, O. (1944). *Theory of Games and Economic Behavior*. Princeton Uni. Press.

Wallace, R. K. (1970). *A Hypometabolic State of Wakefulness*. State University of California.

Weitzman, M. L. (2009). On Modeling and Interpreting the Economics of Catastrophic Climate Change. *The Review of Economics and Statistics*, *91*(1), 1–19. doi:10.1162/rest.91.1.1

WHO. (2020). *Health Technology Assessment*. https://www.who.int/medical_devices/assessment

Wiener, N. (1962): Cybernetics; or, Control and communication in the animal and the machine 2nd Edition Hardcover. Amazon.com.

Wiener, N. (1962). *Cybernetics; or, Control and communication in the animal and the machine* (2nd ed.). Academic Press.

Wilson, T.D. (2004). *Strangers to Ourselves Discovering the Adaptive Unconscious*. Harvard Uni. Press.

Xu, J., Vik, A., Groote, I. R., Lagopoulos, J., Holen, A., Ellingsen, O., Håberg, A. K., & Davanger, S. (2014). Nondirective meditation activates default mode network and areas associated with memory retrieval and emotional processing. *Frontiers in Human Neuroscience*, *8*, 86. doi:10.3389/fnhum.2014.00086

Zhong, W., & Haigh, J. D. (2013). The greenhouse effect and carbon dioxide. *Weather*, *68*(4), 100–105. doi:10.1002/wea.2072

Related Readings

To continue IGI Global's long-standing tradition of advancing innovation through emerging research, please find below a compiled list of recommended IGI Global book chapters and journal articles in the areas of panel data, economic forecasting, applied economics, econometric analysis, time series, microeconomics, and statistical methods for predicting business and finance. These related readings will provide additional information and guidance to further enrich your knowledge and assist you with your own research.

Abduh, M., & Jamaludin, N. (2020). Baitul Maal wat-Tamwil Services for SMEs: Evidence From Indonesia. In A. Rafay (Ed.), *Handbook of Research on Theory and Practice of Global Islamic Finance* (pp. 259–276). IGI Global. doi:10.4018/978-1-7998-0218-1.ch014

Abubakar, M. (2020). Social Empowerment Through Islamic Finance. In A. Rafay (Ed.), *Handbook of Research on Theory and Practice of Global Islamic Finance* (pp. 115–128). IGI Global. doi:10.4018/978-1-7998-0218-1.ch006

Adžić, S. (2019). Financial Systems Reforms in Western Balkans Countries. In D. Ushakov (Ed.), *Global Trends of Modernization in Budgeting and Finance* (pp. 260–279). IGI Global. doi:10.4018/978-1-5225-7760-7.ch013

Agrawal, G., & Jain, P. (2019). Digital Financial Inclusion in India: A Review. In T. Tripathi, M. Kumar Dash, & G. Agrawal (Eds.), *Behavioral Finance and Decision-Making Models* (pp. 195–203). IGI Global. doi:10.4018/978-1-5225-7399-9.ch011

Agyemang, O. S. (2019). Linking Personal Values to Investment Decisions Among Individual Shareholders in a Developing Economy. In T. Tripathi, M. Kumar Dash, & G. Agrawal (Eds.), *Behavioral Finance and Decision-Making Models* (pp. 24–45). IGI Global. doi:10.4018/978-1-5225-7399-9.ch002

Ahmed, J., Collins, P., & Meera, A. K. (2020). Conditional Currency Convertibility Based on Primary Commodities: The Shari'ah-Compliant Grondona System. In A. Rafay (Ed.), *Handbook of Research on Theory and Practice of Global Islamic Finance* (pp. 61–84). IGI Global. doi:10.4018/978-1-7998-0218-1.ch004

Ahmed, M. U. (2020). Financial Reporting of Islamic Financial Institutions: Comparative Analysis of AAOIFI and IFRS. In A. Rafay (Ed.), *Handbook of Research on Theory and Practice of Global Islamic Finance* (pp. 854–873). IGI Global. doi:10.4018/978-1-7998-0218-1.ch043

Ai, T. H., & Ushakov, D. (2019). Taxation Regime and Macroeconomic Systems' Dynamics. In D. Ushakov (Ed.), *Global Trends of Modernization in Budgeting and Finance* (pp. 225–240). IGI Global. doi:10.4018/978-1-5225-7760-7.ch011

Aksoy, E. E. (2019). Individual Factors Affecting the Participation of Turkish People in the New Individual Pension System. In T. Tripathi, M. Kumar Dash, & G. Agrawal (Eds.), *Behavioral Finance and Decision-Making Models* (pp. 104–116). IGI Global. doi:10.4018/978-1-5225-7399-9.ch006

Al-Malkawi, H. N., Pillai, R., & AlShiab, M. S. (2020). Evaluating Microeconomic Factors, Financial Crisis, and Stock Price Dynamics: Evidence From MENA Region. In L. Farinha, A. B. Cruz, & J. R. Sebastião (Eds.), *Handbook of Research on Accounting and Financial Studies* (pp. 131–153). IGI Global. doi:10.4018/978-1-7998-2136-6.ch007

Ali, B., Terzi, C., Mhadhbi, K., & Fakhri, I. (2019). Theoretical Analysis of the Relationship Between Monopoly's Optimal Tariffs and Consumer Utility. *International Journal of Sustainable Economies Management*, *8*(1), 39–51. doi:10.4018/IJSEM.2019010104

Arora, P. (2012). Financial Performance Measures, Efficiency and Indian Banking: Empirical Evidence. *International Journal of Productivity Management and Assessment Technologies*, *1*(2), 43–56. doi:10.4018/ijpmat.2012040104

Ayhan, F. (2019). The Effects of Political and Economic Risk on FDI: A Theoretical Survey. In D. Ushakov (Ed.), *Global Trends of Modernization in Budgeting and Finance* (pp. 44–63). IGI Global. doi:10.4018/978-1-5225-7760-7.ch003

Ayuk, E. T., Fonta, W. M., & Kouame, E. B. (2014). Application of Quantitative Methods in Natural Resource Management in Africa: A Review. In P. V. Schaeffer & E. Kouassi (Eds.), *Econometric Methods for Analyzing Economic Development* (pp. 205–234). IGI Global. doi:10.4018/978-1-4666-4329-1.ch013

Azevedo, G. M., Oliveira, J. D., Ferreira, A. D., & Dias, S. R. (2019). The Use of Financial Graphics as an Impression Management Tool: Evidence of Portuguese Listed Companies. In J. D. Oliveira, G. M. Azevedo, & A. D. Ferreira (Eds.), *International Financial Reporting Standards and New Directions in Earnings Management* (pp. 239–255). IGI Global. doi:10.4018/978-1-5225-7817-8.ch011

Aziz, S., Md Husin, M., & Ashfaq, M. (2020). Harmonising Microfinance With Islamic Banking. In A. Rafay (Ed.), *Handbook of Research on Theory and Practice of Global Islamic Finance* (pp. 240–258). IGI Global. doi:10.4018/978-1-7998-0218-1.ch013

Baber, H. (2020). Crowdfunding Framework in Islamic Finance. In A. Rafay (Ed.), *Handbook of Research on Theory and Practice of Global Islamic Finance* (pp. 307–320). IGI Global. doi:10.4018/978-1-7998-0218-1.ch017

Berguiga, I., Ben Said, Y., & Adair, P. (2020). Islamic and Conventional Micro-Financing in the MENA Region: A Performance Analysis. In A. Rafay (Ed.), *Handbook of Research on Theory and Practice of Global Islamic Finance* (pp. 216–239). IGI Global. doi:10.4018/978-1-7998-0218-1.ch012

Bieri, D. S. (2014). Regional Structure and Economic Development: Growth Empirics for U.S. Metropolitan Areas. In P. V. Schaeffer & E. Kouassi (Eds.), *Econometric Methods for Analyzing Economic Development* (pp. 153–176). IGI Global. doi:10.4018/978-1-4666-4329-1.ch010

Bozkurt, İ., & Hatipoğlu, M. (2019). Does Parasocial Breakup Affect the Stock Market Returns?: Evidence From an Emerging Market. In T. Tripathi, M. Kumar Dash, & G. Agrawal (Eds.), *Behavioral Finance and Decision-Making Models* (pp. 70–87). IGI Global. doi:10.4018/978-1-5225-7399-9.ch004

Burger, R., & du Plessis, S. (2014). A New Keynesian Phillips Curve for South Africa. In P. V. Schaeffer & E. Kouassi (Eds.), *Econometric Methods for Analyzing Economic Development* (pp. 30–48). IGI Global. doi:10.4018/978-1-4666-4329-1.ch003

Carikci, O., & Ozturk, M. S. (2019). Developments in Earnings Management Practices in the IFRS Perspective: An Application in a Public Company. In J. D. Oliveira, G. M. Azevedo, & A. D. Ferreira (Eds.), *International Financial Reporting Standards and New Directions in Earnings Management* (pp. 274–288). IGI Global. doi:10.4018/978-1-5225-7817-8.ch013

Casciello, R., Caldarelli, A., & Maffei, M. (2019). Earnings Management and Mergers and Acquisitions: Empirical Evidence From Italian-Listed Companies. In J. D. Oliveira, G. M. Azevedo, & A. D. Ferreira (Eds.), *International Financial Reporting Standards and New Directions in Earnings Management* (pp. 77–100). IGI Global. doi:10.4018/978-1-5225-7817-8.ch004

Çelik, S., & Koy, A. (2019). Chicken-Egg Dilemma for the Relationship Between Price and Volume in Borsa Istanbul. In T. Tripathi, M. Kumar Dash, & G. Agrawal (Eds.), *Behavioral Finance and Decision-Making Models* (pp. 46–69). IGI Global. doi:10.4018/978-1-5225-7399-9.ch003

Cerqueira, A. M., & Pereira, C. F. (2019). Earnings Management and Stock Market Reaction. In J. D. Oliveira, G. M. Azevedo, & A. D. Ferreira (Eds.), *International Financial Reporting Standards and New Directions in Earnings Management* (pp. 32–52). IGI Global. doi:10.4018/978-1-5225-7817-8.ch002

Chakraborty, S. (2020). Financial Infrastructure and Economic Growth. In Foreign Direct Investments: Concepts, Methodologies, Tools, and Applications (pp. 329-358). IGI Global. http://doi:10.4018/978-1-7998-2448-0.ch013

Chen, N. (2020). Asset Diversification and Efficiency of Islamic Banks. In A. Rafay (Ed.), *Growth and Emerging Prospects of International Islamic Banking* (pp. 117–140). IGI Global. doi:10.4018/978-1-7998-1611-9.ch007

Chhatoi, B. P., & Sahoo, S. P. (2019). A Review on Role of Macro and Micro Banking Environment on Non-Performing Assets Management. In T. Tripathi, M. Kumar Dash, & G. Agrawal (Eds.), *Behavioral Finance and Decision-Making Models* (pp. 281–294). IGI Global. doi:10.4018/978-1-5225-7399-9.ch016

Choudhury, M. A. (2020). PasarMalam and PasarPaghi: Grassroots Application of Islamic Ontological Methodology. In A. Rafay (Ed.), *Handbook of Research on Theory and Practice of Global Islamic Finance* (pp. 150–160). IGI Global. doi:10.4018/978-1-7998-0218-1.ch008

Čulková, K., Csikósová, A., & Janošková, M. (2019). Financing of International Business Through Private Equity: European Industry Case Study. In D. Ushakov (Ed.), *Global Trends of Modernization in Budgeting and Finance* (pp. 83–109). IGI Global. doi:10.4018/978-1-5225-7760-7.ch005

D'Rosario, M., & Hsieh, C. (2018). Predicting Credit Rating Migration Employing Neural Network Models. *International Journal of Strategic Decision Sciences*, *9*(4), 70–85. doi:10.4018/IJSDS.2018100105

Das, C. P., & Swain, R. K. (2019). Determinants of Market Capitalization in India and Its Impact. In T. Tripathi, M. Kumar Dash, & G. Agrawal (Eds.), *Behavioral Finance and Decision-Making Models* (pp. 163–176). IGI Global. doi:10.4018/978-1-5225-7399-9.ch009

Deji, M. S. O. & Salleh, M. C. (2020). Cash Waqf for Entrepreneurship Development. In Handbook of Research on Theory and Practice of Global Islamic Finance (pp. 290-305). IGI Global. http://doi:10.4018/978-1-7998-0218-1.ch016

Dinç, D. T., Gökmen, A., & Soygür, S. (2018). Fresh Fruit and Vegetable Exportation of Turkey and its Contribution to the Economic Growth. *International Journal of Sustainable Economies Management*, *7*(3), 1–18. doi:10.4018/IJSEM.2018070101

Dokas, I., Giokas, D., & Tsamis, A. (2014). Liquidity Efficiency in the Greek Listed Firms: A Financial Ratio Based on Data Envelopment Analysis. *International Journal of Corporate Finance and Accounting*, *1*(1), 40–59. doi:10.4018/ijcfa.2014010103

Dunn, L., & Dunn, R. (2014). Natural Resources and Welfare: A Study of U.S. States. In P. V. Schaeffer & E. Kouassi (Eds.), *Econometric Methods for Analyzing Economic Development* (pp. 235–261). IGI Global. doi:10.4018/978-1-4666-4329-1.ch014

Erdoğan, S. (2015). The Effect of Capital Structure on Profitability: An Empirical Analysis. In U. Akkucuk (Ed.), *Handbook of Research on Developing Sustainable Value in Economics, Finance, and Marketing* (pp. 307–323). IGI Global. doi:10.4018/978-1-4666-6635-1.ch018

Fauzel, S. (2020). Determinants of Islamic Banking in Africa: An Econometric Analysis. In A. Rafay (Ed.), *Growth and Emerging Prospects of International Islamic Banking* (pp. 174–188). IGI Global. doi:10.4018/978-1-7998-1611-9.ch010

Fiodendji, K., Kamgnia, B. D., & Tanimoune, N. A. (2014). Inflation and Economic Performance in the CFA Franc Zone: Transmission Channels and Threshold Effects. In P. V. Schaeffer & E. Kouassi (Eds.), *Econometric Methods for Analyzing Economic Development* (pp. 10–29). IGI Global. doi:10.4018/978-1-4666-4329-1.ch002

Franc, S., & Hladika, M. (2020). Appropriateness of Standard Accounting Tools in Measuring Social Innovation in the New Global Economy. In U. Akkucuk (Ed.), *Handbook of Research on Creating Sustainable Value in the Global Economy* (pp. 332–348). IGI Global. doi:10.4018/978-1-7998-1196-1.ch019

Gazel, S. (2019). The Effects of Macroprudential Policies on Financial Stability in Developing Countries. In A. Behl & S. Nayak (Eds.), *Maintaining Financial Stability in Times of Risk and Uncertainty* (pp. 92–114). IGI Global. doi:10.4018/978-1-5225-7208-4.ch005

Georgantopoulos, A. G., Filos, I., & Poutos, E. I. (2018). Banks, Stock Markets, and Growth Relationships in the EU28 Countries. In C. Zopounidis, A. G. Christopoulos, & P. Kalantonis (Eds.), *Perspectives, Trends, and Applications in Corporate Finance and Accounting* (pp. 129–161). IGI Global. doi:10.4018/978-1-5225-6114-9.ch006

Ghosh, I., & Chakrabarti, S. (2016). Inward and Outward Foreign Investments of the Asian Economies in Transition and India: Determinants of FDI and India's Prospects in CLMV. In V. Erokhin (Ed.), *Global Perspectives on Trade Integration and Economies in Transition* (pp. 212–237). IGI Global. doi:10.4018/978-1-5225-0451-1.ch011

Güngör, S., Demirel, E., & Küçün, N. T. (2019). Personality and Emotional Biases. In T. Tripathi, M. Kumar Dash, & G. Agrawal (Eds.), *Behavioral Finance and Decision-Making Models* (pp. 139–161). IGI Global. doi:10.4018/978-1-5225-7399-9.ch008

Ha, L., & Forgionne, G. (2006). Econometric Simulation for E-Business Strategy Evaluation. *International Journal of E-Business Research*, *2*(2), 38–53. doi:10.4018/jebr.2006040103

Hailu, Y. G., Adelaja, A., Akaeze, H., & Hanson, S. (2014). Explaining International Land Transactions in Africa. In P. V. Schaeffer & E. Kouassi (Eds.), *Econometric Methods for Analyzing Economic Development* (pp. 111–130). IGI Global. doi:10.4018/978-1-4666-4329-1.ch008

Hasan, Z. (2020). Risk and Islamic Finance: A Misconception Corrected. In A. Rafay (Ed.), *Handbook of Research on Theory and Practice of Global Islamic Finance* (pp. 441–454). IGI Global. doi:10.4018/978-1-7998-0218-1.ch024

Holynskyy, Y., & Onyusheva, I. (2019). The Impact of Budget and Fiscal Policy on Entrepreneurial Activity and Country's Competitiveness: The Case of Ukraine. In D. Ushakov (Ed.), *Global Trends of Modernization in Budgeting and Finance* (pp. 280–298). IGI Global. doi:10.4018/978-1-5225-7760-7.ch014

Ibrahim, A. R., & Ashafa, S. A. (2020). Zakat Distribution in the Context of Shari'ah Corporate Governance: Evidence From South-Western Nigeria. In A. Rafay (Ed.), *Handbook of Research on Theory and Practice of Global Islamic Finance* (pp. 161–178). IGI Global. doi:10.4018/978-1-7998-0218-1.ch009

Ibrahim, B. E. (2020). Interest-Free Micro-Finance Without Any Religious Connotation: An Inclusive Global Model. In A. Rafay (Ed.), *Handbook of Research on Theory and Practice of Global Islamic Finance* (pp. 196–215). IGI Global. doi:10.4018/978-1-7998-0218-1.ch011

Iyengar, V., & Bharathi, S. V. (2018). Bibliometric Analysis of Lean, Agile, and Leagile Supply Chains in Automobile Industry (1990 - 2017). *International Journal of Information Systems and Supply Chain Management, 11*(3), 22–45. doi:10.4018/IJISSCM.2018070102

Jackson, R. W., & Court, C. D. (2014). Embedding New Technologies and Extending Time Horizons in Input-Output Analysis. In P. V. Schaeffer & E. Kouassi (Eds.), *Econometric Methods for Analyzing Economic Development* (pp. 192–204). IGI Global. doi:10.4018/978-1-4666-4329-1.ch012

Katsampoxakis, I., Basdekis, H., & Anathreptakis, K. (2018). How the Greek Crisis Determined Firm Profitability and Optimal Debt Ratio. In C. Zopounidis, A. G. Christopoulos, & P. Kalantonis (Eds.), *Perspectives, Trends, and Applications in Corporate Finance and Accounting* (pp. 1–31). IGI Global. doi:10.4018/978-1-5225-6114-9.ch001

Kazakova, N., & Sivkova, A. (2019). Financial Security of Economic Activity: Analysis, Control, Risk Management. In D. Ushakov (Ed.), *Global Trends of Modernization in Budgeting and Finance* (pp. 110–130). IGI Global. doi:10.4018/978-1-5225-7760-7.ch006

Kazi, R. R. (2020). Dual Legal Framework in Islamic Capital Markets: Issues and Problems. In A. Rafay (Ed.), *Handbook of Research on Theory and Practice of Global Islamic Finance* (pp. 524–546). IGI Global. doi:10.4018/978-1-7998-0218-1.ch028

Kchouri, B., & Lehnert, T. (2020). Islamic Banking and Economic Growth. In A. Rafay (Ed.), *Handbook of Research on Theory and Practice of Global Islamic Finance* (pp. 86–114). IGI Global. doi:10.4018/978-1-7998-0218-1.ch005

Keri, I., Gromova, E., & Sinelschikova, N. (2019). Features of Financial Policy Development by Russian Companies in Today's Conditions. In D. Ushakov (Ed.), *Global Trends of Modernization in Budgeting and Finance* (pp. 64–82). IGI Global. doi:10.4018/978-1-5225-7760-7.ch004

Keswani, S. (2019). Emotional Finance Plays an Important Role in Investment Decisions. In T. Tripathi, M. Kumar Dash, & G. Agrawal (Eds.), *Behavioral Finance and Decision-Making Models* (pp. 89–103). IGI Global. doi:10.4018/978-1-5225-7399-9.ch005

Khairiree, K., & Ushakov, D. (2019). Budgeting Administration and Economic Growth Dynamics in Conditions of National Markets' Integration. In D. Ushakov (Ed.), *Global Trends of Modernization in Budgeting and Finance* (pp. 1–21). IGI Global. doi:10.4018/978-1-5225-7760-7.ch001

Kia, A. (2020). Positive Interest Rate, Stationary Economy, and Inefficiency. In A. Rafay (Ed.), *Handbook of Research on Theory and Practice of Global Islamic Finance* (pp. 1–17). IGI Global. doi:10.4018/978-1-7998-0218-1.ch001

Kollias, I. (2014). Optimal Control Indicators for the Assessment of the Influence of Approximate Optimal Feedback in the Baseline RBC Model. *International Journal of Sustainable Economies Management*, *3*(1), 1–15. doi:10.4018/ijsem.2014010101

Köseoğlu, S. D. (2019). Behavioral Finance vs. Traditional Finance. In Behavioral Finance and Decision-Making Models (pp. 1-23). IGI Global. http://doi:10.4018/978-1-5225-7399-9.ch001

Lipovetsky, S. (2018). MaxDiff Choice Probability Estimations on Aggregate and Individual Level. *International Journal of Business Analytics*, *5*(1), 55–69. doi:10.4018/IJBAN.2018010104

Lipovetsky, S., & Conklin, W. M. (2019). Choice Models Adjusted to Non-Available Items and Network Effects. *International Journal of Business Analytics*, *6*(1), 1–19. doi:10.4018/IJBAN.2019010101

Malikov, A. (2020). Sukuk as an Infrastructure-Financing Tool. In A. Rafay (Ed.), *Handbook of Research on Theory and Practice of Global Islamic Finance* (pp. 770–787). IGI Global. doi:10.4018/978-1-7998-0218-1.ch039

Manzoor, A. (2016). Early Warning System for Financial Crises. In Q. Munir (Ed.), *Handbook of Research on Financial and Banking Crisis Prediction through Early Warning Systems* (pp. 22–45). IGI Global. doi:10.4018/978-1-4666-9484-2.ch002

Mariia, E. (2019). Financing at the Housing Market: Analysis of Best Practices in the Selected Countries. In D. Ushakov (Ed.), *Global Trends of Modernization in Budgeting and Finance* (pp. 131–150). IGI Global. doi:10.4018/978-1-5225-7760-7.ch007

Md Husin, M., & Haron, R. (2020). Financial Sustainability of SMEs Through Islamic Crowdfunding. In A. Rafay (Ed.), *Handbook of Research on Theory and Practice of Global Islamic Finance* (pp. 321–337). IGI Global. doi:10.4018/978-1-7998-0218-1.ch018

Mduma, J. K. (2014). Point Density Estimation of Changes in Income Polarization in Tanzania, 1992–2001. In P. V. Schaeffer & E. Kouassi (Eds.), *Econometric Methods for Analyzing Economic Development* (pp. 50–65). IGI Global. doi:10.4018/978-1-4666-4329-1.ch004

Megaravalli, A. V. (2019). Macroeconomics and Its Impact on Stock Markets of India, China, and Japan: ASIAN Markets. In Behavioral Finance and Decision-Making Models (pp. 177-194). IGI Global. http://doi:10.4018/978-1-5225-7399-9.ch010

Mendes, C. A., Rodrigues, L. L., & Parte, L. (2019). An Overall Perspective of Income Smoothing as a Strategy of Earnings Management. In J. D. Oliveira, G. M. Azevedo, & A. D. Ferreira (Eds.), *International Financial Reporting Standards and New Directions in Earnings Management* (pp. 53–76). IGI Global. doi:10.4018/978-1-5225-7817-8.ch003

Michieka, N. M. (2014). Population Dynamics, Economic Growth, and Energy Consumption in Kenya. In P. V. Schaeffer & E. Kouassi (Eds.), *Econometric Methods for Analyzing Economic Development* (pp. 178–191). IGI Global. doi:10.4018/978-1-4666-4329-1.ch011

Miranda, M. C. (2020). Extremal Index Estimation: Application to Financial Data. In L. Farinha, A. B. Cruz, & J. R. Sebastião (Eds.), *Handbook of Research on Accounting and Financial Studies* (pp. 96–130). IGI Global. doi:10.4018/978-1-7998-2136-6.ch006

Mishra, S., & Bansal, R. (2019). Credit Rating and Its Interaction With Financial Ratios: A Study of BSE 500 Companies. In T. Tripathi, M. Kumar Dash, & G. Agrawal (Eds.), *Behavioral Finance and Decision-Making Models* (pp. 251–268). IGI Global. doi:10.4018/978-1-5225-7399-9.ch014

Mohamed, H. B., & Mat Sari, N. (2020). Artificial Intelligence and Blockchain-Driven Islamic Capital Markets. In A. Rafay (Ed.), *Handbook of Research on Theory and Practice of Global Islamic Finance* (pp. 874–888). IGI Global. doi:10.4018/978-1-7998-0218-1.ch044

Mukherjee, S., & Das, R. C. (2019). Reflections on Microfinance: Poverty Nexus From India – An Empirical Inquest. In R. C. Das (Ed.), *Handbook of Research on Microfinancial Impacts on Women Empowerment, Poverty, and Inequality* (pp. 188–207). IGI Global. doi:10.4018/978-1-5225-5240-6.ch009

Mukherjee, S., & Karmakar, A. K. (2019). A Tri-Variate Nexus of Microfinance-Growth-Inequality: The South-Asian Experience. In R. C. Das (Ed.), *Handbook of Research on Microfinancial Impacts on Women Empowerment, Poverty, and Inequality* (pp. 247–265). IGI Global. doi:10.4018/978-1-5225-5240-6.ch012

Mulatinho, C. E., Pereira, D. M., Monteiro, J. A., Leal, L. A., Pederneiras, M. M., Ribeiro, M. V., & Amaro, R. G. (2019). Convergence of Accounting Standards to International Standards and Earnings Management in Brazilian Companies. In J. D. Oliveira, G. M. Azevedo, & A. D. Ferreira (Eds.), *International Financial Reporting Standards and New Directions in Earnings Management* (pp. 256–273). IGI Global. doi:10.4018/978-1-5225-7817-8.ch012

Muriithi, M. K., & Mwabu, G. (2014). Demand for Health Care in Kenya: The Effects of Information about Quality. In P. V. Schaeffer & E. Kouassi (Eds.), *Econometric Methods for Analyzing Economic Development* (pp. 102–110). IGI Global. doi:10.4018/978-1-4666-4329-1.ch007

N'Guessan, C. F. (2014). Asymmetric Equilibrium Adjustment between Employment and Economic Growth in Côte d'Ivoire: A Consistent Momentum Threshold Autoregressive Model. In P. V. Schaeffer & E. Kouassi (Eds.), *Econometric Methods for Analyzing Economic Development* (pp. 1–9). IGI Global. doi:10.4018/978-1-4666-4329-1.ch001

Nadezhda, K., Elena, D., & Larisa, Z. (2019). Financial Behavior of Russian Population under Crisis Phenomena. In D. Ushakov (Ed.), *Global Trends of Modernization in Budgeting and Finance* (pp. 22–43). IGI Global. doi:10.4018/978-1-5225-7760-7.ch002

Naser, H. (2020). The Economic and Environmental Impact of Large Financial Developments in an Oil-Dependent Economy: The Case of Bahrain. In U. Akkucuk (Ed.), *Handbook of Research on Creating Sustainable Value in the Global Economy* (pp. 221–240). IGI Global. doi:10.4018/978-1-7998-1196-1.ch013

Nasir, M. A. (2020). The Relevance of Maqasid al Shari'ah to Anti-Money Laundering and Terrorism Financing. In A. Rafay (Ed.), *Handbook of Research on Theory and Practice of Global Islamic Finance* (pp. 179–194). IGI Global. doi:10.4018/978-1-7998-0218-1.ch010

Nembua, C. C. (2014). Measuring and Explaining Economic Inequality: An Extension of the Gini Coefficient. In P. V. Schaeffer & E. Kouassi (Eds.), *Econometric Methods for Analyzing Economic Development* (pp. 87–101). IGI Global. doi:10.4018/978-1-4666-4329-1.ch006

Ng, W. L. (2013). Improving Long-Term Financial Risk Forecasts using High-Frequency Data and Scaling Laws. In B. Alexandrova-Kabadjova, S. Martinez-Jaramillo, A. L. Garcia-Almanza, & E. Tsang (Eds.), *Simulation in Computational Finance and Economics: Tools and Emerging Applications* (pp. 255–278). IGI Global. doi:10.4018/978-1-4666-2011-7.ch013

Nkoro, E., & Uko, A. K. (2014). Impact of the Volatility of Macroeconomic Variables on the Volatility of Stock Market Returns: Nigeria's Experience. In H. Dinçer & Ü. Hacioğlu (Eds.), *Global Strategies in Banking and Finance* (pp. 218–230). IGI Global. doi:10.4018/978-1-4666-4635-3.ch014

Nogueira, M. F. (2019). The Relationship Between the Quality of Financial Information in Industrial Companies and Discretionary Inventory Management. In J. D. Oliveira, G. M. Azevedo, & A. D. Ferreira (Eds.), *International Financial Reporting Standards and New Directions in Earnings Management* (pp. 179–198). IGI Global. doi:10.4018/978-1-5225-7817-8.ch008

Nondo, C., Kahsai, M. S., & Schaeffer, P. V. (2014). The Role of Governance in Teledensity and Economic Growth: GMM Estimation. In P. V. Schaeffer & E. Kouassi (Eds.), *Econometric Methods for Analyzing Economic Development* (pp. 262–278). IGI Global. doi:10.4018/978-1-4666-4329-1.ch015

Oliveira, J. D., Azevedo, G. M., Ferreira, A. D., Martins, S. P., & Pinto, C. R. (2019). Determinants of the Readability and Comprehensibility of Risk Disclosures: Evidence From Portuguese Listed Companies. In J. D. Oliveira, G. M. Azevedo, & A. D. Ferreira (Eds.), *International Financial Reporting Standards and New Directions in Earnings Management* (pp. 216–238). IGI Global. doi:10.4018/978-1-5225-7817-8.ch010

Oliveira, J. D., Azevedo, G. M., Pinheiro, S. F., & Borges, M. F. (2019). Impression Management Strategies in the Chairmen's Statements: Evidence From the Portuguese Banking Industry. In J. D. Oliveira, G. M. Azevedo, & A. D. Ferreira (Eds.), *International Financial Reporting Standards and New Directions in Earnings Management* (pp. 199–215). IGI Global. doi:10.4018/978-1-5225-7817-8.ch009

Ostovskaya, A., & Pavlenko, I. (2019). Financial Instruments of Regional Economic Policy Implementation. In D. Ushakov (Ed.), *Global Trends of Modernization in Budgeting and Finance* (pp. 177–206). IGI Global. doi:10.4018/978-1-5225-7760-7.ch009

Oyekale, A. S., Adeoti, A. I., & Oyekale, T. O. (2014). Sources of Income Inequality in Nigeria: Decomposition Approaches. In P. V. Schaeffer & E. Kouassi (Eds.), *Econometric Methods for Analyzing Economic Development* (pp. 66–86). IGI Global. doi:10.4018/978-1-4666-4329-1.ch005

Paiva, I. S., & Dias, P. V. (2019). Earnings Management and Audit in Private Firms: The Effect of Financial Recuperation. In J. D. Oliveira, G. M. Azevedo, & A. D. Ferreira (Eds.), *International Financial Reporting Standards and New Directions in Earnings Management* (pp. 154–178). IGI Global. doi:10.4018/978-1-5225-7817-8.ch007

Pamuncak, M. B., Possumah, B. T., & Halim, Z. A. (2020). Integrating Zakat and Microfinance: A Proposed Framework. In A. Rafay (Ed.), *Handbook of Research on Theory and Practice of Global Islamic Finance* (pp. 277–289). IGI Global. doi:10.4018/978-1-7998-0218-1.ch015

Patlasov, O. Y., & Mzhelskaya, O. K. (2019). Scoring Modeling in Estimating the Financial Condition of Russian Agro-Industrial Companies. In D. Ushakov (Ed.), *Global Trends of Modernization in Budgeting and Finance* (pp. 151–175). IGI Global. doi:10.4018/978-1-5225-7760-7.ch008

Patra, S. (2018). Determinants of Participation and Impact of Microfinance: An Econometric Analysis. In R. C. Das (Ed.), *Microfinance and Its Impact on Entrepreneurial Development, Sustainability, and Inclusive Growth* (pp. 156–184). IGI Global. doi:10.4018/978-1-5225-5213-0.ch009

Pimentel, L. M., & Jorge, S. M. (2019). Earnings Quality and Firm Valuation: A "New" Perspective Deriving From the Literature. In J. D. Oliveira, G. M. Azevedo, & A. D. Ferreira (Eds.), *International Financial Reporting Standards and New Directions in Earnings Management* (pp. 1–31). IGI Global. doi:10.4018/978-1-5225-7817-8.ch001

Plaku, D., & Hysa, E. (2019). The Impact of Tax Policies on Behavior of Albanian Taxpayers. In T. Tripathi, M. Kumar Dash, & G. Agrawal (Eds.), *Behavioral Finance and Decision-Making Models* (pp. 219–250). IGI Global. doi:10.4018/978-1-5225-7399-9.ch013

Rab, H. (2020). Money and Monetary Issues in Islamic Finance. In A. Rafay (Ed.), *Handbook of Research on Theory and Practice of Global Islamic Finance* (pp. 38–60). IGI Global. doi:10.4018/978-1-7998-0218-1.ch003

Rabatinová, M., Válek, J., & Kušnírová, J. (2019). Taxation System in Slovakia: National Featues and Prospects of Integration. In D. Ushakov (Ed.), *Global Trends of Modernization in Budgeting and Finance* (pp. 207–224). IGI Global. doi:10.4018/978-1-5225-7760-7.ch010

Rassool, N. H. (2020). Innovation in Takaful: The Musharakataan Business Model. In A. Rafay (Ed.), *Handbook of Research on Theory and Practice of Global Islamic Finance* (pp. 623–641). IGI Global. doi:10.4018/978-1-7998-0218-1.ch032

Rodríguez-Gulías, M. J., Fernández-López, S., Rodeiro-Pazos, D., Faria, A. P., & Barbosa, N. (2020). Effect of Venture Capital on the Growth of Information and Communication Technology University Spin-Offs: Venture Capital Effect on the Growth of ICT-USOs. In B. Álvarez-García & J. Abeal-Vázquez (Eds.), *Emerging Tools and Strategies for Financial Management* (pp. 82–105). IGI Global. doi:10.4018/978-1-7998-2440-4.ch004

Sengupta, A., & Glavin, S. E. (2013). Predicting Volatile Consumer Markets using Multi-Agent Methods: Theory and Validation. In B. Alexandrova-Kabadjova, S. Martinez-Jaramillo, A. L. Garcia-Almanza, & E. Tsang (Eds.), *Simpulation in Computational Finance and Economics: Tools and Emerging Applications* (pp. 339–358). IGI Global. doi:10.4018/978-1-4666-2011-7.ch016

Shaikh, I. M., & Noordin, K. (2020). An Analysis of Determinants to Choose Family Takaful. In A. Rafay (Ed.), *Handbook of Research on Theory and Practice of Global Islamic Finance* (pp. 642–662). IGI Global. doi:10.4018/978-1-7998-0218-1.ch033

Sharmiladevi, J. C. (2020). Cointegration and Causality Study Among Inward FDI, Economic Growth and Exports: An Indian Perspective. *International Journal of Asian Business and Information Management, 11*(1), 63–77. doi:10.4018/IJABIM.2020010104

Singh, R. (2014). *A Survey of Economic Growth*. IGI Global. doi:10.4018/978-1-4666-5848-6.ch004

Singh, R. (2014). *Analysis of Trade-Growth Nexus*. IGI Global. doi:10.4018/978-1-4666-5848-6.ch009

Singh, R. (2014). *Comparative Analysis and Robustness Tests*. IGI Global. doi:10.4018/978-1-4666-5848-6.ch008

Singh, R. (2014). *East Asian Growth Controversy*. IGI Global. doi:10.4018/978-1-4666-5848-6.ch003

Singh, R. (2014). *Growth Accounts of the Asian Economies*. IGI Global. doi:10.4018/978-1-4666-5848-6.ch006

Singh, R. (2014). *Growth Experiences of the Asian Economies*. IGI Global. doi:10.4018/978-1-4666-5848-6.ch002

Singh, R. (2014). *New Method New Estimates*. IGI Global. doi:10.4018/978-1-4666-5848-6.ch007

Singh, R. (2014). *Overview of Global Development Patterns*. IGI Global. doi:10.4018/978-1-4666-5848-6.ch001

Singh, R. (2014). *The Empirical Growth Literature*. IGI Global. doi:10.4018/978-1-4666-5848-6.ch005

Singh, V. V., Pandey, M., & Vashisht, A. (2019). Employees Perception Regarding CSR Initiatives of the Companies in India. In T. Tripathi, M. Kumar Dash, & G. Agrawal (Eds.), *Behavioral Finance and Decision-Making Models* (pp. 204–217). IGI Global. doi:10.4018/978-1-5225-7399-9.ch012

Sinha, M., & Sengupta, P. P. (2017). FDI and Trade in Services Towards Sustainable Economic Growth: An Empirical Evidence from India. *International Journal of Sustainable Economies Management*, *6*(1), 22–33. doi:10.4018/ijsem.2017010102

Sohail, H., & Arshed, N. (2020). Cost-Efficiency Analysis of Mudarabah Companies. In A. Rafay (Ed.), *Handbook of Research on Theory and Practice of Global Islamic Finance* (pp. 568–592). IGI Global. doi:10.4018/978-1-7998-0218-1.ch030

Sousa, A., Góis, C. G., & Viseu, C. (2019). Earnings Management in SMEs: Evidence From Portugal and Spain. In J. D. Oliveira, G. M. Azevedo, & A. D. Ferreira (Eds.), *International Financial Reporting Standards and New Directions in Earnings Management* (pp. 101–126). IGI Global. doi:10.4018/978-1-5225-7817-8.ch005

Spaseski, N. (2018). *Fractal and Wavelet Market Analysis in Pattern Recognition*. IGI Global. doi:10.4018/978-1-5225-3259-0.ch007

Spulbar, C., & Birau, R. (2019). *Estimating Long-Term Volatility on National Stock Exchange of India*. IGI Global. doi:10.4018/978-1-5225-9269-3.ch011

Spulbar, C., & Birau, R. (2019). *Financial Nexus: Efficiency and Soundness in Banking and Capital Markets*. IGI Global. doi:10.4018/978-1-5225-9269-3.ch004

Spulbar, C., & Birau, R. (2019). *Investigating Long-Term Behavior of Milan Stock Exchange*. IGI Global. doi:10.4018/978-1-5225-9269-3.ch017

Suprijanto, T. (2020). The Role of Profit Rate in Islamic Monetary Policy. In A. Rafay (Ed.), *Handbook of Research on Theory and Practice of Global Islamic Finance* (pp. 18–37). IGI Global. doi:10.4018/978-1-7998-0218-1.ch002

Szczerbicki, E., & Waszczyk, M. (2006). Modelling of Complex Economic Systems: Toward Conceptual Platform. *International Journal of Enterprise Information Systems*, *2*(1), 67–78. doi:10.4018/jeis.2006010105

Tomar, D. S., & Tomar, R. S. (2019). Comparative Analysis of Service Quality Perception Between Public Sector and Private Sector Banks of India. In T. Tripathi, M. Kumar Dash, & G. Agrawal (Eds.), *Behavioral Finance and Decision-Making Models* (pp. 117–138). IGI Global. doi:10.4018/978-1-5225-7399-9.ch007

Triantafyllou, A. (2020). Investing in Commodities in Times of Uncertainty and Lax Monetary Policy. In C. Zopounidis, D. Kenourgios, & G. Dotsis (Eds.), *Recent Advances and Applications in Alternative Investments* (pp. 1–36). IGI Global. doi:10.4018/978-1-7998-2436-7.ch001

Tripathi, T., & Dash, M. K. (2019). An Impact Assessment of Goods and Services Tax in India Through Strategic Analysis Approach (SAA). In T. Tripathi, M. Kumar Dash, & G. Agrawal (Eds.), *Behavioral Finance and Decision-Making Models* (pp. 269–280). IGI Global. doi:10.4018/978-1-5225-7399-9.ch015

Vieira, E., & Madaleno, M. (2019). Earnings Management and Corporate Governance in Family Firms: Evidence From a Small Market. In J. D. Oliveira, G. M. Azevedo, & A. D. Ferreira (Eds.), *International Financial Reporting Standards and New Directions in Earnings Management* (pp. 127–153). IGI Global. doi:10.4018/978-1-5225-7817-8.ch006

Wajeetongratana, P. (2019). Environmental Accounting Implementation and Stimulation of National Business Global Competitiveness: The Case of Thailand. In D. Ushakov (Ed.), *Global Trends of Modernization in Budgeting and Finance* (pp. 299–324). IGI Global. doi:10.4018/978-1-5225-7760-7.ch015

Wan Jusoh, W. N. (2020). Corporate Social Responsibility: Conventional and Islamic Perspectives. In A. Rafay (Ed.), *Handbook of Research on Theory and Practice of Global Islamic Finance* (pp. 129–149). IGI Global. doi:10.4018/978-1-7998-0218-1.ch007

West, G. R., & Jackson, R. W. (2014). Simulating Impacts on Regional Economies: A Modeling Alternative. In P. V. Schaeffer & E. Kouassi (Eds.), *Econometric Methods for Analyzing Economic Development* (pp. 132–152). IGI Global. doi:10.4018/978-1-4666-4329-1.ch009

Related Readings

Zeldner, A., Osipov, V., & Skryl, T. (2019). Model of Socioeconomic Development Based on Market Economy and Public-Private Partnership (PPP) Mechanism: Key Approaches and Terms for Implementation. In D. Ushakov (Ed.), *Global Trends of Modernization in Budgeting and Finance* (pp. 241–259). IGI Global. doi:10.4018/978-1-5225-7760-7.ch012

About the Authors

Torben Larsen has a MSc Econ from University of Aarhus and an international Degree in Strategic Management from University of Maryland-Tietgenskolen Dk. He has broad experience in regional planning of healthcare with Academic Awards from 1) Association of Hospital Managers in Norway, Lundbeck Fonden Dk and MIE96. He is a former Chief Research Consultant at University of Southern Denmark which included leadership of an EU-sponsored research project in Integrated Homecare. He has been involved with various courses and conferences and has written research papers in Health Economics, Neuroeconomics, Meditation and Biofeedback. He is giving guest lectures in cybernetic economics.

***

Ulla B. Bendtsen is MSc (Econ) from University of Aarhus with 30+ years of working experience in the field of environment, energy and climate change. Currently she is Director for international affairs at the Secretariat for the Danish Council on Climate Change.

Are Holen is Professor Emeritus, MD with plenty of research in meditation. He and others founded 1966 ACEM as a secular NGO for meditation. Are has written the ‘Psychology of Silence’ which is a masterpiece in a modern lifestyle including meditation.

Ole D. Nielsen is a Danish author, lecturer and entrepreneur. He is a master in history and Danish from University of Copenhagen, and has written several textbooks on teaching, pedagogy, stress management and slow living.

Anna Pacak-Vedel is postdoctoral researcher (PhD 2018) at the Department of Psychology and Behavioral Science at University of Aarhus, Denmark. Also she is a consultant for private test companies and glectures for the Human Resource sector.

Hiltrud Schinzel is restorer from Academy of Fine Arts in Vienna, Austria, PhD in Arts History from Bochum University, Germany and Artist (Drawing and Painting on Paper). Her research focuses on mediation between arts and science.

Louis B. Stewart is MSc (Econ) from University of Aarhus. He has formerly worked with economic modelling of climate policies at the Secretariat of the Danish Economic Council. Currently, he is an economic and climate analyst at the Secretariat for the Danish Council on Climate Change

Index

L

M

N

O

P

R

S

T

U

W

Y

www.ingramcontent.com/pod-product-compliance
Lightning Source LLC
LaVergne TN
LVHW080856300926
849162LV00003B/440